VISION

Sonia N

Teachers Speak Up!
Stories of Courage, Resilience, and Hope in Difficult Times
Sonia Nieto & Alicia López Nieto, Eds.

Embracing Diversity:
Teachers' Everyday Practices in Secondary English Language Arts Classrooms
Sarah Bickens, Frances Bittman, & David J. Connor

Families With Power:
Centering Students by Engaging With Families and Community
Mary Cowhey

Teachers Speak Up!

Stories of Courage, Resilience, and Hope in Difficult Times

Edited by
Sonia Nieto and Alicia López Nieto

TEACHERS COLLEGE PRESS

TEACHERS COLLEGE | COLUMBIA UNIVERSITY
NEW YORK AND LONDON

Published by Teachers College Press,® 1234 Amsterdam Avenue, New York, NY 10027

Copyright © 2024 by Teachers College, Columbia University

Front cover photograph by Matt Hoffman / Unsplash.

Library of Congress Cataloging-in-Publication Data is available at loc.gov

ISBN 978-0-8077-6952-2 (paper)
ISBN 978-0-8077-6953-3 (hardcover)
ISBN 978-0-8077-8230-9 (ebook)

Printed on acid-free paper
Manufactured in the United States of America

We dedicate this book to our late husband/father, Angel Nieto Romero, an exemplary teacher who quietly demonstrated affection and undying support for his family, friends, and students, and who believed in the power of love to transform and guide. His death delayed the writing and publication of this book as we dealt with our deep grief, but his life reminded us to come back to it and motivated us to finish.

Contents

PART III: THE MANY FACES OF SOCIAL JUSTICE

PART IV: TEACHING AND ACTIVISM IN
THE CLASSROOM AND BEYOND

PART V: TEACHING, HEARTBREAK, AND REDEMPTION

Introduction

This book is about some of the many forces that have turned the lives of teachers and other educators upside down during the fraught past few years. Due to the stresses facing the teaching profession, many educators left their positions in droves, some reluctantly, others never to return. According to one story, teacher turnover had reached new highs by the spring of 2023 (Chalkbeat, 2023). The stories of teachers who stood up to face the numerous challenges of these years have not yet been fully documented, at least not through the words of educators themselves. As the editors of this volume, we know and have worked with many teachers facing daunting circumstances. Impressed by their resilience, courage, and creativity, we collected some of their stories for this book.

WHO WE ARE

We are a mother–daughter pair of educators and writers with many years in education. We know that most teachers rarely get to tell their own stories, particularly pre-K–12 teachers who work in public schools. Other educators, some of whom work not only as classroom teachers but in other teaching roles as well, have also impressed us with their strength and commitment to education and to students, including school librarians, school board members, union activists, district administrators, entrepreneurs, and others. Because the challenges in educational spaces are neither new nor related only to the pandemic, we decided to reach out and ask some of them to write about their experiences, not just during the past several years but also throughout their careers because we know that their experiences are not new or novel. We are hopeful that their stories will inspire, teach, and motivate those who are beginning their educational journeys, those who are veterans in the field, and those who may be losing hope.

Sonia Nieto

I spent over 50 years as an educator. Most of my teaching, research, mentoring, and service were dedicated to teacher education with a specialization in teaching immigrant and marginalized students, and a research focus in multicultural education, literacy, and ESL.

Beginning my professional career as a teacher of Spanish, English language arts (ELA), and English as a second language (ESL) in an intermediate school in Brooklyn, NY, I later spent several years teaching at the first bilingual school in the Northeast, and then as a curriculum specialist in the same school in the Bronx. My career in higher education started at the Department of Puerto Rican Studies at Brooklyn College in 1972, where I remained for 3 tumultuous years during the height of the ethnic studies movement and, realizing that I needed a doctorate to continue in the field, my family and I picked up stakes and moved to Massachusetts where I could pursue my doctoral degree. After completing my doctoral degree at the University of Massachusetts, Amherst, I worked for the Massachusetts Department of Education's Bureau of Equal Educational Opportunity for a year, but it became clear that being a bureaucrat did not suit me because I missed my true calling, teaching. I was recruited back to UMass in 1980, where I progressed from assistant to associate to full professor before retiring in 2006. I am now a professor emerita. I loved my career and my time at UMass. Though I received numerous invitations from other universities to relocate, I had not wanted to be anywhere else. I remained at UMass for 26 years.

Each of these experiences in education shaped the educator I am today.

Alicia López Nieto

I went into teaching when I was 25, after years of thinking I did not want to be a teacher. I started teaching French in an all-girls independent school in New York, a place where I found wonderful mentors, small class sizes, and a great deal of financial support for professional development. After 7 years there, I worked at another independent school until my husband and I were expecting our third baby. Wanting to be close to family, I accepted a position as a Spanish and French teacher at a public school near my parents in Massachusetts. Soon afterwards, I decided to study for my master's degree in bilingual, ESL, and multicultural education. With the support of my husband and parents, I managed to get my degree while raising three children under the age of 4 and working full-time. At that time, the English as a second language teacher and curriculum leader at my school was leaving her position. It was the perfect opportunity for me to shift gears from world language teacher to ESL teacher. I immediately loved this position, feeling that I could develop stronger relationships with smaller numbers of students and their families.

A few years ago, I decided I wanted to take the next step in my education, and I began the path toward a PhD. I currently work in administration in an elementary school, and that has been gratifying because I can work with students and teachers in a different way. Years ago, you could not have told me that I would follow in both my father's and my mother's footsteps, and yet here I am, happily doing so.

ABOUT THIS BOOK

Few years have been as challenging for the United States, and indeed for the entire world, as the period from 2020 through 2023. Faced with a deadly pandemic that killed millions, the world shut down and commerce came to a shrieking halt, with businesses and schools shuttered. In the midst of this tragedy and uncertainty in the United States came the killing of numerous African American men and women by police officers, a trend that had been evident for many years but became more dramatic after the death of George Floyd on May 25, 2020. The reaction to this event was more intense than previous killings because Floyd's death was caught on video and broadcast around the world, sparking mass demonstrations and universal calls for a racial reckoning. As a result, and in tandem with the pandemic, enormous inequities in all areas of life in poor and marginalized communities were laid bare. For teachers and other educators, these years signaled an unprecedented period of both distress and new questions about whether education as we know it could survive. At the same time, the pandemic ushered in new opportunities for both educators and students to learn new ways of teaching, learning, and using technology.

Given the tumultuous past several years, teachers and other educators have been at the forefront, and in the crosshairs, of what it means to be an educator today: The continuing pandemic with disastrous consequences for students, teachers, schools, and our society in general; the racial reckoning that began after the police killings of George Floyd and many others since then, that resulted in an increasing awareness among the general population—especially young people—of the ravages of racism throughout our history; the devastating and destructive effects of climate change through hurricanes, tornadoes, and fires, among other natural and man-made disasters; the increasingly virulent attacks on public education and teachers by those who would dismantle it in favor of privatized and for-profit schools; the dramatic changes in our nation's demographics and its implications for the future of education; the contentious debates over culture issues such as Critical Race Theory, book banning, and other matters related to diversity and social justice: All of these have changed the nature of teaching and learning today.

As a result of these conditions, and because of our longstanding interest and experience in educating the next generation of students and teachers, we decided to explore how teaching and learning have changed in the past decade or so, and the implications of these changes. Each of us has written about the work of teachers and students, both individually and together: Alicia through her *Maestra/Teacher* blog and our co-authored book, *Teaching, a Life's Work* (Nieto & López, 2019), and Sonia through a series of books, most recently *Why We Teach Now* (Nieto, 2015) and her co-authored book cited above (Nieto & López, 2019). The current book follows on the heels of these as well as our continuing dedication to the field of teaching and learning and the influence of students and teachers. Thus, we reached out to educators—some of whom we knew and had previously worked with as teachers and colleagues, and others whom we did not know but who had been recommended by other educators as having interesting stories to tell about their experiences in the field. Most were classroom teachers while the others included educators both in and out of classroom settings. In our invitation to educators, we encouraged them to write about how the issues surrounding the state of education today have affected their vision of teaching and their practice. The book includes essays by not only K–12 classroom teachers but also others who work with learners in a wide capacity of roles. Hence, we see it as broadening the definition of who is a teacher, and what it means to teach.

We received enthusiastic affirmative responses from 18 of the educators we invited to participate (please note that Chapter 4 has five authors). The authors reflect a broad range of teaching experiences from elementary, middle, and high school. Some have been teaching for many years and others are newer to the profession. These educators work in urban, rural, and suburban schools and other educational institutions, and they teach a variety of subject matters from English, mathematics, the arts, social studies, ESL, ethnic studies, and more. Some are not classroom teachers at all, though some were in the past. (We decided to keep the word *teachers* in the title because all of them, despite some of them having other roles at present, are still teachers in different ways.) What all of them have in common is a profound belief in the power of public education to make a difference in students' lives, as well as in their own. Like the educators, the students they teach are also diverse in ethnic and racial identity, social class, gender identity, native language, ability, and in other ways. Some are immigrants or refugees, while others have families who have been here for generations.

Major Themes Addressed in the Essays

- Teaching through a pandemic
- Becoming an educator in turbulent times
- Confronting issues of identity, race, and history through curriculum and pedagogy
- Welcoming all students into schools and communities

Sections

We have categorized the essays into five sections that best fit the major ideas the authors address in their essays:

I. Identity, Family, and Community
II. Love and Affirming Practices
III. The Many Faces of Social Justice
IV. Teaching and Activism in the Classroom and Beyond
V. Teaching, Heartbreak, and Redemption

Although all the essays include most of these issues, some delve more deeply into one or another of the themes. Nevertheless, although they share similar themes, each essay differs from all the others: some authors reflect on their lives as teachers; others focus on specific pedagogical practices; a few present actual curricula. The essays vary in tone from jubilant to wary.

We begin our book with a preliminary chapter, written by Sonia, that frames the remainder of the book by addressing such questions as:

- What is the role of classroom teachers and other educators in unprecedented and challenging times?
- What is the context of public education in the United States today, and what impact are public schools having on young people?
- What are the obstacles to preparing young people for engaged lives in a democratic society?
- What visions do the authors have about public education, and how do they put these visions or ideals into practice?
- What can readers learn from the visions and practices of the teachers and other educators in these pages?

The final chapter, written by Alicia, draws several fundamental conclusions from the previous chapters, envisioning a more hopeful course for the future.

REFERENCES

Nieto, S. (Ed.). (2015). *Why we teach now.* Teachers College Press.
Nieto, S., & López, A. (2019). *Teaching, a life's work: A mother–daughter dialogue.* Teachers College Press.

CHAPTER 1

Facing a New World in Teaching and Learning

Sonia Nieto

The field of education has become especially contentious since the dawn of the 21st century. Most of the challenges are not new; in fact, many have been around for decades, but they have worsened steadily since the complicating factors of the pandemic, the culture wars, and deepening racial and economic inequality, among others. In what follows, we describe some of these. We begin with what the pandemic has meant for educators, students, and our country.

THE PANDEMIC AS A CATALYST FOR INCREASING INEQUALITY AND ADDRESSING LEARNING CHALLENGES AND MENTAL HEALTH CONCERNS

Shortly after March 2020 when COVID-19 began to be felt in the United States, almost all schools in the country closed. Inequality—economic, educational, experiential, and other—was quickly felt across the board, though some communities were better able than others to withstand the pressures associated with the pandemic. It was especially families with higher levels of education, greater economic and cultural resources, and access to more opportunities who could provide financial and educational help for their children, while poor and working-class families struggled mightily to do so.

Even before the pandemic, however, perceptions of inequality differed depending on one's politics and material position in society. Just as the pandemic was beginning, a PEW Research survey found that although most Americans agreed that there was too much inequality in our society, they did not necessarily view it as a priority to be addressed (PEW Research Center, 2020). For instance, a notable divide existed between Democrats and Republicans on whether inequality required major changes to our economic system: Republicans were much more likely to blame inequality on the personal choices people make, while Democrats were more likely to claim that discrimination against some racial and ethnic groups and lack of opportunities were responsible. Not surprisingly, these differences were also visible among people at different income levels, with low-income families saying that addressing inequality should be a top priority, while higher-income families believed it was not. The situation worsened after the pandemic took hold.

Student Learning

Inequality has also left an indelible mark on student learning, mental health, and other issues related to the pandemic. According to the National Academy of Education, the nation's premier research organization, which includes some of the most eminent scholars in the field, early evidence suggests that the closing of schools and migration to online learning in 2020 had a detrimental effect on student learning. According to the report,

> The health crisis has surfaced for a broader public what many educators and policy makers have known for decades, namely *growing disparities of resources and educational outcomes for historically marginalized, disadvantaged, and underserved students.* (National Academy of Education, 2020, p.1; emphasis added)

The report, released after a 2-week period in July 2020 when educators and policymakers in reading, mathematics, and well-being convened to discuss how to address education inequities in the face of the COVID-19 epidemic, continues to be relevant. Focusing on this troubled period, the panel chose to include not only the issue of academic achievement, but also the trauma and social-emotional harm caused by the pandemic and the ongoing crisis in racial injustice. Rather than provide simple answers for these formidable problems, the report instead highlighted some "best bets," that is, strategies and actions to address them. These included providing all children who needed them with meals, reaching out to families that schools had not heard from since the start of the pandemic, providing grade-level instruction and academic rigor for all students, giving them access to technology to advance their learning, providing teachers and staff with the professional development and support they needed, while making the social–emotional well-being of students a top priority. Importantly for our work in this book, recognizing "teachers' efforts as they work to educate children through these challenging times" was also addressed (NAEd, 2020, p. 4).

Ever since the pandemic took hold in early 2020 and sent most students to continue their schooling from home, a major concern among educators, families, and policymakers was the impact of remote learning on students. A study of high school students in a large urban school district in which families were able to select either in-school or remote learning for their children found that students attending school remotely did indeed suffer socially, emotionally, and academically more than their in-school peers (Duckworth et al., 2021). The findings were consistent across gender, race, and socioeconomic subgroups. Although the researchers themselves noted several limitations of the study, its findings should be kept in mind when similar circumstances arrive in the future.

The largely touted "learning loss gap" proclaimed by politicians has been a reality not only in the United States but also throughout the world. However, these claims are often overblown, as headlines suggest they are historic, devastating, and irreversible, and that students are left critically behind. To counteract this assertion, the editors of Rethinking Schools devoted an entire issue to what they call "the learning loss trap" (The Editors of Rethinking Schools, 2023). They write,

> It is a narrative meant to distract the public and discipline teachers. Here's the recipe: 1. Establish that closing schools hurt students using a narrow measure like test scores; 2. Blame closure of schools on teacher unions rather than a deadly pandemic; 3. Demand schools and teachers help students "regain academic ground lost during the pandemic"—and fast; 4. Use post-return-to-normal test scores to argue that teachers and schools are "failing"; 5. Implement "teacher-proof" (top-down, standardized, even scripted) curriculum or, more insidiously, argue for policies that will mean an end to public schools altogether.

While it is obvious that the most vulnerable students have always borne the brunt of unresponsive bureaucracies and that the pandemic certainly added to the stresses, to blame teachers and schools in extravagant claims for the problem will not solve it. Rather, more resources need to be devoted to the most marginalized students, schools, and communities.

Student Mental Health

From the beginning of the pandemic, the crisis of student mental health has loomed large in numerous reports and research studies. Mental health challenges impacting young people have included depression and anxiety, and suicide among youth has also increased dramatically. Already occurring at unprecedented rates before the pandemic, these issues became even more critical due to the isolation suffered by students. Many pre-school-to-grade-12 educators around the country discovered that mental health challenges were worse than they had believed.

Adding to the concern, according to federal data, more than 75% of schools surveyed in spring 2022 said that although teachers and staff were concerned about depression, anxiety, and trauma among their students, only half of all schools surveyed could provide teachers with the training or other resources they needed to tackle these issues (Meckler, 2022). Many health professionals and organizations, including U.S. Surgeon General Vivek Murthy, the American Academy of Pediatrics, the American Academy of Child and Adolescent Psychiatry, and the Children's Hospital Association, warned the public in general, and schools in particular, about these problems. In 2021, the Centers for Disease Control found that almost 45% of high school students were so sad or felt so hopeless that they were unable to engage in regular activities (St. George & Strauss, 2022).

In a groundbreaking 2023 article, "America's Teenage Girls Are Not Okay" (Thompson, 2023), *The Atlantic* called the situation a national crisis; others have called it an epidemic. The extent of the crisis is evident in striking ways; for example, the share of girls who said they've contemplated suicide increased 50% in the past decade. There is no universally agreed upon cause of this predicament: Some believe it has to do with social media, others blame the pandemic, or the lack of personal connection with others. The situation is no doubt a combination of all these factors and others, making it clear that girls are especially having a hard time with social and emotional problems for which most are not receiving adequate care (Thompson, 2023).

The mental health effects of the pandemic seem to have lasted beyond the pandemic in various nations. In a post-pandemic study, a team of researchers from Iceland and the United States sought to find out more about the long-lasting effects of COVID-19 on students' mental health. The team found that elevated depressive symptoms and worsened mental well-being across girls and boys aged 13–18 years were maintained up to 2 years into the pandemic. Although alcohol intoxication initially decreased during the beginning of the pandemic, it increased again as social restrictions eased. In contrast, better mental health outcomes and less substance use were associated with higher levels of parental and social support and an average sleep duration of 8 hours or more per night. The researchers' recommendations? That population-level prevention targeting adolescent depressive symptoms be prioritized in health policy in the wake of COVID-19.

The Pandemic's Impact on the Most Vulnerable Students

Students of marginalized populations have always been the hardest hit by school policies and practices, an especially evident trend during 2020–2023, the worst years of the pandemic. District-wide, city, and national policies have had an especially chilling effect on these students. These include standardized testing and lack of early childhood education and other benefits enjoyed by more prosperous students (see, for example, Thorisdottr et al., 2023).

In a wide-ranging review of the effects of COVID-19 on center-based preschool programs for 3- and 4-year-olds, researchers Robert Hahn and W. Steven Barnett found that many low-income children of color, both in the United States and globally, were at risk for poor educational trajectories and outcomes because of a lack of preschool services (Hahn & Barnett, 2023). These outcomes include health and health-related issues, as well as cognitive development.

Because center-based preschool programs are not available to all children, access has been a major impediment for many families. Specifically, the report revealed that the families of the most vulnerable children were unable to access preschool education to advance their children's learning and development. The researchers made clear that although early childhood education is not a panacea for the future lives of these children, providing cognitive and socioemotional skills is at least a buffer that might shield them from the worst effects of poverty and disadvantage. A specific example of the benefits of center-based preschool education comes from Boston, Massachusetts (Gray-Lobe et al., 2023). It is the only randomized study of a large-scale universal preschool with long-term educational follow-up mentioned in the extensive review. Using a lottery system for admission because of a lack of funding for all interested families, the researcher was able to follow more than 4,000 students, some enrolled in preschool and others not enrolled. Unlike other preschool programs, the Boston program required all teachers to have a bachelor's degree, something that no doubt also had an impact on the findings: The researchers found that the benefits of attending preschool were associated with a 6% increase in high school graduation, an 18% increase in on-time college attendance, and a 5.5% increase in attendance of a 4-year college, while differences among racial groups were small (Gray-Lobe et al., 2023).

A major conclusion of the review of the many projects that the researchers studied is very clear: "Because resource deprivation is concentrated in low-income and minority communities, publicly funded universal ECE can also be a powerful instrument for the promotion of social equity" (Hahn & Barnett, 2023, p. 75).

THE POLITIZATION OF EDUCATION

Politics have been in the crosshairs of public education for many years, and the situation has only degraded in the past decade or so. Discord and contention have ensued, from a rapidly escalating number of book bans to the uproar over Critical Race Theory (CRT) and the rejection of the College Board's African American History Honors course, among other curriculum issues. An interrelated and ever-growing host of factors have created chaos in classrooms, schools, and communities, making these spaces more toxic and vulnerable to conflict than ever. The past several years have added to the political and social divisions that have characterized the nation for some time, resulting in a further cleavage in the national divide and an expansion of the so-called culture wars. But are these the major concerns of most families or teachers? A 2022 survey of parents, guardians, and teachers by Learning Heroes, a nonprofit education organization, found that parents' and guardians' greatest concern (68%) was with politicians who are not teachers making decisions about what their children learn, followed by concerns about their children's happiness and well-being. These, and not so-called wokeism and other culture war issues, were high on the lists of families and teachers (Learning Heroes, 2022).

Below are a few of the issues that have most created and perpetuated the politization of schooling. We begin with the ongoing legacy of the 1983 report, *A Nation at Risk*.

Privatization and the Lasting Effects of *A Nation at Risk*

Vouchers, the debate over charter schools, and whether public funds should be used for private, primarily religious schools, have raged since the 1980s, especially after the release of *A Nation at Risk*, a report produced by the National Commission on Excellence in Education (1983). An initiative created by President Reagan and propelled by right-wing interests, the report's language was meant to strike fear into the hearts of educators and citizens alike. According to the authors, the report primarily decried the decline of the United States due to its declining public education system. In turn, the report became the guiding metaphor for much of what has happened in public education since that time, including a drastic increase in standardized testing, privatization, prayer in schools, and other neoconservative ideas. An incisive commentary by James Harvey, a former member of the commission, called the report "the forty-year educational disaster that is the modern education reform movement" that he says was based on "shockingly shoddy logic" (see Strauss, 2023c). The harsh criticisms have continued to the present day: A recent analysis titled *Accountability 3.0* concludes that the outcomes of both No Child Left Behind and the Elementary and Secondary Education Act concluded that

> this key federal law has been framed as an effort to strengthen schools and close opportunity gaps, yet it has constrained state and local officials, produced a host of unintended consequences, and largely failed to realize its aims. Moreover, whatever their benefits in data transparency and attention to student subgroups, these ESEA iterations have failed to meaningfully address systematic inequalities affecting racially minoritized students, low-income students, students with disabilities, emerging bilingual students, and others.

A Nation at Risk morphed into other examples of privatization. A 2023 report from the Network of Public Education is blunt in its assessment of the corrupting influence of privatization on public education. One example focuses on the funding of so-called parent groups:

Political interests use crises to turn politics and policy their way. This has happened during the COVID pandemic as right-wing "parent" groups came out of nowhere to protest health measures such as masking and vaccine requirements in schools, then moved on to Critical Race Theory, then LGBTQ issues, book banning, and an endless stream of other ginned-up culture war issues (Cunningham, 2023, p. 3).

Cunningham, author of the report, cites an impressive number of sources to verify this claim. He explains, for instance, how neoliberal conservative education groups use parents as a "front" while, behind the scenes, real power is held by billionaire funders who support the undermining of teacher unions and public schools. Most of these organizations are tied to ultraconservative activists who spout the benefits of vouchers and other privatization schemes. These groups serve as an echo chamber for one another, appearing on all manner of conservative media outlets and, eventually, on more mainstream outlets. In the meantime, legitimate parent groups rarely get this kind of attention or exposure.

In a post reprinted in Valerie Strauss's *Washington Post* column, James Harvey, the aforementioned senior staff member of the commission, has not been timid in his harsh assessment of the report's impact, which he claims was bombastic and based on "ignorance and pride" (Strauss, 2023c). Harvey maintains that the final draft cherry-picked and misinterpreted data to fix the facts in support of its argument (Strauss, 2023c). Despite its many faults, the report has driven much of what has been defined as "education reform" for the past 40 years, indicting teachers, administrators, and teacher unions for most of the problems in the public education system. According to Harvey, the report came very close to blaming them as "enemies of the United States." And yet, the steamroller of so-called education reform was largely accepted by education policymakers and the public for many years.

And thus was born the modern standardized testing movement.

National Standardized Testing

The use of yearly standardized tests has become a ubiquitous, and largely accepted, presence in most public schools in the nation. But more recently, teachers, the general public, and even politicians have joined the chorus of critics of using tests as the be-all and end-all of educational progress.

Scholar and activist Diane Ravitch is a case in point. An early proponent of the *No Child Left Behind* legislation and school reform movement that began in the 1980s and continues today, she has become one of the fiercest critics of the accountability movement that has been largely based on standardized testing and its deleterious effects on teaching and learning. In 2013, she cofounded the advocacy group Network for Public Education to oppose the privatization of public education and high-stakes standardized testing. In a 2021 article featured in Valerie Strauss's *Washington Post* education column, Ravitch reviewed the racist history of standardized testing and subsequent national and state testing policies that have led to the widespread deterioration of public education. In a post on her own blog, Ravitch writes,

> The tests now required by federal law are worthless. The results are reported too late to matter. The reports to teachers do not tell them what students do or do not know. The tests tell students whether they did well or poorly on a test they took six months ago. They do not measure "learning loss." (Ravitch, 2021)

That is, Ravitch rebuts the claim that the annual tests are helpful to teachers, schools, and the public because they do little to provide relevant and important information about student progress. "This is wrong," she states bluntly, because the tests are a "measure, not a remedy" and thus not very helpful to either teachers or school systems. She adds, "The tests are a boon for the testing corporations. For teachers and students, they are worthless" (Ravitch, as cited in Strauss, 2021). Her conclusion is both stunningly simple and eminently doable: "American education," she writes, "will improve when the federal government does what it does best and allows highly qualified teachers and well-resourced schools to do what they do best" (Ravitch, cited in Strauss, 2021).

In a related vein, education scholars Gibbs, Pivovarova, and Berliner (2023) argue that, in many states, the reason that information obtained from standardized tests is of limited use to teachers is because data on individual students are typically not available until well after students have moved on to the next grade. These researchers maintain that states are wasting billions of dollars every year on such tests, a position vehemently opposed by the nation's largest testing companies as well as fans of testing, including many politicians on both sides of the aisle who view tests as at least providing concrete numbers to support their argument that students are not learning as much as they used to, and that teachers' skills have not kept up with the changing times. But the authors argue that the nation is spending too high a price on standardized testing not just in dollars but also in lost teaching and learning time, by using standardized tests as the major way to assess student learning (Gibbs et al., 2023). Another criticism of yearly high-stakes standardized tests comes from Jamaal Bowman, a former teacher, the founder of a highly regarded public charter school in the Bronx, and a current member of Congress. Bowman sponsored the More Teaching Less Testing Act, which would eliminate the yearly testing regime and instead offer states more flexibility in assessing student progress and, thus, more time for teaching. Endorsed by both national teacher unions, the NEA and the AFT, as well as by the NAACP and many Democrats, as of this writing the passage of the bill is uncertain (Strauss, 2023b).

The Assault on Teachers

Across the nation, teachers have been among the first to feel the politization of education. Rather than being applauded and respected for their work, teachers frequently find themselves as targets of the media and the public at large. Some are afraid to offer their students award-winning books that may violate laws because they touch on the history of racism, or that may appear to ultraconservatives, many of whom might not even have read the book, as too sexually explicit. As a result, teachers' very ability to do their job is under threat.

A recent report characterized the changing status of the teaching profession in the past 50 years, focusing on the loss of prestige and teacher satisfaction (Kraft & Lyon, 2022). In a January 26, 2023 article *Washington Post* columnist Valerie Strauss summarized some of the report's key points:

> Teachers are underpaid, grossly in some places. Teachers are under threat of legal action in some states if they discuss with students the truth about race and institutional racism in the United States. Teachers are blamed for school closures during the coronavirus pandemic, accused of being groomers by ultra right-wing politicians, expected to spend their own money on basic classroom supplies and denied the respect other professions receive. (Strauss, 2023a)

A major finding of the Kraft and Lyon report is that "the current state of the teaching profession is at or near its lowest levels in 50 years" (Kraft & Lyon, 2022). Exploring a range of issues that may help explain the downfall of the teaching profession, the authors identify and explore some of the factors that might explain these historical patterns, including education funding, teacher pay, outside opportunities, unionism, barriers to entry, working conditions, accountability, autonomy, and school shootings. Little surprise, then, that attrition in the teaching force has reached new heights: For instance, a 2023 study across eight states found that teacher attrition has increased by as much as 30% since the pandemic began (Barnum, 2023).

Despite all the dire warnings about teacher shortages—many of which are realistic and are, in fact, taking place—Jay Mathews, who writes about education for *The Washington Post*, takes a different approach. After speaking with many teachers about the low pay, little prestige, and the many sacrifices that teachers make, he concludes,

> We need a better understanding of why good, smart people choose those jobs and stick with them. I'm glad we appreciate the value of what teachers do. It might help to listen more carefully to what teachers say about their work before having anxiety attacks when our offspring say they might try it. (Mathews, 2022)

The Assault on Curriculum

The curriculum, that is, the content that is taught in schools, has also come under increased scrutiny and criticism, especially in Republican-led states. The assault has been particularly evident in topics having to do with what and how to teach American history, especially if it highlights the most egregious and unpleasant aspects of our history such as slavery, racism, and the sometimes violent treatment of ethnic and racial populations that put the nation in a negative light. Even the mention of LGBTQ communities, whether in history books, novels, or poetry books, has become enormously contentious.

One of the most controversial issues became a lightning rod for conservative groups. Critical Race Theory, or CRT, refers to a set of ideas that address the systemic nature of racism in American history and life. Until recently, it had been an academic subject largely confined to higher education settings, but it became one of the most polemical issues in education from fiery talk shows to winning strategies in political campaigns. As of the end of the 2021–2022 school year, 16 states had banned the discussion of CRT in schools. Tennessee was one of those states.

This phenomenon was scrutinized by four researchers and teacher educators. In a 2022 article by Laura Beth Kelly, Laura Taylor, Cara Djonko-Moore, and Alixa Marchan, the authors review the impact of the issue on schools, teachers, and politics. According to the article, "Such laws, many have argued, are intentionally designed to prevent K–12 teachers and students from engaging in critical conversations about race, gender, and oppression" (Kelly et al., 2022). The authors, researchers, and teacher educators in Memphis, wanted to find out how teachers interpreted what many considered the vague language in the legislation. In their study, they engaged with 31 practicing and prospective teachers in focus group conversations about the legislation that had recently been passed in the state. They maintain that, ironically, the ban is in reality a perfect illustration of the racist policy structure that the theory explains. Their research found that the law has had a significant negative impact on classrooms and what teachers believe they can address, and what they should avoid. Yet, in many cases, the teachers' perceptions went beyond what was stipulated in the legislation. In one of many examples, a kindergarten teacher was even afraid of teaching her students the Rosa Parks story, a topic that has been one of the few relating to racism to pass muster in many school curricula for the past several decades. But, as she mused, how can she teach about Rosa Parks without discussing racism?

Book Bans

Closely related to curriculum challenges are widespread complaints about books, both in schools and public libraries. Book banning has a long history in the United States. In fact, the practice goes back to 1637 in Quincy, Massachusetts, when Thomas Morton's *New English Canaan* was banned for its supposedly harsh and heretical critique of Puritanism (Book Banning in the United States and Beyond, n.d.) Thus, it can be said that book banning, as we have seen it from Puritan times to the present, is "as American as apple pie." But the practice has grown exponentially in the past several years, particularly concerning books related to LGBTQ and racial and ethnic topics. In what it calls "an alarming trend," a 2022 report from PEN America found that 1,586 books were banned in the United States (PEN America, 2022). Banning books in public schools and school libraries has climbed to unprecedented levels as all kinds of books—fiction, nonfiction, and poetry—have received the sledgehammer of censorship. In addition, some state legislatures have already, or plan to, enact laws to censor teachers, librarians, and others who dare challenge these bans. The state of Florida's law SB 775 (commonly called the "Don't Say Gay" law that criminalizes explicit sexual material) has taken this culture war to new and often ridiculous levels: According to a blog by Christine Sleeter and Francesca Lopez, under the statute, "providing such material to students in class is a misdemeanor, punishable by up to one year in jail and a $2000 fine" (Sleeter & López, 2022).

Similar bans have taken place in other school districts, cities, and states. Such challenges did not originate from a large number of people, as one might suspect: Instead, individuals who filed more than 10 complaints were *responsible for two-thirds of all the challenges*. Moreover, one analysis of book challenges from across the country found that the majority were filed *by just 11 people* (Natanson, 2023). Books concerning race and racism were included in the bans, but most have focused on the right's newest boogeymen, LGBTQ content, storylines, and characters. In terms of their reasons for wanting to ban LGBTQ books from libraries and schools, those responsible cited several reasons, ranging from their fear of exposing children to sexual content, to the idea that the books might give children the idea that they too might be gay, to the belief that children could be "groomed" by such books.

As a result of the many attacks on books and curricula, teacher organizations have begun to hit back. The question of whose story is told has been in dispute since the founding of the republic, but the issue is neither new nor limited to the United States. However, in our nation, given the strength of teacher professional organizations, several of them have started to respond. For example, a coalition of organizations representing teachers of various subject matters and grades warned Republican-led states to end restrictions on what teachers can teach in the wake of laws that limit the curriculum, particularly as related to race, gender, and other contentious issues. The statement below, used with permission from the collaborating organizations, demands that teachers be allowed to do their jobs. In the interest of making this unprecedented statement more widely available, we share it in its entirety here.

Freedom to Teach Statement

School districts, the most active battlefield in the American culture wars today, are facing an unprecedented number of calls to remove books from schools and libraries; false claims about "obscenity" invading classrooms; the elimination of teaching about evolution and climate change; challenges to the need for making sense of and critiquing our world in mathematics classrooms; and legislation redlining teaching about racism in American history. These actions are putting excessive and undue pressure on teachers, who are caught in the crossfire of larger political conflict, motivated by cultural shifts and stoked for political gain.

Teachers are being maligned as "harming" children and are subjected to constant scrutiny (and even direct surveillance) by many parents, school administrators, and activist groups. Some are afraid to offer their students award-winning books that may violate vaguely stated laws about teaching the history of racism or that may be misleadingly labeled as pornographic. As a result, teachers' very ability to do their job is under threat.

In their zeal, activists of the current culture wars unfortunately treat teachers as if they are enemies. The truth is that teachers are uniquely important leaders who, in educating current and new generations of students, bear responsibility for this country's future. They are trained professionals with one of the hardest and most demanding jobs, a job that requires deep commitment, but brings little financial reward.

Teachers need our support; they need our trust; they need to have the freedom to exercise their professional judgment. And that freedom includes the freedom to decide what materials best suit their students in meeting the demands of the curriculum, the freedom to discuss disturbing parts of American history if and when they judge students are ready for it, and the freedom to determine how to help young people navigate the psychological and social challenges of growing up. In short, teachers need the freedom to prepare students to become future members of a democratic society who can engage in making responsible and informed contributions and decisions about our world.

The stakes are too high. We cannot let good teachers leave the field because they no longer have the freedom to do their jobs. We cannot let the education of our children and young adults become collateral damage in partisan political machinations.

Authored by the following professional organizations for teachers: National Council for the Social Studies, National Council of Teachers of Mathematics, National Council of Teachers of English, National Science Teaching Association, and the National Coalition Against Censorship.

CONCLUDING THOUGHTS

This chapter has just scratched the surface of the multiple factors defining the sociopolitical context of public education today. Nevertheless, we have attempted to provide ample evidence that the pandemic with its many consequences, a stark and worsening economic and social inequality, the racial reckoning that continues unabated, and a relentlessly divided civic polity are among the issues that have made education an incredibly difficult terrain for students, teachers, and schools to navigate. Although in this book we focus primarily on teachers, we are equally cognizant of the impact of these forces on everyone else who cares about education and the future of young people.

In the sections that follow, we focus our attention on 18 educators who have faced these struggles valiantly. Their essays document their vision of truthful, socially just classrooms, schools, and communities to make education more consequential for the young people with whom they interact, and for the profession of teaching. Though small in number, their aspirations for education, and their practices, whether in classrooms or out-of-school settings, reflect the lives of many other educators who remain hopeful despite it all.

REFERENCES

Barnum, M. (2023, March 6). *Teacher turnover hits new highs across the U.S.* Chalkbeat. https://www.chalkbeat.org/2023/3/6/23624340/teacher-turnover-leaving-the-profession-quitting-higher-rate/

Book banning in the United States and beyond. (n. d.). Harvard University, Gutman Library. https://guides.library.harvard.edu/c.php?g=1269000&p=9306840.

Cunningham, M. T. (2023, February). *Merchants of deception: Parent props and their funders* [Report]. Network for Public Education.

Duckworth, A. L., Kautz, A. D., Satlof-Bedrick, E., Talamas, S., Lira, B., & Steinberg, L. (2021). Students attending school remotely suffer socially, emotionally, and academically. *Educational Researcher, 50*(7), 479–482.

The Editors of Rethinking Schools (2023). The "learning loss" trap [Editorial]. *Rethinking Schools.* https://rethinkingschools.org/articles/the-learning-loss-trap/

Educational accountability 3.0: Beyond ESSA [Joint report]. (2023). Beyond Test Scores Project and National Education Policy Center.

Gibbs, N. P., Pivovarova, M., & Berliner, D. C. (2023). Same tests, same results: Multi-year correlations of ESSA-mandated standardized tests in Texas and Nebraska. *Education Policy Analysis Archives, 31*(10). https://doi.org/10.14507/epaa.31.7696

Gray-Lobe, G., Pathak, P. A., & Walters, C. R. (2023). The long-term effects of universal preschool in Boston. *The Quarterly Journal of Economics, 138*(1), 363–411. https://doi.org/10.1093/qje/qjac036

Hahn, R. A., & Barnett, W. S. (2023). Early childhood education: Health, equity, and economics. *Annual Review of Public Health, 44*, 75–92 https://doi.org/10.1146/annurev-publhealth-071321-032337

Kelly, L. B., Taylor, L., Djonko-Moore, C., & Marchand, A. D. (2022). The chilling effects of so-called critical race theory bans. *Rethinking Schools, 37*(2). https://rethinkingschools.org/articles/the-chilling-effects-of-so-called-critical-race-theory-bans/

Kraft, M. A., & Lyon, M. A. (2022). *The rise and fall of the teaching profession: Prestige, interest, preparation, and satisfaction over the last half century.* (EdWorkingPaper: 22-679). Annenberg Institute at Brown University. https://doi.org/10.26300/7b1a-vk92

Learning Heroes. (2022). *Hidden in plain sight: A way forward for equity-centered family engagement (Parents 2022).* https://bealearninghero.org/2022/06/23/parents-2022-i-hidden-in-plain-sight-a-way-forward-for-equity-centered-family-engagement/

Mathews, J. (2022, September 6). Analysis: Despite what you've heard, plenty of teachers still love what they do. *The Washington Post.* https://www.washingtonpost.com/education/2022/09/04/teacher-shorage-great-resignation-quitting/

Meckler, L. (2022, May 31). Schools are struggling to meet rising mental health needs, data shows. *The Washington Post.* https://www.washingtonpost.com/education/2022/05/31/schools-mental-health-covid-students/

Natanson, H. (2023, May 23). Objection to sexual, LGBTQ content propels spike in book challenges. *The Washington Post.* https://www.google.com/search

?client=firefox-b-1-d&q=Objection+to+sexual%2C+LGBTQ+content+propels +spike+in+book+challenges

National Academy of Education. (2020). *COVID-19 educational inequities round-table series summary report.* https://naeducation.org/covid-19-educational-inequi ties-roundtable-series-summary-report/

National Commission on Excellence in Education. (1983). *A nation at risk: The imperative for educational reform.*

PEN America. (2022). *Banned in the USA: Rising school book bans threaten free expression and students' first amendment rights (April 2022).* https://pen.org /banned-in-the-usa/

Pew Research Center (2020, January). *Most Americans say there is too much eco-nomic inequality in the U.S., but fewer than half call at a top priority* [Report]. https://www.pewresearch.org/social-trends/2020/01/09/most-americans-say -there-is-too-much-economic-inequality-in-the-u-s-but-fewer-than-half-call-it-a -top-priority/

Ravitch, D. (2021, February 4). What you need to know about standardized testing. *Diane Ravitch's blog.* https://dianeravitch.net/2021/02/04/what-you-need-to -know-about-standardized-testing/

Sleeter, C., & López, F. (2022, December 5). Confronting book bans. https://www .tcpress.com/blog/confronting-book-bans/

St. George, D., & Strauss, V. (2022, December 5). The crisis of student mental health is much vaster than we realize. *The Washington Post.* https://www.washington post.com/education/2022/12/05/crisis-student-mental-health-is-much-vaster -than-we-realize/

Strauss, V. (2021, February 1). What you need to know about standardized testing. *The Washington Post.* https://www.washingtonpost.com/education/2021/02/01 /need-to-know-about-standardized-testing/

Strauss, V. (2023a, January 26).The basic rights teachers don't have. *The Washing-ton Post.* https://www.washingtonpost.com/education/2023/01/26/basic-rights -teachers-dont-have/

Strauss, V. (2023b, March 23). This educator turned lawmaker wants to end misuse of standardized testing [Analysis]. *The Washington Post.* https://www.washing tonpost.com/education/2023/03/23/a-bid-to-end-standardized-testing

Strauss, V. (2023c, April 26). Gaslighting Americans about public schools: The truth about "A Nation at Risk" [Perspective]. *The Washington Post.* https://www .washingtonpost.com/education/2023/04/26/how-nationatrisk-report-hurt -public-schools/

Thompson, D. (2023, February 16). America's teenage girls are not okay: Rising teen anxiety is a national crisis. *The Atlantic. https://www.theatlantic.com /newsletters/archive/2023/02/the-tragic-mystery-of-teenage-anxiety/673076/ ?utm_source=apple_news*

Thorisdottir, I. E., Agustsson, G., Oskarsdottir, S. Y., Kristjansson, A. L., Asgeirsdottir, B. B., Sigfusdottir, I. D., Valdimarsdottir, H. B., Allegrante, J. P., & Halldorsdottir, T. (2023). Effect of the COVID-19 pandemic on adolescent mental health and substance use up to March 2022 in Iceland: A repeated cross-sectional, population-based study. *The Lancet, 7*(5), 347–357. https://doi.org/10.1016/ S2352-4642(23)00022-6

IDENTITY, FAMILY, AND COMMUNITY

Identity, family, and community are the foundation of what educators do every day. Whether it is establishing a community in the classroom, or being a part of a school, or sharing insights about our neighborhood community and learning about our students' families, backgrounds, passions, and goals, it is all essential to building relationships at school. And identity and family are inextricably tied into the idea of community.

Alicia and Sonia both established communities in their classrooms where student identities were highlighted, and where families, biological or chosen, were welcome. Alicia's first step in creating community in her classroom was to write an introduction letter to her students. Key aspects of the letter were: sharing that she is multilingual and has family in different countries; naming her family members; talking about her favorite kinds of music, hobbies, and books; pasting a photo of her large family in the classroom with people of every age and many colors; and telling her students that she loves teaching. Each of these parts of the letter are placed with intention. For example, sharing about her languages and cultural background prompts students to do the same. Pasting a photo of her family is her way of indicating to her students that all colors in her family, and therefore theirs, are accepted and celebrated. Talking about her favorite foods, such as mofongo and arroz con gandules, sparks recognition among her Puerto Rican students. The first assignment she gives students is for them to answer her letter. While building community, with this activity she hopes to begin creating a safe space for her students to share about themselves and to feel welcome and seen.

As a professor, Sonia did a similar activity with her students. On the first day of class, she asked them about their names, using questions prompting them to reflect on the origin of their name (first, middle, or last), what it meant, who named them and any special traditions surrounding naming babies in their culture. Names bring both positive and negative memories to all of us, so this affirming way to begin class is another example of how educators can begin to create community in a positive and nurturing way. By participating in these activities as educators, and being somewhat vulnerable, we can open pathways for our students to get to know us as well.

In this section, we read powerful accounts of other ways educators can engage with students in a culturally affirming manner. Sonie Felix, an educator of Haitian origin, begins with a personal story that gives us a glance into her background and upbringing and sets the stage for her essay. Through her accounts, she shares her views on the importance of friendship and culture, and the influence her background has had on her role as an educator. The title of her essay (You Lead Who You Are), reaffirms that we cannot separate who we are from how we do what we do as educators. As the principal of the Community Academy Alternative High School in Boston, Massachusetts, she had to lead the school through the challenging COVID-19 pandemic. She found that the educators in her school were frustrated and stressed to the point of near burn-out. Firmly believing that she must listen to understand rather than listen to hear, she asked her staff to participate in a writing activity that basically allowed them to vent, telling her their difficulties, but also their successes. Having a safe space in which to express their feelings and frustrations while supporting them by sharing her own challenges with them helped rebuild a sense of trust and community. She likens this space to the "huddles" community members would have in Haiti, which in her mind were similar to circle practices. Opening up so her staff did the same—being honest and vulnerable, sharing stories and inviting them to write—was a compelling way to connect and to unload stress and anxieties about teaching during the pandemic. Sonie then followed up with a similar activity with some students, where they engaged in writing poetry about their experiences during the pandemic.

Nadla Tavares Smith also begins her essay with an anecdote, a memory of her mother ironing school uniforms late at night, and then of hearing clanging pots and pans in the early morning hours at her childhood home in Brazil. Reflecting on the memory now, she realizes that her mother was working incredibly hard as a single mom who had not had many opportunities herself to help her children reach their potential through education. Her recognition that her mother's hard work propelled Nadla into her career as a teacher show her pride in her mother's efforts. Living in Brazil, Nadla always identified as Black, but when she immigrated to this country, her identity was put into question, as often happens for many Afro-Latine* people when they arrive in the United States. While teaching her students about their own identities through children's literature, she eventually began to embrace her newer identity as an Afro-Latina. As she helped students learn about the less obvious parts of heritage through lessons, they all learned a great deal about the students' countries and families. Nadla found that she had tremendous empathy for them because of their shared experiences. While Nadla teaches her students to embrace their culture and background, she also emphasizes that educators and administrators must recognize and respect cultural differences. For example, educators must understand that some families cannot participate in school in the traditional White, middle-class ways of engaging, such as joining the PTO, and yet this does not mean they are not involved in their child's education. Nadla's lessons about teaching are powerful reminders to all educators about embracing identity and diversity at the same time.

Chapter 4 brings us Cabo Verdean scholars and educators living in a Cabo Verdean community in Boston, where the authors discuss their trajectory in founding the Cabo Verdean Center for Applied Research (CVCAR). Cabo Verde (also known as Cape Verde) is an archipelago of ten islands in the Atlantic Ocean, west of Senegal. Cabo Verdeans have a long history of immigration to the United States, particularly in eastern and southeastern Massachusetts. In Cabo Verde, Portuguese is the language of government and schools (the "official language") while the everyday language people use is known as *Kriolu*. Prompted by the passage of the Look Act in Massachusetts in 2017, community activists recognized that there was a dearth of information and resources about Cabo Verde among the people of the Cabo Verdean community. The Look Act, signed into law by Governor Baker in 2017, was designed to replace the previous more restrictive law mandating English immersion programs. The goal of the newer law is to provide districts with more flexibility as to the language acquisition programs—including ESL, Sheltered Immersion, or Bilingual Education—they choose to meet the needs of English learners while maintaining accountability for timely and effective English language acquisition.

The CVCAR group banded together to design a curriculum for high school students of Cabo Verdean heritage. Called the Cabo Verdean Heritage Language and Culture Curriculum, it is comprised of three modules: Module 1 teaches the Cabo Verdean alphabet and the history of the language; Module 2 delves into identity as a general concept and then as applied to Cabo Verdean culture; Module 3 explores Cabo Verdean immigration and looks at American citizenship. The authors found that several of the challenges they faced in teaching the curriculum were related to Cabo Verde's colonial history and the depreciation of the Cabo Verdean language; at times they even found it difficult to convince other Cabo Verdeans of the validity of teaching a language that was once unofficial and unwritten. However, they persisted, making tweaks to the curriculum as needed. Although they rolled it out during the pandemic and classes were online, they found successes and learned valuable lessons, one of them being the importance of engaging with the community when writing curriculum about that community.

As you read the essays in this section, we encourage you to ponder how you embrace and highlight identity, family, and community.

NOTE

*According to Hispanic Executive (Méndez, 2023), "Latine is used when referring to a group of people of multiple genders or for someone identifying as nonbinary, gender fluid, genderqueer, bigender, agender, and gender nonconforming. Latine is what's commonly used among Spanish speakers as it's more easily pronounced than Latinx and can be used in plural forms."

REFERENCE

Méndez, L. (2023, June 5). *A brief explainer on Latine and Latinx*. Hispanic Executive. https://hispanicexecutive.com/latinx-latine-explainer/

CHAPTER 2

You Lead Who You Are

Sonie Felix

My leadership journey into education began as a young girl growing up in Côtes-de-Fer, Haiti.

IN THE BEGINNING: IDENTITY AND VISION FORMING

Growing up in the countryside helped to set the foundation for my leadership development. Côtes-de-Fer is a beautiful mountainous terrain located on the tropical island of Haiti. The sun rays from back home are like no other; *soleil lakay* is love, innocence, and the beginning of my journey into leadership. I remember waking up on Saturday mornings and tending to my daily chores of prepping the kitchen for breakfast and making sure that all of Mama's provisions were ready before I would dash off, like a flash of lightning, to Nani's house. We would have the entire day to ourselves to dream, to escape our current reality, to be whatever we wanted to be in the world.

Nani and I pretty much grew up together. We were both born in July and went to the same school in the village. Our walks to and from school were everything to me! I was always amazed at how well-put-together Nani was. She wore her navy blue uniform with a white shirt detailed with lace on the collar. Two ponytails adorned her head with crisp white ribbons tied into perfect bows. But it was her eyes that intrigued me. Her big brown eyes would hypnotize me to do anything that she wanted. One day while walking home from school, Nani dared me to enter Madame Moise's yard. We were both warned to never, ever enter her property and if she was on one side of the road, we would have to cross to the other side to avoid her. Everyone stayed away from Madame Moise's. She was known to do bad things to little kids, and if they entered her property they might not ever return to their families.

That day I felt courageous, and because I was getting into mischief all the time, I had nothing to lose. Nani gazed into my eyes and whispered, "I dare you to enter the yard and grab that bowl and bring it back to me."

I was not going to back down from Nani's challenge. After all, I was a full year older than her, and Mama and the church ladies, hoping to help me change my ways, prayed over me every Sunday. Besides, I had to show Nani that I had courage and that I didn't allow fear to consume me. Needless to say, I took on the challenge and ended up face-to-face with Madame Moise. As I tip-toed into the chaotic yard filled with tin cans, buckets, and old rubbish I noticed Madame Moise standing erect on the porch, wearing a look of anger and malice. Her piercing eyes met mine and I stood there frozen, not knowing what to say or do. Each time I tried to muster up the courage to say *bonjour*, fear overtook me.

Madame Moise slowly walked down the porch stairs and each time she took a step toward me, I took a step back. All of a sudden, she lunged toward me and grabbed me by the arms. I yelled out a loud shriek and out came Nani out of nowhere.

"Let her go!" she yelled. Nani grabbed a rock from the ground and threw it at Madame Moise with all her might. In an attempt to dodge the flying rock, Madame Moise released me from her grasp and I ran out of the yard as fast as I could and onto the main road toward home. After a full five minutes of sprinting, we finally made it to the village, and Nani and I went to our favorite spot under the mango tree to recap our great escape from Madame Moise and conjure up a story to tell our parents.

That day I realized that not only was Nani my neighbor, she was my best friend in the whole wide world. She knew me inside and out, and there wasn't a secret that I could hold inside without telling her. Saturdays were our days. We would have the entire afternoon to ourselves sitting under the mango tree and dreaming of all the possibilities in the world, such as, What if we moved to the United States? We would imagine all of the possibilities that we would have if we escaped our impoverished island. What would we do, who would we become? I admired Nani's courage to stand strong in the face of fear and her relentless drive to want and do better for the village and her people. When I gazed into her eyes all I could see were promising possibilities for the future. Her mischievous ways were simply a bonus.

As I reflect on moments that left imprints on my life and in my work, I always find myself going back to Haiti, back to my childhood days, back to the lessons that my mother and the church ladies instilled in me. We knew we were poor people monetary-wise, but we were rich in our traditions and values. I remember vividly the nights when we would huddle by the fire behind the hut and the elders would tell us stories of the past. There was always a message for us to ponder and discuss. Messages of hope, communal work, and genuine love for the betterment of people. You see, when a neighbor didn't have, it was the responsibility of the village to come together and lend a helping hand by sharing coffee and sugar, or by praying together; and if a family had loved ones in the United States, then we would reach out for support when all else failed. These traditions are a way of life in the village; the acts are not done for glory or esteem. It is just a way of life.

OUR CURRENT REALITY: COURAGE IN THE MIDST OF COVID-19

Fast-forward to the year 2021. I am now the principal of Community Academy Alternative High School in Boston, Massachusetts, in the midst of a global pandemic. And while I am committed to the work of educating young people well, I often wonder how I can use the lessons and the traditions from my village to navigate and inspire students and staff to see the possibilities in the midst of all of this darkness and to exercise courage in the midst of fear as we navigate this tough terrain. I firmly believe that you lead who you are. The idea that your core beliefs are influenced by who you are, where you are from, and the struggles that you have encountered helps me to define and sometimes redefine my purpose in this work.

Using Restorative Justice Circles With Adults

Lately, I find myself creating structured spaces through restorative justice (RJ) circles for the adults in my school to engage in the discourse similar to the huddles we used to use in Haiti. This practice has allowed for communal work and the promotion of oral literacy/traditions. I thought to myself, if we are to become a "Restorative Justice School" in the truest sense, then the adults must practice what we preach and engage in these practices as well, especially during the pandemic. As many of our students and families struggled with the effects of the pandemic on their schooling and home life, so did the adults (including me).

Many of the adults at the school were experiencing loss at a rapid pace, and also levels of anxiety due to the pandemic were at an all-time high. Staff meetings via Zoom were becoming a space for unproductive work, and sometimes the professionalism flew right off the screen. This caused me to think deeply about the needs of the adults: I mean, if we weren't okay, how could we give our best to our respective communities and to our students? In addition to the services that the Boston Public Schools district provided, the leadership team and I made the conscious decision to create and structure safe spaces for the adults to address challenges in teaching and learning brought on by the pandemic and to gather to celebrate small wins and successes. The Leadership Team unanimously voted to incorporate circle processes for the adults (including families) as a structure and a practice to gain understanding and to support our work of creating a caring climate for all. Now, I have to say that I am no expert in using RJ circles, but I am on the journey of learning how to use these practices to address harm and also celebrate successes as a school community. But what I have learned is that the rituals and routines involved in the RJ circles mirror my experiences in Haiti as a child living in the village. As I continue to grow in my understanding of how to utilize the RJ circle processes, I am learning that they are not only being used in schools to help create positive classroom climate, but they are also being used in neighborhoods and detention centers as part of the peacemaking process and a way of restoring health and productive relationships. Based on *The Little Book of Restorative Justice* (Zehr, 2002), the restorative movement has been around for a long time, with a main goal of helping victims and communities heal, but the RJ circles originated with Indigenous people as a process for addressing community issues and as a response to violence and harm.

Leading in the pandemic allows for opportunities to reassess the human condition and the state of well-being of our most vulnerable and marginalized students.

The pandemic has made it crystal clear that in America the rich continue to get richer and the poor continue to suffer from injustice, biased curricula, and policies that have put our students at a disadvantage instead of creating possibilities that are equitable and specifically catered to meet their needs. These inequities affect our most marginalized students directly and indirectly, and yet we expect them to thrive and continue as if they are not living these realities. These issues cannot be overlooked any longer in light of the national conversation about a racial reckoning and anti-racist education.

There is more than "learning loss" to worry about during these times. Many of our Brown and Black students and their families are truly hurting, so it was important for my school team to first acknowledge the crisis and then to pivot our thinking and our way of being to understand what is going on in the community. It was important for the team to engage in deeper conversations with the community to learn about their needs and resources (or lack thereof) before developing an action plan to help keep our students safe and healthy during these challenging times. I had to dig deep and reflect on my leadership work at the school to assess if what we were doing aligned with the needs of our students. I had to not only lead with a purpose, but with love and return to Maslow's hierarchy of needs, a framework used in psychology based on a 5-tier model of human needs (see McLeod, 2007).

This mind shift had to also be applicable to the adult staff. What was their frame of mind concerning all that has happened? Were they okay, and what are their needs? Are they able to reimagine teaching and learning at our school during the pandemic? In the world of politics, it is easy to get side-tracked by the noise and lose sight of the goal. I had to prioritize the basic human needs of my school community (Tier 1 of Maslow's Hierarchy of Needs) in order to not only survive the pandemic but thrive throughout the experience. I believe that it is the responsibility of schools to support students and families in eradicating the inequalities not only in our schools but also in communities at large.

If you listen to understand instead of listening to simply hear, then you will have begun the process of getting at the core of the matter. I took this idea and ran with it and started my listening tour at school. I met one-to-one with teachers and staff members, simply listening to them share their hopes, fears, points of pride and the areas they needed support with. I then created a Google Doc where we committed to reflect in writing and capture our thoughts. I wanted to understand what the adults in my school were thinking and doing during the pandemic. Little did I know that the document would reach other educators outside of my school community.

Below are some sample thoughts and ideas captured from the adult perspective of COVID-19.

COVID-19 Files, September 2021

Sonie: It's impossible to capture the wave of emotions circulating through me at this time of uncertainty. This is my attempt to capture what is real and what this pandemic has revealed to be true. All the facade, gone! All the bullshit, gone! Thinking about how to be in tune with my creative urge to blow this shit up into something special to capture all the human stories that have ended without true endings or lives that have awakened! To all I have hurt, I'm sorry! To all whom I've hurt, please accept my apologies. I still choose to wrap my arms around you virtually and embrace the human experience beyond Zoom meetings and such. So, to this end, let poetry reign . . .

Donna: I sit here crying as I tell this story. I received a call from one of my student's parents. The call started with her seeking support during this time of her family's homelessness. I helped her with what I could. Then she asked me if I could confide in you, Ms. Lashus. I said, sure. She said, "My son has not been sleeping through the night since this whole pandemic has started. He cries often and is unable to express himself to others. I worry about him and I'm not sure how to help him. I wanted to say when I mentioned your name and said I was going to call you, his face lit up. It was the first time in a long while that I had seen that smile."

I said, "I will call him or have a Zoom meeting with him so we can talk." We tried both but he refused to come to the phone or get on the computer. He said, "I want to see Ms. Lashus like I do at school." She asked me, "Is there any way he can personally see you, I think it will help." I said, "Yes, if you come by my house. I will stay on the porch and he can be on the sidewalk and we can talk from there. Let's see if that works."

The next day they came. I was waiting on the porch. I was so excited to see him and he was excited to see me. We gave air hugs and laughed together as we would when we were in school. He said to me, "I remember when I first came to the school you greeted me with a smile and a hug. You told me everything was going to be all right now that I was at Taylor and I was one of yours. I have been so sad since we left school because I haven't been able to see you and things have not been right. I need to know you are ok. If you're ok, I'm ok because you are mine too, Ms. Lashus."

My heart broke because I was not able to go down those stairs and wrap my arms around his tiny little body. We talked some more and made a plan to call in one week and see each other the following week the same way. We said our goodbyes and I watched him walk down the street with his mom. The next morning the mom called me to tell me he slept through the night and he had already started his schoolwork on Zoom today. She said, "Thank you for all that you do. It really makes a difference to our little ones. Thank you, Sonie, for letting me be able to record this somewhere; it was too precious to just stay in my heart."

Sonie: My mother called me today all the way from Côtes-de-Fer, Haiti, and shared her news of joy. She received the small offering I was able to share with her. She was able to have Easter joy at her church and provide coffee. As small as it was to her and the village, it was huge for me here in the U.S. where I was suddenly able to shake out of my funk and self-pity! I'm blasting Kompa music for the rest of the day!

Lisa: Hello Sonie. Thank you for the invite. I believe "what is meant to be will be." As the protector of my family I never thought we would be going through something so devastating. It's silent, deadly and unpredictable. As a mother, I always worry about my children from the oldest to the youngest. I try not to show fear but this is my reality right now. So I try to inform them concerning what information is out there about this pandemic. They say you are your child's first teacher. During this time I give props to the educators out here because I'm trying to be Mom, Teacher, Homemaker, Lunch Lady, Doctor, Hairdresser, Pharmacist, Therapist and everything in between. I'm tired and my office is starting to look like a 1st grade classroom. Much love though because EDUCATION will continue!!!! My family has been blessed and I will pray that we continue to be. I would like to say, "Everyone please stay safe and healthy and we will all get through this as long as we continue to support and encourage one another. Blessing from My Family to Yours."

Linda: Thank you for the invitation to write. I feel fortunate to know you. Perhaps what I've learned from this pandemic is that, although we all like to plan, we cannot always plan or know what's in store for us . . . But what we *can* control is our ability to reach out to others and express our love and virtual connections and gratitude. That's what I've been mindful of . . . who are the people I haven't been in touch with, and can I connect now?

Jean: I would like to thank Sonie for this invitation. This is a good initiative during a rather difficult period. The world is currently experiencing a rather painful pandemic (COVID-19). This is a dangerous virus because the coronavirus kills so many people around the world, despite the great scientific research. At this point, we have to be careful in order to fight the virus. I wish all people and their families would stay strong during this dangerous moment. It's better to follow the hygienic rules to avoid any problem.

Sonie: The days transition swiftly into nights and the nights into weeks. It's hard to believe that a month has passed and with no end in sight to this pandemic. I worry for my family and friends and I worry about my students. I haven't been feeling well lately but I take each day on as a blessing to learn something new about myself and about life. I've been avoiding writing and capturing my thoughts on paper, but I find solace and peace in letting the words pour onto the screen. I am definitely taking a new perspective on life.

Finally feeling better with a new focus and purpose. I want to first cut this hair off and do more for my loved ones and for those less fortunate. I'm thankful for my blessings and for the opportunity to even write this essay! I have been ill physically and have questioned all of my moves and intentions in the past decade. What has been constant for me is my spirituality and my love for true family and friends. I've come to realize that not everyone is on the same path or journey that I am on and that's okay. I value the importance of knowing that I have the power to make a difference in my own, small and unique way and that's all that needs to happen. It's best to work within your sphere of influence.

Tracy: "Fear Not." Over the past few weeks I have meditated on these two simple, yet profound words. They appear in the Bible quite frequently and for me represent God's desire for us to trust him. Fear can be a powerful force. After all, we can look at many of society's ills and recognize that fear is at the base of each. For example, at the base of racism is fear of losing power and privilege, or of just not being good enough. At the base of greed is the fear of not having enough resources. Fear causes both actions and inactions that can be debilitating. How many times have we let fear rule in our lives? At no point has fear ever brought anything of value into my life. During this time of uncertainty, I have decided to "fear not!" I have simply decided to trust God! I have used this time to recognize and thank him for his many blessings. I have food, shelter, family, friends, and the ability to continue doing his work through connections with my students. As I look back over my life, I can see how trusting him has always resulted in an outcome that has brought some level of joy, even in the midst of sorrow. COVID-19 will do what it will, but I will trust God as I embrace its challenges. I will learn new things and seek to polish the old. Thank you for the opportunity to share my thoughts, Sonie! Blessings!!!

Sonie: Tracy, thank you for sharing your thoughts. My faith is also getting me through this time of darkness.

Wow, I am in the process of flipping through my phone and listening to Phil Collins's "In the Air Tonight" and it amazes me of all the memories I have captured on my phone. Memories of happy moments; moments of hurt and growth; moments that may have been lost in the midst of living. I am now learning how to live and celebrate in my space of being known as a "weirdo." I smile at the thought of knowing how to slow time down and capturing moments that have shaped my life. I want to encourage each of you to think and reflect on how you have captured significant moments in your life, whether through writing, pictures or mementos. Reflect and grow!

Starting my first Zoom fitness for the kids on 4/30 @ 5pm. I wanted to try and get the little ones moving too. I hope it goes well. I miss seeing their little faces and bright smiles. I really want them to teach me how to TikTok.

What About the Children? Youth Voices and Advocacy

Leading through a pandemic can also take its toll on the work of leading a school. I found myself more tired than ever before, even questioning the line of work that we're in. I often worried about the mental state of our students and the school community and I leaned heavily on Social Emotional Learning strategies and our schoolwide counselors for support in providing a space to check in with students and staff. But were we actually elevating our student voices or were we silencing them through procedures and policy? Everything relating to school seemed to be a paradox. The same system in which we are working to become change agents is the one we must dismantle. I found myself questioning everything about the work and spending more time with the students to simply listen to their experiences and learn about the courageous work they were doing outside of school. I often thought about the educational experiences that we were creating for the students and adults at the school. Are we set up to fail our communities of color? I had to reassess my priorities and find ways to bring joy to the work and to capture courage during COVID-19. I asked several students to capture their thoughts on COVID-19 and courage using the following prompts:

1. What were some of the biggest challenges I faced this year?
2. What strengths did I show in addressing those challenges?
3. Who or what helped me address those challenges?
4. What opportunities did those challenges create?

5. What did I learn about:
   - my family, and past experiences?
   - my school community?
   - my local community?
   - myself?
     » How did I take care of and nurture myself this past year?
     » What would I say to my beginning-of-the-year self if I could go back in time? "If I knew then what I know now . . ."

Below are sample student writings written during COVID-19.

"Racism 2023!"

Living in a tornado of hate,
where all of the . . . isms rear its' ugly head!
Bullets flying through the streets . . .

Fighting a war that I know nothing of.

By Kobe Watson (Class of 2024)

It came in like a wave of darkness washing over the world. Separating families and friends and welcoming death wherever and whenever possible. Masks became the new "must-have" accessory and hand sanitizer flew off the shelves. Isolation became a close friend, reminding us of the human condition and the need to reconnect with others. In the midst of this darkness, courage lives. It peeks out in crevices when no one is looking and allows a glimpse of light to shine; to let us know that there is hope.—Jenny

The pandemic was a difficult time for me because I had to adjust to things I wasn't used to. I used to be able to go to the park, movie theaters, gyms, or restaurants but a lot of those places were shut down due to the pandemic. Waiting for the phases to finish was depressing because you would think things would be better but we would be in each phase for at least a month or 2.—Jenny

Schoolwork online was something I had to adapt to since it was my first time taking classes online. At first, it was awkward but after a week or so I was able to feel comfortable.—Jean

A challenge I was facing the most was not being able to play basketball. When the pandemic first started I would see at least 1 or 2 people play at the outdoor courts but about 3 months later they took down the rims since we were entering a different phase.

Because the rims were taken down, I was basically forced to play on my ps4 (video game console) but after a while, I was tired from repetitive gaming and wanted to do something else.—Jakaree

After about another month things were a lot more lenient and I ended up being able to enjoy some of my old hobbies. Aw, the things we take for granted.—Jeff

THE LEGACIES WE LEAVE BEHIND

As educators, we are always taught to lead our lessons with the question of, "What is it that we want our students to know and be able to do by the end of the lesson, unit of study, and eventually the year (Wiggins & McTighe, 1988). What if that same question is posed to leaders regarding their work of legacy leading? What would your response be? What would your body of work represent? What would you leave behind for others to carry on the torch? What impact would it have on current social issues that are crippling communities and closing opportunity gaps for communities of color? I have been thinking about these questions as they relate to my *why*, the purpose of doing this work, and in this season I am fueled and motivated to return back to where it all started for me, back to Côtes-de-Fer, back to where it all began.

My legacy work is directly connected to the legacies that my family is trying to leave for the village of Côtes-de-Fer to continue the work. My

Picture of the newly built hotel in Cod De Fe, Haiti (Madame Moise's old land). The space can be used to hold conferences and teach classes.

family just recently built a space for gathering in the village, right where Madame Moise used to live, and my plan is to have that as a site for service-learning trips that connect students from the United States with students in CDF, Haiti. The site would support experiential learning trips and ceremonial gatherings in the village. "Soleil Lakay!"

To sum it up: Leading during the pandemic has allowed me the courage and freedom to scream in a world that wants to silence the voices of diverse communities. I am often reminded of the leadership quote by Lao Tzu when I begin to lose sight of the "real" work:

> Go to the people. Live with them. Learn from them. Love them. Start with what they know. Build with what they have. But with the best leaders, when the work is done, the task accomplished, the people will say "We have done this ourselves."

REFERENCES

McLeod, S. A. (2007). *Maslow's hierarchy of needs*. Retrieved from http://www.simplypsychology.org/maslow.html

Wiggins, G., & McTighe, J. (1998). Backward design. In *Understanding by design* (pp. 13–34). ASCD.

Zehr, H. (2002). *The little book of restorative justice*. Good Books.

CHAPTER 3

Who Is That in the Mirror?

A Journey of Self-Discovery, Resilience, and Pride

Nadla Tavares Smith

"There is, in fact, no teaching without learning."

—Paulo Freire

MY FAMILY IN THE MIRROR: EDUCATION AS A POWERFUL TOOL FOR CHANGE

One of my most vivid memories from my childhood is one of my mother, late at night, ironing my school uniform for the next day. Then there was the clanging of pots and pans at 5 a.m. At that time, I didn't put much thought into it, but now as an adult, educator, and mother, it all makes sense. My mother, a single mother of six children, a low-income Black woman, who had only been given the opportunity to complete 4th grade, was doing everything in her power to ensure that I would have opportunities denied her.

I was born and raised in Salvador, Bahia, Brazil. I attended public school my whole life and, later on, a public university. I am the second person in my family to pursue a college degree. My oldest brother, Henrique, was

My Mother and Me

the first. This is a critical piece of information because this is the very thing that drives me and the reason I became an educator. That's also what is in my mind when I plan, collaborate with colleagues, teach my students, seek to improve my teaching and advocate for my students and their families. I know that thanks to my mother, my brother could have a better life than she had; consequently, I did too, and my nieces and nephew did, too. Our family could move up the social ladder because one of us paved the way. That's the responsibility I carry daily for my students and their families, and I am fully aware of it because I am a product of it.

WHY DID I BECOME A TEACHER?

Speaking of being an educator, let me take you on a journey about how the power of causing change seduced me. My interest in education sparked when I started working as an educational secretary for a governmental program that served young and older illiterate adults. The program adopted a Freirismo (Paulo Freire) pedagogy of teaching reading and writing based on learners' experiences and what was tangible to them. Right there, I could see how education could be empowering and life-altering. I remember the joy and the sense of empowerment from those mature students who didn't think they would be able to read and write. The changes impacted everyday affairs, from reading the drug information leaflet and taking the right bus, to organizing in their communities to demand long overdue changes.

After that, I worked in public and private schools and another governmental program that prepared low-income young and older adults for the university entry exam. All these experiences helped me understand that I had finally encountered a way to fight against the oppressive system that had denied education and, with that, social mobility to my mother, my aunts, uncles, my ancestors, and many others that looked like them. That's when I realized being an educator was my calling.

Looking in the Mirror: Identity Development, Awareness, and Pride

When I permanently moved to the United States in 2011, I faced many challenges that many immigrants from developing countries face. For example, people think that you don't have an education, that your education is not up to American standards, that all immigrants are illiterate and, therefore, do not possess any knowledge, and so forth. Unfortunately, deficit is a prevalent word to use when describing immigrants.

When I decided and dared to follow my heart to get my master's and become an educator in the United States, I found many oppositions. People would walk up to me and say that it was a terrible idea, that I would never find a job, and that I would waste my money and time. Sadly, many of my students hear the same arguments. People can't see beyond the fact that one does not know English YET; they can't see the value of other languages, ways of living, and knowledge. It was difficult for me as an adult to assert myself and move forward without letting people's perceptions and prejudices hold me back, and I can only imagine what it is like for the children I work with and care deeply for to have to deal with this at such a young age. I wish more people had an opportunity and openness to see my children and everything they bring as assets. You would be amazed! They truly possess a wealth of knowledge, and I constantly learn from them.

Another interesting aspect of moving to the USA is the shift in identity. Throughout the year, my students and I talk, write, discuss, and reflect on our identities, which can be pretty challenging and revealing to people from other countries. Before moving to the USA, I always identified as Black. I feel Black; my experience growing up was of a Black person, from the music I listened to, the religion my family practiced, the dance, and many other cultural elements, but also the adversities of living in a racialized society. As in the USA, many white Brazilians like to think there is no racism, even when actively perpetuating it.

In the USA, I had to embrace a new identity as Latina, which I did not feel that I completely fit in. Having to negotiate who you are and how people perceive you in your new country is another experience I share with my students. And that's where the books my colleague Blanca Osorio-Castillo and I use to develop our social justice projects are pivotal in facilitating these conversations in which students engage with stories that serve as mirrors, reflecting their own experiences, as well as other stories that serve as windows or sliding glass doors to the experiences of other people. (Bishop, 1990). The projects, the discussions, and the constant critical thinking are ways we found to develop awareness and pride; to break through the box

My Identities

that society forces us in; speak for ourselves; dazzle society with all of our colors, sounds, hearts, and minds; tell our own stories; and affirm who we are while pushing back on their narratives about us. I am, along with my students, learning about myself and how the different parts of me intersect to make this unique individual.

I remember one particular project that I developed with my colleague Blanca. I think this project marked me so much because I understood how heritage is somewhat tangible and abstract for my multilingual learners. The project was to celebrate Latinx Heritage Month, which happens from September 15th through October 15th. We started the project by discussing the word *heritage* and what it meant to have a heritage. Then we read two books and discussed big ideas, such as family and cultural heritage. We noticed that students were aware of their traditions and ways of being as a family and individuals but needed to be more knowledgeable about their country of origin or heritage. That may be because some of them were born in the United States and came here very young. Through the projects, our Latinx multilingual learners developed a deeper awareness of their cultural practices and knowledge about their country of origin/heritage. Seeing their awe and pride was very moving, mainly because we often only hear violent and sad stories about El Salvador. We learned a bit about history, geography, and Spanish and Indigenous contributions. We watched videos of people walking on the streets and doing everyday things as all of us do but on the streets of El Salvador. El Salvador, which seems so far from their daily life and somewhat abstract, became more vivid and understood as part of who they are.

Here is an example of a poem by an Salvadoran student:

I am Adrianna Alvarado,
I am Julia, my mom, too

Bulletin Board on Latinx Identities

After reading the books "**Alma and How She Got Her Name**" by Juana Martínez Neal and "**Where Are You From?**" by Yamile Saied Méndez, some of the Latinx students from Crocker Farm wrote a poem as a way to reflect on their identities and celebrate their heritages.

One of our school bulletin boards is showcasing these poems written by Latinx Multilingual students

Making tortillas, laughing, and
pranking my dad

I am cobbled streets of
El Salvador
firm, strong, and reliable
I am Adrianna

My Reflection in the Mirror: My Students and Their Families

I see myself and my family in my students and their families. I see my mother in their parents and guardians who work long hours to provide basic necessities such as food, clothes, and shelter. I see my mother when I see my students come to school because, although she did not have the opportunity to finish elementary school, she knew the value of education and ensured I was at school every day. And that's why we must push back on the narrative that immigrant and low-income families don't care about their children's education because they do care a lot. They have aspirations for their children as any other parents, and they want their children to have a life with fewer struggles and more financial security. We need to have a less white-middle-class lens when examining the realities of low-income families. Many of my students' parents work two or three jobs to provide for their children and help their families back in their home country. They might not be checking their children's backpacks every day or being able to attend school functions. However, they show up for their children every day by sending them to school, entrusting educators with their children's future, and providing for their families. In addition, in many countries, parents are not as involved in school matters as they are expected to be here. On the other hand, the level of involvement depends on the individual as well. My own mother, for example, would check my grades, read any notes sent home, attend some events (her working schedule permitting), and trust that the school was doing its job. So cultural differences ought to be taken into consideration when working with families from different cultural backgrounds.

I see my young adult self in my students, full of knowledge and eager to share but unsure about the words in English. My experience as a graduate student was challenging and humbling. The language of academia was very difficult and, to be honest, I would find myself constantly looking up words. It would take me three times the hours to read the required reading of the week than it would for my native English speaker counterpart. I knew a lot and read a lot, but I couldn't say a lot; I often found myself isolated. Even though I think of myself as someone who knew quite a bit, had a genuine desire to learn, and who always put forth her best effort, all my professors and peers saw was someone who could not say much. There has not been a single day in my teaching career that I have not been amazed by my students' wealth of knowledge. I remember this 3rd-grade multilingual learner from China who could not speak a complete simple sentence in English YET, but could talk about world history, geography, and science through translation. His math skills were outstanding too. However, what his peer could see was a Chinese student who did not speak English. That always has bothered me for two reasons. First, I wondered how that affected his self-esteem as a learner and individual. Second, it affected his relationship with his peers; they often saw him as inferior. ESL classes have always been a safe space for multilingual learners because we have become a community that shares similar experiences about being new to the United States and speaking a language other than English. We also can see each other as capable individuals because we know that we possess knowledge, unique experiences, and linguistic competence in a language(s) other than English. However, I constantly think about how to build up my multilingual learners' self-esteem and provide opportunities for them to show off their capabilities, knowledge, and just who they are. Over the years, I have brainstormed ways to highlight multilingual learners' assets in the classroom with the co-teachers I work with. That is a task that has to be done deliberately and becomes second nature for teachers. It is a shift in our mindsets. Through doing that, we are improving the multilingual learners' self-esteem and hopefully changing preconceptions that other students might have about people from other countries.

As a school with a diverse population, we celebrate different traditions and empower students to have ownership of their cultural practices. But that is not enough; we must highlight multilingual learners' language(s) and subject content knowledge in math, science, ELA, and social studies, among others. How do you solve a math problem in El Salvador? What are some animal adaptations from wild goats from Afghanistan? What folktales from

China tell us about a specific period in that country? How are people developing sustainable cocoa bean production in Brazil?

I see myself in my students negotiating new parts of their identities while upholding who they are. What are the parts of me I want to show? What is the part of my identity that is most important? One of my most beautiful moments this school year was a read-aloud with a 3rd-grade refugee multilingual student from Afghanistan. I am constantly drawing my students' attention to the plurality of religions in our world. For this lesson, I chose to read the book *In My Mosque* by M. O. Yuksel because it would serve as a mirror for my Muslim student and a window for my Christian students. This text would also facilitate conversations about religious traditions, family, and community. Ahmad and I did a shared reading of the book in which I read the parts in English, and he read all the words in Arabic. Ahmad had so much to share about his experience going to mosques in Afghanistan with his family. I could feel the pride emerging from him as he read and pointed to pictures. There was one time in particular when it was very powerful and moving: when Ahmad stood up and read the call to prayer. He was clearly reminiscing about his home and was proud to share his traditions. Ahmad is a funny, energetic, talkative little boy who, at the same time, can be very in tune with his feelings. He often talks about things he likes in the United States, but Ahmad also misses the freedom he had back home, family, and friends in Afghanistan. He is also trying to navigate all the holidays celebrated in the United States, such as Christmas—he brought us gifts—and Halloween—he dressed up as Spider-Man.

Finally, I see myself in the people who stand for what's right and work ceaselessly to build an equitable and just society. It is our duty to continue the work of those who came before us. Thanks to the brave people from the past, we have a better world today than what they experienced. Nonetheless, their work is not done. As an educator, I treasure each of my students and deeply respect their individuality, and I care for them with the hope for a better future because that's what they represent.

REFERENCE

Bishop, R. S. (1990). Mirrors, windows, and sliding glass doors. *Perspectives: Choosing and Using Books for the Classroom, 6*(3), ix–xi.

CHAPTER 4

Cabo Verdean Kriolu, From the Community to the Classroom

Ambrizeth H. Lima, Dawna Marie Thomas, Abel Djassi Amado,
Marlyse Baptista, and Lourenço Garcia

In 2017, Massachusetts enacted the Language Opportunity for Our Children Act (Look Act) to support certified dual language programs to help students graduate with proficiency in a world language and English. Dual language programs for Spanish, Haitian, and Vietnamese students in the local district were implemented in 2017. However, the dual language program for Cabo Verdean students was delayed several times. In 2020, Dr. Ambrizeth Lima (lead author of this chapter) was told by her school district that the reason for the many delays was that "there are no Cabo Verdeans who can do that type of work or have that kind of expertise." Dr. Lima knew this was not the case, so she requested a meeting with school administrators. Many Cabo Verdean scholars and practitioners who work in education attended the meeting. We filled the room, and, when we were introduced to the meeting facilitator, she was overwhelmed by the number of Cabo Verdeans who showed up ready to go to work. She responded, "Wow, what a glorious moment! This is amazing!" Clearly, this was the first time that these administrators had met a cadre of Cabo Verdean professionals ready to advocate for the rights of Cabo Verdean children.

A CALL TO ACTION

From that meeting, the Cabo Verdean Center for Applied Research (CVCAR) was created and we developed the Cabo Verdean Heritage Language and Culture curriculum for high school students in the local school district. This chapter provides a synopsis of the events that led up to the Cabo Verdean Heritage Language and Culture curriculum, the many challenges along the way, and lessons learned from the process.

WHO ARE WE? THE CABO VERDEAN CENTER FOR APPLIED RESEARCH

"Who are we?" is a common theme, not only for the Cabo Verdean Center for Applied Research, but also for the Cabo Verdean community in general. CVCAR evolved from the call for action during that first meeting. Our membership includes two Massachusetts public school administrators and three university professors. Dr. Lima, who brought us together, emigrated from Cabo Verde as a teenager and has firsthand experience as a student in the public school system. She also has been an educator in the school system for more than 20 years. She was our guide throughout the process. Three other members emigrated as adults; the fifth member was born in the United States and her ancestors emigrated from Cabo Verde in the 1800s, during what is known as the Whaling Era. We bring a wide range of educational backgrounds and expertise, including education, political science, sociology, linguistics, and women's and gender studies.

We are all community activists working from the grassroots to the university and across the Cabo Verdean community here in the United States and in Cabo Verde. Our specific objective and primary purpose are to promote and facilitate the inter-, multi-, and trans-disciplinary study of Cabo Verdean history, culture, language, and people. Together we represent the Cabo Verdean immigration journey from the whaling era to the present time. Our vision for the Cabo Verdean Heritage Language and Culture curriculum was not only to teach Cabo Verdean children to be proficient in both Cabo Verdean and English, but also to immerse them in their history and to strengthen their cultural pride.

Members of the Cabo Verdean Center for Applied Research: From left to right—
Lourenço Garcia, Dawna M. Thomas, Marlyse Baptista, Ambrizeth H. Lima,
Abel Djassi Amado

DEVELOPING THE CURRICULUM

The struggle for the recognition and legitimization of the Cabo Verdean language within the local community and school district has been an arduous journey. CVCAR, as a newly formed organization, began by advocating for equitable education for Cabo Verdean children by requesting that the school district acknowledge the Cabo Verdean language. Throughout the chapter, we use the term Cabo Verdean (also known as *Kriolu*) not only to assert its language-hood status but also to follow recommendations from the Cabo Verdean government to call the country and language by using their native labels.

In 2021, the district acquiesced and partnered with CVCAR to create the *Cabo Verdean Heritage Language and Culture* curriculum for high school students in the local public school system. As a team, we spent hours discussing our approach and were especially aware that the language could not be taught as stand-alone content; instead, it had to be taught in conjunction with other features of the Cabo Verdean culture. The resulting course, which includes three modules divided into different units, highlights the historical and social experiences of Cabo Verdeans in the United States. The teacher's guide is written in English and the teaching materials are in Cabo

Verdean. The modules are (1) Cabo Verdean Language; (2) Negotiating Identity: Then and Now; and (3) Immigration: Past and Present. The course is inter- and multidisciplinary, combining insights from several academic fields, among them sociolinguistics, history, political science, sociology, immigration studies, and women's and gender studies.

Module I: Cabo Verdean Language

We wanted the students to learn about the key facets of the Cabo Verdean language and to understand that Cabo Verdean is one of many Creole languages in the world. In addition, it was important to teach the students about the history of the Cabo Verdean writing system and the motivations that guided the various orthographic choices behind the written representation of Cabo Verdean. Students learned how to draw connections between written and oral platforms to understand the literary tradition of Cabo Verdean. The module's key topics comprise the scientific study of language; the concept of Creole languages; the origins and development of the Cabo Verdean language; heritage language speakers; the history of writing the Cabo Verdean language; and the Cabo Verdean alphabet (formerly known as ALUPEC), seen below in Figure 4.1. We intentionally included materials concerning the rise of Cabo Verdean from its subordinate status to now being recognized as a viable language of instruction. We also highlighted that until recently there was no standardized writing for the Cabo Verdean language. Since 1994 a government-sanctioned standardized

Figure 4.1. The Cabo Verdean Alphabet

(Da Composição do ALUPEC)

O ALUPEC é de base Latina e compõe-se de vinte
e três letras e quatro dígrafos, com a representação
maiúscula, e minúscula, na seguinte ordem de apresentação

*ALUPEC is Latin-based and consists of 23 letters and
four digraphs, with upper and lower case representation,
in the following order of presentation*

A B C D DJ E F G H I J K L LH M N N NH Ñ
O P R S T TX U V X Y Z

A b d dj e f g h I j k l lh m n nh ñ o p r
s t tx u v x z

Source: **Decree-Law** number 67/98 (*Boletim Oficial da República de Cabo Verde*, the official gazette of the government)

alphabet for writing Cabo Verdean has emerged. The language module also includes aspects of identity such as code-switching. The goal is for students to learn that the use of their native language in their education is a linguistic human right.

Marlyse Baptista, the trained linguist in CVCAR, helped us express the importance of using the Cabo Verdean language. Her work on Module I drew from years of experience and expertise in the field of linguistics. She believes that "to teach community members how to read and write in Cabo Verdean by using an orthographic script, which had been officialized by the Cabo Verdean government (the ALUPEC), was essential." In the lead-up to the implementation of the curriculum, she presented community workshops aimed in part at sensitizing the community to the idea that their language can be read and written and hence used in the classroom. Community members' writings (prose and poetry) and all the proceedings of the workshops were published in *Cimboa*, a community journal of letters, arts, and studies produced by the Cabo Verdean Consulate in the late 1990s and early 2000s. This publication further supported the community's language—*Cabo Verdean*. We applied the model to Creole languages, showing how colonial powers have catapulted colonial languages to the top of the language hierarchy by imposing them in the classroom while subordinating Creoles and their speakers by trivializing them, marginalizing them, and keeping their languages out of education. Opening students' eyes to the mechanics of how language subordination operates provides them with effective tools to dismantle it (Lippi-Green, 2012). Students in the Heritage Language course echo this sentiment. For example, a student in the Heritage Language course shared (in Cabo Verdean), "I never expected that in the United States, I would learn about my own language. Instead of learning it in my country, I learned it in the United States. One of the most important things I learned was to learn my own language because they don't teach it to me in my country. They only teach Portuguese. I learned about how my language came about and how to write it grammatically correct." This quote, however short, has many implications. It indicates the continuity of colonial language ideology, lack of linguistic human rights, and linguistic supremacy of the Portuguese language in Cabo Verde. It also reinforces the need to implement the Cabo Verdean dual language program, along with the Heritage Language course.

Module II: Negotiating Identity, Then and Now

This module is centered on students' understanding and exploring through the prompt of "Who Am I?" Identity is not only valuable for students' own social, moral, and intellectual development; it also serves as a foundation for examining the choices individuals and groups make (Nieto, 1999). Students explore various facets of their identities. They begin by building a working definition of identity. They explore their own identities by framing the concept through cultural identifiers—race, culture, age, and gender. We felt this was very important because of how our societies through culture, customs, and institutions provide us with the language and labels we use to describe others and ourselves. These labels are based on beliefs about race, ethnicity, religion, gender, sexual orientation, and economic class. This instruction is critical because of how Cabo Verdean identity has historically been misunderstood and made invisible within the United States White/Black binary racial categories (Nieto, 1999; Sánchez Gibau, 2005). Beliefs about these categories are so strong that they prevent us from seeing the unique identities of others. These beliefs can also contribute to suspicion, fear, and sometimes hatred toward some members of our society.

While the vast majority of the students in the dual language program have some knowledge of Cabo Verdean culture and history, many do not realize that Cabo Verdeans have been immigrating to the United States since the late 1800s. Similar to the experience of CVCAR member Dawna, many students born in the United States have lost their language and cultural identity as second-, third-, or fourth-generation Cabo Verdeans. Thus, we felt it was important to connect students to Cabo Verdean history both in Cabo Verde and in the United States. In addition, this module explores gender roles and the differences between how girls and boys are socialized in Cabo Verdean families. For example, girls are protected and expected to help at home while boys are given more freedom to explore the world. Again, our goal is to bridge the traditions between the Cabo Verdean and American cultures. A student noted, "I really enjoyed this class because we talked about the culture. Cabo Verde was where I was born and I have so much pride sitting in a class and learning about my culture. During the class, I learned so many things about Cabo Verde and things that I had never learned about the history of Cabo Verde." Another student stated, "I found this class very, very interesting because we had fun telling stories, and doing research about our ancestors. Most importantly, I learned so much about our country, culture, and traditions. We learned about our singers and writers because they are part of our music. This class is so good because [it is] about our past, our culture, and how we should continue to support our country. We are a very intelligent race, we learn very fast, and we love to learn new things. We will continue to fight to learn and survive."

Cabo Verdean immigration to the United States has been eloquently captured in Cabo Verdean folklore, especially song lyrics and poetry. When we shared the module with teachers, we began the presentation with the *morna*, a traditional genre of music from Cabo Verde:

"Oli-m na meiu di mar, ta kunpri nha distinu na kaminhu di Amerika"
(Here I am in the middle of the ocean on my way to America)

The song goes on to say that it is sad to "leave my mother" and *sodadi* (longing) overcomes me, let me go, or I will perish." Yet, Cabo Verdeans continue to leave the islands and travel to places unknown. How did we arrive at these shores? How has the Cabo Verdean immigrant community thrived in the United States?

Module III: Immigration, Past and Present

This module delves into the history of immigration to the United States from Cabo Verde to understand the "push and pull" factors (e.g., drought, famine, better jobs) that have brought, and that continue to bring, Cabo Verdeans to this country. The curriculum covers the early Cabo Verdean immigration, which began with the onset of the whaling era (the mid- to late 1800s) and continues to the present day. Students analyze Cabo Verdean immigrant experiences vis-à-vis the experiences of different ethnic and racial groups that have immigrated both voluntarily and involuntarily to the United States. They explore key immigration landmarks such as Ellis Island as an entry checkpoint and Lady Liberty as a beacon for millions of immigrants. Students examine immigration timelines and zero in on various immigration acts that included and/or excluded many prospective immigrants based on race and/or ethnicity. Students conduct their own research; for example, they interview their family members to identify the push and pull factors that brought them to the United States. As one student related in his mother tongue, "I came here so that I can have the profession of my dreams, which is becoming a nurse. I am so happy that my mother and my brothers came with me." This student saw the United States as the proverbial "land of opportunity."

The module includes directions for the teacher to provide an environment conducive to the social and emotional well-being of students. It is imperative that students feel safe speaking about their immigrant experience (especially their status) without fear of reprisals. Students can present their research findings to their classmates and compare and contrast their experiences as a group. One student shared in Cabo Verdean, through a writing assignment, "I learned why there are so many Cabo Verdeans in the United States. I learned that the first Cabo Verdeans came to the United States through whaling ships that stopped in Cabo Verde." Another student added in Cabo Verdean, "I had so much fun in this class sharing folktales and researching my ancestors. I learned a great deal about my own country, my culture, and my heritage." Students continued to make connections between the past and present within their culture; for example, a student described Memorial Day as a day to remember the soldiers who fought for the United States. She then added, "This day reminds me of the Day of the Freedom Fighters in Cabo Verde when we remember those who fought for our freedom in Cabo Verde." She added by writing in English, "God Bless America!"

The third module concludes with a unit titled The Path to Citizenship. The reasoning behind the unit is that immigrant students need to understand immigration laws, as they pertain to the risks of deportation and the right to become a citizen in their new country. After completing the unit, students in the Heritage class were able to share their understanding of the path to citizenship, and one student said, "citizenship is a condition whereby a member of a state can enjoy the rights and privileges and participate in the political life of the state." This student was able to articulate one of the essential precepts of citizenship and went on to add, "To be a citizen is to have a right to live with freedom, prosperity, and equality." When asked what specific right an American citizen has, she answered, "the right to vote and the possibility to get better jobs." In terms of the responsibilities that come with citizenship, another student responded "to make decisions based on ethical principles and determination." The curriculum, therefore, begins with the exploration of early Cabo Verdean immigrants who came through the whaling industry and culminates with the students sharing their dreams for the future. They see themselves as nurses, professional athletes, police officers, and military personnel, thus following the path of so many Cabo Verdeans who came to these shores looking for a better life.

ONGOING CHALLENGES

We encountered several challenges as we developed the curriculum. These ranged from implementing the course during the COVID-19 pandemic to the lack of knowledge regarding the Cabo Verdean community in general to the debate over what language(s) we should teach our children. The bureaucracy within the school system also presented obstacles for teachers, administrators, students, and families.

This course was inaugurated during the COVID-19 pandemic, with students attending classes remotely. As with many schools, the pandemic challenged even the best teachers to create a sense of community and an engaging classroom environment. We continuously coached the teacher as he implemented the curriculum. From our discussions with the teacher and students, we gathered that they had a positive experience learning the content of the three modules in the Cabo Verdean language.

We encountered other challenges in implementing the curriculum. The first step was educating the district about the pernicious effect of language policies in Cabo Verde and in the United States. Many times we found ourselves reiterating that the Cabo Verdean language plays a crucial role in everyday interactions and is an identity marker. Furthermore, we argued that the Cabo Verdean language is a viable language of instruction, and we engaged in dialogue with the small segment of our community who still sees Cabo Verdean as naturally subordinate to the Portuguese language. Thus, many believed that Cabo Verdean students would be better served by the existing Portuguese dual language curriculum.

School administrators suggested that the Cabo Verdean community itself was confused about what language to use in the curriculum. Cabo Verdean teachers and administrators argued that because the Cabo Verdean language has variations across the country's ten islands, it would be difficult to choose which variation to teach. This is a longstanding argument that is rooted in a deeper sociopolitical and historical struggle. This resistance toward the Cabo Verdean language is due to our enduring colonial history. To counteract such challenges, our team employed linguistic tools that demonstrate that Creole languages follow the same rules and principles that govern the grammar of any natural language (Baptista, 2002). We taught students about the different linguistic components that can be found in any natural language, that is phonology (sound systems), morphology (the form of words), syntax (the structure of sentences), and semantics (the meaning of words). Our team also introduced students—and administrators—to the fact that Creole languages are acquired in the same way as any other natural language (Baptista, 2002).

As mentioned above, another major challenge was the language variation. The variation that characterizes any language has been used by opponents of the representation of *Kriolu* in education, as a major excuse for stalling any effort at using *Kriolu* in the classroom. In response, we introduced students to the official alphabet of the language (formerly known as ALUPEC) not only to show them that they can use it to read and write in their variety of languages but also to make them aware of the variants of the same word in their language. We showed them that the same variation observable in *Kriolu* can also be witnessed in English. Addressing the perennial questions of "which Creole variety?" and "which alphabet?" allowed us to demonstrate that all varieties of the language can be represented while discussing the notion of standardized language.

Another recurring challenge was the school system bureaucracy, including access to funds, ethnic power or lack thereof, and resistance from stakeholders such as school principals. Our eagerness to produce materials and begin to implement the curriculum was squelched by the relentless lack of access to funds that had been allocated to Cabo Verdean students by the state. We were told numerous times that the funding had been appropriated for other activities; while other groups enjoyed budgets that enabled them to develop their curricula, we tirelessly put the curriculum together with no guarantee of remuneration. In addition, it seemed that stakeholders such as principals were empowered to deny access to Cabo Verdean students; some of them refused to allow the implementation of classes in their buildings and it appeared that the district did not challenge them. The district spoke incessantly about equity and touted linguistically and culturally responsive education. To illustrate the disparate treatment of Cabo Verdean students, we gave a presentation to the district on the theme of equality versus equity. The district promoted equality in the sense that all linguistic groups should have equal access to funds for dual language programs. The Spanish-speaking students (the largest language group in the district) had their dual language programs. Then, the district established a dual language program for Haitian-speaking students (the third largest language group). Next, the Vietnamese students were able to secure their dual language program (the fourth largest language group). The Cabo Verdean children (the second largest language group) were not provided with a dual language program; instead, we were given the option of having a Heritage Language class. We continue to assert that, yes, there is equality in the sense that everyone in the district understands that Cabo Verdean children deserve to have a dual language program, but the district continues to perpetuate inequitable practices whereby some linguistic groups get what they need, and others do not. The perennial question is "Why?" We tend to look at disparities from a binary perspective (Black and White, American and immigrant), and we fail to examine inequities that are inter-ethnic in nature. When members of an ethnic group acquire resources, they tend to guard the resources and believe that they have them because they "worked" for them.

To illustrate, when a particular linguistic group was invited to speak at the Office of Multilingual Education, the group related that it had established a strong dual language program that was thriving. The speaker for the group attributed it to the group's community mobilization. One of the authors came across the speaker as he was leaving and he looked at her and said, "Cape Verdeans need our help to get their program going. We will help you organize yourselves." However, the problem is not that Cabo Verdeans have not mobilized or advocated for resources that their children deserve; the problem is a lack of institutional support.

Three professional development sessions were conducted for teachers, parents, and administrators. The goals of the professional development sessions were to ensure that the teachers have the knowledge, skills, and understanding to engage their students with a high-quality, culturally and linguistically relevant curriculum that is well-rounded for success in life. Each 2-hour session focused on the curriculum's modules and was held virtually. Participants in the session were diverse in gender and race. The professional development sessions included topics related to the lesson plans that the teachers would implement during class. The sessions provided an opportunity for teachers to learn about Cabo Verdean history and the journey to the United States. They also established a framework for understanding how languages do not exist in a vacuum but are an integral feature that intersects with race, culture, ethnicity, gender, and nation. While all the sessions went well, the session on Module II—Negotiating Identity: Then and Now is noteworthy and highlights challenges in discussing race in the United States. It also offers the context to better understand the struggle many Cabo Verdeans continue to experience with race, ethnicity, and culture in the United States.

POWER OF AN ILLUSION—PBS SERIES

The exercise on race in Module II was based on the Power of An Illusion curriculum from the Public Broadcasting Service (PBS). It includes episodes that focus on race and how the concept of race has evolved in the United States. This series is designed for educators and presents exercises and questions about what race is. "Sorting People" is an activity that includes ID cards showing a diverse group of people (i.e., in terms of race and gender) in two rows. The top row includes boxes of ID cards with people's faces and in the row below are racial categories. The participants (the teachers) are supposed to "match" the people by putting each person into a racial box. Two participants (both White teachers) objected to this exercise, suggesting it was racist, and the group fell silent. We sat amid the silence and tension. Another teacher (teacher of color) broke the silence by saying "I am put in a box every day and I think this exercise is important." We continued with the exercise, and everyone selected correct and incorrect categories, which is to be expected. Many participants shared ideas and moving stories about how they have experienced race and racism. It showed how we all are asked to define or identify ourselves racially on a daily basis and, if we are not asked, assumptions are made about us based on how we look, our accents, and our names.

While the exercise was challenging for us all for many different reasons, it was worthwhile not only to better understand the Cabo Verdean community, but also because discussions about race, privilege, and systems of power can empower us all to know "where we came from, who and where we are, and what we can do" (McIntosh, 2009, p. 8). The different levels of (dis)comfort demonstrated by white teachers and teachers of color is an all-too-familiar disconnect between how some whites perceive race and how communities of color experience it. For example, due to the complaint from the teacher, administrators called a meeting with our CVCAR member who works for the school system. The intent was to review the next professional development presentation to ensure that it did not have any content with potential controversy or discomfort. Due to the coercive tone of the request, our member did not feel safe attending this meeting alone. In solidarity, all the CVCAR members attended the meeting with the administrators. During our discussion of this exercise, one white teacher said: "I didn't know I had white privilege." This meeting shed light on the entrenched issues related to race and the contradictions associated with trying to provide equitable and meaningful education.

Working on educational standards presented another challenge, especially for university professors. While the university professors certainly have standards and assessment protocols to follow, they are like entrepreneurs in the classroom and do not have to adhere to standards like teachers in the K–12 system. Thus, we relied on CVCAR's members who are public school educators to guide us. The university professors felt they were in a master class on education. Praxis, in essence, took center stage, as professors saw their theoretical frameworks put into practice. At the same time, the practitioners were able to frame their practice within theoretical frameworks. This was extremely powerful because these two realms are not mutually exclusive: Our practitioner member shared that as a teacher many times she has been told in professional development that she does not need to understand the theories that frame classroom activities or strategies. In fact, she was repeatedly told, "Don't worry about theory. Here are the activities for you to use in class." She also heard many of her colleagues say dismissively, "Oh, I don't care about that. It's all theory. Just give me the activities." During the development of this curriculum, the dichotomy between theory and practice was bridged and we truly saw praxis in practice, where theorists and practitioners brought their expertise together to frame the content of the curriculum.

LESSONS LEARNED

The curriculum development process and implementation taught us many things. Below are some of the major lessons we hope you will keep in mind, whether or not you teach Cabo Verdean students.

Students embraced the learning process regarding their cultural history along with the language. For example, students saw their identities mirrored in their instructional materials; this has been shown to promote positive social identity development by increasing pride, confidence, and healthy self-esteem. A mirror approach supports their recognition of the distinctions in the traits of the dominant culture, their home culture, and other cultures. It further allows students to be exposed to the lived experiences of others, expanding their understanding and empathy while exploring diverse social, cultural, political, and historical contexts.

Another important lesson we learned is that curriculum developers have to engage and sustain close relationships with the Cabo Verdean community members, teachers, and students. Community engagement included meeting with community members, conducting professional development sessions for staff members, meeting regularly with administrators, and doing ongoing public outreach. In addition, we organized and promoted Cabo Verdean Heritage Celebration events that brought together scholars, artists, musicians, writers, and the community.

Part of our mission was to inform the Cabo Verdean community about the value and full functionality of its language. During the Decade of Indigenous Languages declared by UNESCO, our team noted that, despite growing recognition of the value of mother tongues, we encountered resistance to the Cabo Verdean language. However, our success was found in the students and participating teachers, who expressed deep satisfaction with the curriculum, which in turn has motivated us to continue to promote CVCAR's mission.

The Cabo-Verdean language deserves recognition not only as a medium of instruction but also as a language that affirms our students' culture, history, life experience, identity, and dignity. This requires educators to leverage students' first languages as assets and resources to engage them academically. It is a well-known fact that there is a dearth of linguistically and culturally relevant instructional materials for Cabo Verdean students. This curriculum not only establishes Cabo Verdean as a language of instruction but also provides culturally relevant resources for the education of Cabo Verdean children both in the diaspora and in Cabo Verde.

REFERENCES

Baptista, M. (2002). *The syntax of Cape Verdean creole: The Sotavento varieties.* John Benjamins Publishing.

Lippi-Green R. (2012). *English with an accent: Language ideology and discrimination in the United States* (2nd ed.). Routledge.

McIntosh, P. (2009). *White privilege: An account to spend.* The Saint Paul Foundation. Available at https://www.whitworth.edu/cms/media/whitworth/documents/administration/diversity-equity--inclusion/peggy-mcintosh-white-privilege-an-account-to-spend.pdf.

Nieto, S. (1999). *The light in their eyes: Creating multicultural learning communities.* Teachers College Press.

Sánchez Gibau, G. (2005). Contested identities: Narratives of race and ethnicity in the Cape Verdean diaspora. *Identities: Global Studies in Culture and Power, 12*(3), 405–438.

Part II

LOVE AND AFFIRMING PRACTICES

We write a great deal about love in this book. Love is at the forefront of our practice as teachers. Yet love alone cannot sustain either students or teachers. Love must be accompanied by hope, justice, creativity, high expectations, respect, and critical thinking. Love for our students and our practice must also work in collaboration with more concrete practices such as consistent support for teachers, financial investment in education, time to work with colleagues in meaningful ways, and quality professional development that does not talk down to teachers. In this section, you will read the thoughts, ideas, and experiences of three educators from diverse areas of teaching about how to sustain love, hope, and joy in teaching. The teachers in this section exemplify what it means to have love for our students while also sharing and learning about ourselves and having culturally responsive, rigorous expectations for students. In a way, these essays serve as a primer for how to be a successful culturally literate and sustaining educator, providing readers with tips and advice without being pedantic.

As an ESL student herself until 4th grade, Odalis Amparo has never forgotten how it felt to struggle with a new language. As a young student, she also found math quite challenging, and she notes the irony of becoming a math teacher to dual language and ESL students. Odalis's parents immigrated to Western Massachusetts from the Dominican Republic, and they underscored the importance of her being bilingual and biliterate. While learning English was difficult for her, she is now proud to share with her students that she was an English learner, and that she is a first-generation, bilingual Dominican woman who grew up in the same city as her students. In her essay, Odalis outlines her core beliefs, highlighting helpful classroom strategies and practices after each one. She firmly believes that we need to honor and sustain the humanity of our students. Connecting with students by sharing ourselves with them and listening to them is a key aspect of Odalis's teaching. She models for them what it means to bring one's whole self to the classroom, and then leaves them the space to do the same. Odalis emphasizes bringing joy into the classroom—yes, even the math classroom!—by being joyful herself and by sparking students' curiosity and natural love of learning. In her classroom, students' funds of knowledge are respected; their languages and ways of being are nourished; their activism is kindled; their critical thinking is nurtured. A true believer in asset-based teaching, Odalis reflects on being the teacher she wishes she had while growing up.

Suzanna Dali-Parker, an ESL teacher, addresses the state of professional development for teachers, suggesting that teachers need a "detox" of sorts from the rigid, canned kinds of training that often are "prescribed." She recognizes the importance of professional development while reminding us that teachers are critical thinkers and educated people and are often willing and even desire to delve more deeply into matters that affect their practice and their students. The need to humanize professional development practices is highlighted through her writing. While she acknowledges that there are gaps in teacher knowledge, she also calls attention to the importance of retaining an asset-based perspective of teachers and to honor their intellectualism, while also deeply examining their own relationships to education. Suzanna believes that we can learn a great deal from children's play, that it can foster imagination and encourage creativity. According to her, creating beautiful spaces for students—even in a basement closet classroom—promotes learning. She shares a poem that reads like a devastating list of commands to a student, but then ends her chapter with precious vignettes from her classroom that show critical thinking, kindness, joy, creativity, and hope among her students.

A multitalented and fiercely dedicated teacher, Mary Jade Haney has taken on many and varied roles as an educator. But whatever the role, her love for her students and their families and communities, as well as her creativity and enduring commitment, are legendary. From her experience with her own parents, whom she calls her "first teachers," Mary Jade has learned to engage with a wide range of people in the educational arena. Entreating teachers to "journey on," she uses her own journey as an example of resilience and courage despite the many challenges teachers face today.

Acting alternatively as a classroom teacher, art teacher, summer camp director, school librarian, and adjunct professor and teacher educator at a local university, Mary Jade understands that leadership must always be a fundamental aspect of education. Whether it is working on her own education—for instance, going through the arduous process of earning the designation of Nationally Certified Teacher—or focusing on her students by selecting appropriate books for them, creating innovative curricula, mentoring aspiring educators, leading a flash mob, collaborating with other teachers, or hosting family members at a school activity, Mary Jade exemplifies what it means to be an educator who knows how to imbue each activity with a social justice perspective.

The three essays in this section demonstrate what it means to keep hope and joy at the center of teaching, salient messages in this era of education. We hope that they will motivate you, our readers, to do the same.

CHAPTER 5

The Art of Intention

Odalis Amparo

The thread of core truths outlined below captures the essence of *who* I am as an educator, *why* I do what I do, and most importantly, *how* I go about doing it. My hope is that by the end of your journey through this essay, you will ultimately understand that honoring and sustaining the humanity of students and educators is imperative.

CORE TRUTH 1

The opportunity to matriculate and enter the field of education is a privilege for which my mother crossed an ocean. Therefore, I lean into the work that much more deeply.

The ability to get the education necessary to teach, in the first place, has been and always will be a privilege. I am a first-generation college graduate who has access to opportunities for which my mother bravely crossed an ocean. My mother came to the states from the Dominican Republic, in hopes of finishing her high school education and attending college. The realities she had to confront were not aligned to her original hopes; nonetheless, these realities paved the way for me to accomplish my own. Being in this field at all is high stakes. Not just professionally because the work matters, but personally because of the sacrifice it took for me to have the opportunity to be here in the first place.

I have recently transitioned into a role outside of public education and am now working for a problem-based core curriculum built on the principle that all students are capable learners of grade-level mathematics. Prior to my current role, I was an instructional mathematics coach for the Holyoke Public Schools, the same district I attended as a student. Before that, I taught a variety of grades at the elementary level, including Kindergarten, Grade 2, and Grade 4. One of the highlights of my career thus far has been teaching 4th grade in a dual language program. It has been an interesting journey so far, one that has been very fulfilling. I think a lot of the impact I had as a teacher was directly related to the path that led me to teaching in the first place. Growing up, I struggled immensely with learning a second language. In the early 2000s, the educational climate in Massachusetts was not one that welcomed all parts of my linguistic repertoire. As a child, I felt a deep-rooted pressure to acquire "good" English. I wanted to fit in. I placed incredible amounts of pressure on myself to speak without an accent and write in a way that was aligned to what I believed at the time was grammatically correct. Although I was born here in the United States, my mother really felt it important to make sure I was bilingual and biliterate. When I entered kindergarten, I did not know any English. In fact, I was not in a mainstream classroom until 4th grade. Being in this role now as a math coach is somewhat ironic, as I struggled with math, in addition to learning a second language. Quite honestly, I never truly enjoyed the subject until starting my teaching career.

For a long time, mathematics has been viewed as the "universal language." But whose? Numerically speaking, yes, it is a set of universal truths. The symbols might be the same in much of the world, but the context the numbers live in, and the content-specific language that surrounds the numbers on a page and/or hides them in plain sight, varies. I was one of those children who struggled with accessing mathematics in part because of the language barrier, but mostly because the understanding of translanguaging was not yet widely known in the field (see García & Wei, 2014) and bilingual education was falling out of favor. What I may have known did not count unless I knew it in English.

I always viewed myself as someone who was not innately a "math person," and who never could be. Mathematics felt rigid and disconnected from the world outside of the classroom, and from *my* world in particular. References to apple orchards and baking were not culturally responsive to Odalis and the rote and procedural approach widened the lack of connection between me and the content. It was not until I stepped foot into the classroom that I realized how important it was to remember that language itself was the universal thread, weaving together all content areas.

When I began to teach upper elementary grades, I quickly realized that many students struggled with mathematics in the same way I once did. Between the unfinished learning, high stakes assessments, and rigidity that some students associated with mathematics, there was little to no room for the joy and wonder that belong at the very core of the discipline. This became the launching pad to many of the successes I had in my classroom each year. I felt it was crucial to do whatever was necessary to support students in truly internalizing the content and seeing its significance outside of the classroom.

CORE TRUTH 2

There are many important factors that impact the quality of education, but arguably, the most important elements of impactful teaching and coaching are intentional relationship building and authentic connection.

Although there are many factors that directly impact the efficacy of education, it is my belief that connection and relationship-building are the heart of authentic teaching and meaningful learning. Education is *love in action.* Love in education is multifaceted. It can take many shapes, depending on the scenario and students. There are many approaches one must have in order to connect with each individual child. Remembering that students are human beings first is integral to genuinely connecting with them. It takes a network of stakeholders with great communication to help students learn and grow, and educators must intentionally make connections and build relationships with everyone accordingly. This includes caregivers and honors the fact that the "grown-ups at home," as I used to say to students, were experts in a way I could never be as their teacher. Being intentional in building a relationship also means having to respect students, just as I would respect any other person. Although still children, students deserve to be spoken about in the same way one would speak if they were in the room. This applies to caregivers and families as well. Every year I tried my best to attend the extracurricular activities in which students participated. Doing this provided opportunities to connect with families because connecting with caregivers that students most interacted with outside of school was vital to the success of the child.

The depth and breadth of teaching is all encompassing and should always take into account the students in front of us, meaning it changes each year, with every cohort of students. Every decision has an impact on the humans that are the literal *future*. Everything we say and do directly affects how a student sees themselves not only as a learner, but as a whole being. A lot of their identity is cultivated in the elementary school classroom, and keeping this at the forefront of all decision-making is important. In fact, I believe that I made the most impact in my practice by truly inviting the whole child into the classroom, and nurturing a one-on-one relationship with each and every one of them. In order for me to be an effective teacher, I needed to understand at a deep level all the layers that made up each child that walked through the door. Students are not empty vessels waiting to be filled, and we as educators should never view ourselves as "givers of knowledge." What were their likes and dislikes? What experiences have they had both inside and outside of school that have shaped them as learners? What funds of knowledge, that is, what knowledge, skill sets, and assets do families in the community have that can enhance the learning experiences for all students? What are the elements that shape their culture? What does their name mean to them and their identity? Who do they look up to? What subjects do they enjoy? Which do they find challenging? Why? What is their communication style? How do they feel best supported?

I tend to be reflective by nature, but I have found that it is definitely one of the most important aspects of being in this field. How can I improve my practice if I am not constantly thinking deeply about the decisions I am making during the day? I would encourage my students to self-reflect frequently and I would challenge myself to facilitate their reflection in a variety of ways. At times I would have a "Food for Thought" quote or statement written on the board and have them free write while they enjoyed breakfast. This was a great way to shine light on a variety of figures not so widely known or celebrated in our society, such as Jaime Escalante, Sylvia Méndez, and Dolores Huerta. Other times I would pose simple questions such as, "If you could go back to the start of the week, what are two things you would do differently?" and "What does success look like in math? During lunch? At recess?"

I found it crucial for students to understand that the learning that took place in the classroom was pertinent to their lives outside of school, both while they were in school and later in life. I tried to connect everything we did to life beyond the classroom. This would keep students engaged in a way that no curriculum could on its own. For example, at the start of the school year I would frequently launch mathematics with a thought-provoking task. I would ask all students to add an item of their choosing to an anchor chart posted at my easel. I would then tell them that *everything* in the world somehow connects to mathematics. Students would usually respond with phrases such as, "Yeah, right!" or "No way! Then I would proceed to draw connections between a few of the items on the list to mathematics (e.g., a piece of paper can be connected to weight, angle measurements, geometry, etc.). It usually only took a handful of connections before little to no prompting was needed for them to continue the process. By the end of the launch, almost everyone was usually excited about mathematics the next day.

I also found facilitating weekly classroom community meetings to be restorative and reflective. It provided me with ample opportunity to celebrate classroom successes, empower students to share ideas and solutions, and increase student agency. Sometimes simple things were honored and acknowledged, such as students being actively involved in a particular activity or persevering through a challenging math center. Other times, we would dig into areas of growth in our classroom community. Weekly meetings provided space for other conversations to take place. I encouraged students to provide their suggestions on how certain topics could be addressed or solved, and they were given the opportunity to reflect on their own choices throughout the week.

Honoring student voices and letting them be active members of the relationship I was building with them was paramount. That said, relationships are a two-way street. That meant that I too had to invite myself wholly into the classroom. My moral imperative, the journey to the field, mattered. My interests, joys, and experiences outside of teaching mattered and students deserved to get to know about them. I would start every first day of school with a "Get to Know Your Teacher" presentation. I would prepare slides ahead of time with images that visually captured who I am. I would then welcome any comments or curiosities about what I shared. This would always serve as a perfect transition to them sharing important things about themselves. I would then invite students to create some sort of visual to share at a later morning meeting, following the guidance I modeled. This activity always felt *good*. It felt *good* to share that English was my second language, and that I knew exactly how some of them felt. It felt *good* to share that I was a mom, daughter, and sister. It felt *good* to share that I was Dominican and talk about my first name being Odalis and how to pronounce it. This mindset and approach to the launch of the school year inadvertently invited students to feel comfortable with the vulnerability it sometimes took to not just take social risks, but academic ones too. As a teacher I found it important to share my truths with students. I also found it important to answer the question— *why am I here? What led me to where I am today?* Inviting myself wholly into the classroom is when my most authentic teaching took place because it set the stage, so to speak, for the experiences I facilitated for my students.

Regardless of age, it feels good to be seen and heard, to be invited into a conversation and listened to. At the end of the day, my students were human beings first, and in order for anything academic to take place, we all had to get to know one another authentically first. And *that* truly made all the difference.

CORE TRUTH 3

Education at all levels and in all forms is the single most important catalyst for change.

Society is imperfect; therefore, so are districts and schools. In many cases, one must adhere to expectations that disadvantage some of our students and at the same time think outside the box about how to best advocate for them. There are vast opportunities both inside and outside of the classroom that can promote change at a larger scale. Each educator has the opportunity to cultivate a child's desire to learn, think critically about the world around them, and chase after their individual hopes and dreams, which more than likely stretch far beyond any given school year.

Several years ago I put together a short persuasive writing unit in the early fall for my 4th-graders that focused on Indigenous Peoples' Day. Unfortunately, at that time, the district's calendar still listed the holiday as Columbus Day. This presented itself as the ideal, real-life situation to launch the unit. Rather than pose all the reasons why the holiday should be named Indigenous Peoples' Day and not Columbus Day, I shared information from varying perspectives and encouraged students to form their own opinion. I gathered a plethora of materials, including videos, books, letters, newspaper articles, and interviews that both supported and challenged using Columbus Day as the name for the holiday. Most students were only familiar with one narrative, the one connected to Christopher Columbus. The task at the end of the unit was for students to write a letter to the superintendent sharing their stance on what the name of the holiday should be. They were to support their opinion with evidence grounded in all the primary and secondary sources I had shared with them. At the end of the unit, they wrote letters that defended one side or the other, but regardless of what side was "chosen," all students were made aware of the broader narrative and set of truths attached to the holiday.

Although it is more than likely that the work we did had nothing to do with the change the district made to the calendars a few years later—that is, changing the name of the holiday to Indigenous People's Day—there was a sense of empowerment in knowing that something completed in class was of significance to the world beyond the brick and mortar. It was evident that students were inspired and it made an impact. Students that school year were able to exercise the right to be critical consumers of information presented and form their own opinions, rather than being told what to believe.

CORE TRUTH 4

Teaching is a tapestry, threaded together by skillful educators with varying perspectives, making education the most complex and beautiful field to work in.

On a superficial level, the classroom experience is informed by district and state-driven expectations and standards. But the fullness of the true classroom experience is shaped by many other external factors. Some of these include, but are not limited to, state policies, the current political and racial climate, societal "norms," social movements of any kind, inequities of all types, and geographic location. All of this layered in with the individuality of each student, their varying needs, and teachers' unique teaching styles, creates the textured, complex field of education.

Teaching that allows learners to thrive entails student-centered instruction where all learners feel valued and understood. Learners thrive when their needs are met in a way that is conducive to their own learning style. As a teacher I put in the effort necessary to stay up to date on research and theories relevant to classroom instruction and implement them in my practice. This is the part of teaching where theory and practice come together beautifully if we think about it intentionally.

I held high academic expectations for all my students but had a firm belief that it was my responsibility as an educator to provide multiple entry points to the content, making it accessible to all students regardless of their socioeconomic, linguistic, and academic background. This goes beyond providing scaffolding and implementation of appropriate teaching strategies and relies heavily on equitable instruction. The "one size fits all" approach in teaching is antiquated, and my teaching style is reflective of a compilation of other approaches more appropriate for the classroom now. I aimed for instruction and learning in my classroom to feel like an experience that is well-rounded and student-driven.

There was one activity in particular that really made all of this come to life. I designed a spiral review math project for my 4th-graders that also served as an opportunity for them to share about themselves and their culture. Students were prompted to choose their favorite dish or one that was popular at a holiday with their family. I then supported them with finding a recipe online that best captured the dish they chose. I went to the local supermarket and picked up flyers. Students were tasked with figuring out how much it would cost to purchase all of the ingredients for their dish if they were to make it for the number of people they lived with. This project prompted students to actively add and multiply fractions, whole numbers, and decimals. At the end of the week-long project, I encouraged them to make a poster that would depict the math behind "making the dish," as well as a picture or illustration of what they chose. Many students took it a step further and included facts about where the dish came from, if applicable, and why it was their favorite. The recipes chosen represented my students in ways that I had not yet known about. I learned all about pierogies, flan, sancocho, pumpkin pie, shepherd's pie, Irish stew, arroz con gandules, empanadillas, homemade cookies, and many other delicacies.

"Great teachers don't break the rules; they know when and how to bend them" has been a statement that grounded my teaching for a long time. While in the classroom, I found that in order to meet the academic expectations placed on my shoulders, while also teaching students the standards that need to be taught, I needed to be flexible and creative in the output of my information. There has to be a balance between following the curricula and holding students to high expectations, while also presenting the content in a way that does not count out or marginalize any groups of people and gives all students an entry point to the academic standards. As a teacher it is my responsibility to think critically about everything I present to my students *before* presenting it. At times this means being a disruptor, especially if working for an administration that is not open to learning and internalizing new practices or pedagogies. When in that type of environment, one must be prepared to professionally justify certain academic decisions and adjustments made to curricula. As a coach I supported educators in doing this by empowering them to internalize the Common Core State Standards. If an educator is well versed in understanding the standards, it makes it easier to make adjustments necessary without compromising the rigor of the content.

CORE TRUTH 5

Diversity, equity, and inclusion are the very fibers that make up high-quality instruction and should be the cornerstone of all pedagogical approaches.

Education is the means by which we provide students with access to the world beyond the classroom. It is the right of every child to be nurtured in a way that prepares them as global, well-rounded citizens. Diversity, equity, and inclusion are the very fibers that make up high-quality instruction and should be the cornerstone of all pedagogical approaches. Without attention to all three, it is impossible to provide students and educators with adequate learning experiences. For historically marginalized students to thrive mathematically, instruction must be rooted in culturally sustainable practices.

Students are diverse in countless ways. Socioeconomic status, racial and ethnic background, taste in food, music, extracurricular activities, linguistic repertoires, academic strengths and areas of growth, funds of knowledge of both the child and their families—these are all part of the diversity students bring to the classroom. As a teacher I provided students with ample opportunities to engage in meaningful discourse and share their ways of thinking. I consistently made intentional adjustments to the core curriculum in hopes of providing students the space to collaborate and engage with one another and productively struggle through authentic math tasks. As a coach, I have had the privilege of working with many educators and supporting them in addressing their own personal challenges with mathematics, as well as fostering an inclusive learning environment for their students that is in alignment with their needs.

Unfortunately, equity in *theory* and in *practice* can sometimes look starkly different. In theory, it is providing students with what they need to help them access the content. But without a shift in paradigm on *how* we are doing that, there will be continued missed opportunities in our teaching and student learning. Disrupting the antiquated approach to teaching mathematics is what I am most passionate about. Cultivating positive student mathematical identities, eliciting student thinking, and providing a platform for students to share and revise that thinking is crucial.

In my time while completing my graduate degree in teaching English as a second language at Mount Holyoke College, I discovered that my passion lies in how mathematics and language are interconnected. I learned that language development goes beyond solely supporting students learning English as a second language. Mathematics is a language in itself, and its instruction should be treated as such.

CORE TRUTH 6

Teaching matters.

Every decision made in the classroom has a direct impact on a student's trajectory as a human being. The impact is far beyond simply academic. When something's importance weighs this heavily, the investment in doing it well is immense.

Reflecting on my time in the classroom, I now see that the way I approached certain things, even in the slightest of ways, is what made the experience what it was. I created a student pledge several years ago that captures the essence of the classroom climate toward which we all worked to co-create. I would kick off each morning with everyone reciting this pledge, or simply listening to their classmates recite it. By the end of the year, many students would have it memorized by heart. The most popular section of the pledge went as follows, "I will learn something today because today matters and my future is built one 'now' at a time." I think students liked this part the best because it served as a daily reminder that life is a collection of moments, and that the moments in school, the decisions they made, all contributed to life beyond the classroom. Year after year, this idea intrigued students. Starting the school day with the student pledge helped cultivate a culture of importance. They mattered. Their decisions mattered. How they treated one another mattered. Their hopes and dreams mattered, both long term and short term. When students were taking any type of independent classroom assessment, I would leave notes for them as they were working in order to encourage and motivate them. Every note I wrote was always specific to the student and what they needed at the moment. Often, by the end of the day, I would have a collection of Post-Its on my desk with student responses or simple thank-yous for notes received.

CORE TRUTH 7

If not me, then who? If not now, then when?

I taught in a way that I wished teachers had taught me when I was a student, and I coached teachers the way I hoped someone coached and supported me when I was in the classroom. I value education because without it, we would not have any other profession or the skill set to be the critical consumers we need to be. I did my best work both as a classroom teacher and mathematics coach when I maintained my focus on the humanity of the people I was serving. I find joy in learning, growing, and creating a space where both students and educators discover the same joys. I find fulfillment and validation in the complexity of the field and the students and educators I have had the privilege of serving. Successful teaching and learning can be defined in a variety of ways. Personally, I believe that true magic happens when students are encouraged to bring their own thoughts and experiences to the classroom, prompted to actively make connections with new content and knowledge, and supported to think critically about how it all culminates and connects to the world around them. As educators, we must create a learning space that honors and sustains pre-existing funds of knowledge, while also nurturing and cultivating new rigorous experiences.

REFERENCE

García, O., & Wei, L. (2014). *Translanguaging: Language, bilingualism and education.* Palgrave Macmillan.

CHAPTER 6

From Prescriptions to Descriptions
Shaping Teacher Practice for Equity and Justice Through Aesthetic Experience

Suzanna Dali-Parker

After so many attempts at protocols meant to create safe spaces for hard conversations, many teachers appear today more resistant than ever to engage in professional development that requires a sourcing from within to improve their practice, a reaching for the heart, and its power to pull us deeper into the internal rhythms that regulate our beliefs and values, our understanding of each other and of the world. What's at stake is the extent to which teachers are encouraged to visit their internal landscapes in search of an aestheticism, a reconnection to hope, that place where the will for what's good and right can be felt deeply, the place that distinguishes a teacher's practice with a unique vibrancy focused on the desires that constitute the goals of a socially just and inclusive society and that makes a lighthouse of hope on the horizon.

Rarely are teachers encouraged to source from within themselves, to professionally develop from the inside out, rather than on the continuous gorging of programmatic strategies and the routine binging on prefabricated preservative-filled lesson plans and activity sets. Instead, teachers need serious detoxification from the boxed-in professional-development plastic containers to which they have grown addicted and, more sadly, on which they depend.

This new wave of professional development focused on racial equity and social justice that beckons teachers to examine their biases and learn to teach with race and diversity in mind is beginning to feel to so many teachers like a spoon-fed bitter elixir. Just recently, I overheard a colleague of mine ask, "Why are they force-feeding us all this race stuff?"

ON IMAGINATION AND EMPATHY IN TEACHING

Professional development around racial equity and social justice is struggling to get teachers to the other side, that is, to the humanizing side of practice. The excavation into the heart and the calling upon our mind's capacity to see in images and to hear through poetry, to discern the differences between the red and blue of our nation and the red and the blue of a heart that beats for empathy and compassion—this is what is most needed in the hard conversations. The work of Maxine Greene (1995) is essential to this task as her life's work reminds us that continuing to entertain racial equity for social justice with an "I" will do little to lessen the uncomfortable emotions that come from needing to make oneself vulnerable.

> I would suggest again, however [that] it may well be the imaginative capacity that allows us also to experience empathy with different points of view, even with interests at odds with ours. Imagination may be a new way of decentering ourselves, of breaking out of the confinements of privatism and self-regard into a space where we can come face to face with others and call out, "Here we are." (Greene, 1995, p. 31)

"Here we are" . . . these three simple words unite us because in the end, as teachers and educators, aren't we all truly in the same boat? Drowning in the same waters? Trying to swim upstream when the current won't let go? And wouldn't we prefer to have each other in those waters than be alone? If one is drowning, the instinct of the other is to save, and to save fiercely without thought, because in that instance the common denominator is life. This we can all agree upon. How, then, can teachers develop the urgency to reach out to each other in solidarity, not to save education, or children, but rather to nurture a practice that is first and foremost humane, and deliberately situated within a sociocultural and sociopolitical context?

What is sorely missing from professional development on racial equity for social justice is the explicit critical examination of empathy, the need to ask how we can connect the rational conceptualization of empathy with the vulnerable landscape of the heart. Brené Brown's (2018) work on empathy can be useful here. In her book *Dare to Lead* (2018) she studies the intersection of courage, vulnerability, shame, and empathy, and distinguishes between sympathy and empathy. "Empathy is feeling with people. Sympathy is feeling for them. Empathy fuels connection. Sympathy drives disconnection" (p. 152). Sympathy is not a bad thing, by any means, but it lives closer to our heads than to our hearts. Knowing more about empathy as social practice embedded in culture and systems of power can prepare teachers to more fully embrace the goals of professional development centered on issues of racial equity and social justice.

Professional development (PD) intent on inspiring self-transformation in teachers must engage them in self-study while simultaneously acknowledging the fear and shame that may surge from such reflective activity. The process of confronting one's biases and one's life narrative can be both painful and liberating; it can strengthen, but can also pool into a space of resistance.

PD for racial equity and social justice must account for the affectual responses of teachers, often characterized through guilt and defensive attitudes. It must secure the consideration of the complexities of what it means to surrender one's beliefs and experiences, many of which may be in direct conflict with the goals of the PD. Brown addresses the affectual challenges one may face when being asked to work from the place she refers to as "wholeheartedness,"

> Rather than protecting and hiding our heart behind bullet proof glass, wholeheartedness is about integration. It is integrating our thinking, feeling, and behavior. It's putting down the armor and bringing forth all the scraggly, misshapen pieces of our history and folding in all of the different roles, that when falsely separated, keep us feeling exhausted and torn, to make a complex, messy, awesome, whole person. (Brown, 2018, p. 72)

For these reasons, far more attention must be paid to understanding the levels of empathy as described by Brown, and to the conscious engagement of empathy into social practice through depth of understanding, the development of metacognitive abilities, and always with a willingness to reflect on oneself critically and creatively.

The work of Brown can assist teachers in understanding the role that vulnerability plays in becoming a "wholehearted" educator (Brown, 2018). Vulnerability and empathy are intrinsic to each other. So, while the task of PD for racial equity and social justice is of paramount importance to education reform, it nonetheless must be redesigned with the understanding that what is being asked of teachers is complex. It calls for the integration of interdisciplinary research that seeks to uncover human social behavior across all levels of human experience with the goal of constructing pathways from the self to the multiple layers that comprise society. As I see it, too much is assumed, especially at the level of language, that is used to discuss and participate in the theoretical underpinnings that frame research and knowledge in culturally relevant and critical pedagogies. Without consideration of these gaps in teacher knowledge, the end result is that the hard conversations teachers are being asked to engage in fail to rise beyond heated opinions.

Safir and Dugan take it a step further in their book *Street Data: A Next Generation Model for Equity, Pedagogy and School Transformation* (2021), arguing that simply engaging in self-study and learning to adopt the discourse that speaks to equity in teaching often falls short of any tangible effects in teacher practice or school culture. They refer to this as "navel-gazing equity," described as "keeping the equity work at the level of self-reflection and failing to penetrate the instructional core and school systems and structures" (p. 37). They further contend that

> transformation requires investment in personal and interpersonal development, awareness and creation of shared cultural practices, and the redesign of inequitable systems—all at the same time. (Safir & Dugan, 2021, p. 37)

Therefore, the role of school and district leaders, of community social agencies, and of families cannot be undermined; all stakeholders have equal levels of obligation and a responsibility for equity work to have an impact on a systemic level. Yet with school principals taxed with insurmountable levels of administrative tasks, the hardest, deepest levels of work around equity inevitably falls on the shoulders of teachers. All the more reason to consider the suggestion that teachers engage in self-study that includes interdisciplinary perspectives such as that described by Brown's work on empathy, and the development of vulnerability in public and professional spaces. As I see it, empathy without imagination is not possible, and "working towards equity" (Safir & Dugan, 2021, p. 29) is not possible without imagination.

A CULTURE OF COMPLACENCY IN TEACHER PRACTICE

In the end, teachers' complacent attitudes concerning professional development, irrespective of the topic, prevail: "Just tell me what you want me to do, how you want me to do it, and for how many minutes a day." I put this in quotes because there isn't a teacher in America who wouldn't confess to these sentiments at some point in their career when introduced to yet a new district initiative that makes no sense, myself included. However, this cannot be the attitude used to engage in professional development for racial equity and social justice: One cannot simply go through a series of steps for x number of minutes daily. "Tell me what to do and for how long" cannot apply. One cannot simply "do equity as a series of tools, strategies, and compliance tasks versus whole-person, whole-system change process linked to culture, identity, and healing" (Safir & Dugan, 2021 p. 33).

Changing the attitude of complacency in teachers must happen for all professional development activity first, before it can be eradicated from professional development that centers around one's way of doing and seeing the world. All district and state professional development needs re-visioning from programs that provide "teacher friendly" manuals and toolkits in favor of approaches that encourage teachers to develop critical observation and recording skills, that can be contrasted against numerical data, and that will endow conversations around student achievement and inclusivity with a critical reflection of practice.

Yet, getting to those deep conversations is not so easy when prescriptive literacy programs, and the metrics-driven progress monitoring tools that accompany them, do little to inspire teachers toward conversations that attend deeply to the daily joys and successes, frustrations and challenges that students of color and English language learners (ELLs) may experience in their learning. Most importantly, when such milestones or challenges are acknowledged, many teachers are not guided into the ways in which such knowledge can be used as "data" that informs practice and promotes creative and alternative instructional and curricular choices. Acknowledging the dehumanizing nature of metric data, and its persistent conclusions that children of color continue to perform poorly in literacy and math, Safir and Dugan (2021) propose educators shift toward "an equity driven change process" (p. 57) that starts from the bottom up:

> Street data are the qualitative and experiential data that emerges at eye level and on lower frequencies when we train our brains to discern it. These data are asset based, building on the tenets of culturally responsive education by helping educators look for what's *right* in our students, schools, and communities instead of seeking out what's *wrong*. (p. 57)

In addition, PD should provide teachers with access to rich complex texts that will lead to a practice characterized by depth of mind and powerful intentions. No one articulates this regard for a practice of hope embodied through scholarship more succinctly than Sonia Nieto, who in measuring her initial experiences as an educator, recognized that

> the marriage of hope with critique was not only possible but in fact indispensable for true learning to take place. As educators who believe in and work with students, it seems to me that an attitude of hope and critique is our only option. (Nieto, 2010, pp. 30–31)

MY PROFESSIONAL DEVELOPMENT JOURNEY

Unlike the static prefabricated mountains of checklists and templates and guidelines, my inner spirit breathes life into my teacher practice. My distant textual mentors have given me permission to never lose myself scouring through the state-produced toolkit, but rather to use my belief in the power of individual and social change through critical reflection (Freire, 1998), aestheticism and the arts (Greene, 1995), and creative mal-adjustments (Kohl, 1994), the dimensions of human experience that foster the humanization of public education. Love and beauty and hope, empathy and compassion, along with the single human capacity to imagine and reimagine one's life, is precisely what I am suggesting have shaped my practice and continue to motivate my energies as a teacher.

Many might argue against the heady conceptual nature of my internal resources, the core of which is surely theoretical and too ethereal to serve practice in, well, any practical terms. In a field characterized by atomization, standardization, and quantification, many would be quick to brand me an idealist, a hopeless romantic. So be it. I'd be proud to sit on the bench alongside Herbert Kohl, who described himself as an "incurable romantic" and in the service of "peddling hope" in his book of essays *I Won't Learn from You* (1994, p. 87). I believe, as Kohl does, that teaching is a romantic act, one that inspires hope and shapes desires for self and social change. However, to be clear, hope, as I conceive of it, is not a vacuous, ornamental desire that gushes out contained by nothing and with no direction. Sonia Nieto (2010) warns against an "uncritical and idealized brand of hope," stating that "an uncritical hope is neither useful nor liberating" (p. 28). This is what I call in Spanish the "ay bendito, pobrecito" kind of hope that is well meaning, but prevents teachers from setting high expectations for students of color, and from believing that they possess home and community "funds of knowledge" (González et al., 2005).

While it has taken me a very long time to accept my romantic inclinations as a teacher, today I respect the role this perspective has played in shaping my teacher practice. There is nothing hopeless in believing and feeling deeply the joys and the lows of being in the service of others; in holding steadfast to the belief in the human capacity to love and in creating change that leads to a more inclusive and just world. My romanticism for teaching has allowed me to bring a vulnerability to my practice characterized by desire to create and to transcend the mundane through the critique of experience.

In his book *Teachers as Cultural Workers: Letters to Those Who Dare Teach* (1998), using himself as an example, Freire states, "I know with my entire self: with my critical mind, but also with my feelings, with my intuitions, with my emotions. What I must not do is stop at the level of emotions, of intuitions" (p. 30). To this point he further adds the teacher's need to read critically and deeply and in dialogue with the author to "place the objects of my intuition under serious and rigorous investigation" (p. 30). Freire further explains "lovingness" (p. 40) as not only the love one has for one's students, but also the love one has for the very human processes of learning and living within a sociohistorical moment wherein the self, wholly intertwined in concert with others, and through social and cultural experience, transforms.

Within this space of "lovingness" is where Herbert Kohl would agree lies the ability to "creatively maladjust," a concept inspired by Martin Luther King's famous 1958 speech in which he calls upon his followers to never adjust to institutional and social racism but rather instead "to be maladjusted to such things" (speech excerpt quoted in Kohl, 1994, p. 129). Reflecting on his own experience as a teacher, and the challenges he faced between institutional agendas that promoted inequities in education, and his instincts to do right by his students, Kohl found the value in "creatively maladjusting," explaining that

> creative maladjustment becomes a sane alternative to giving up altogether. Creative maladjustment consists of breaking social patterns that are morally reprehensible, taking conscious control of one's place in the environment, and readjusting the world one lives in based on personal integrity and honesty— that is, learning to survive with minimal moral and personal compromise in a thoroughly compromised world and of not being afraid of planned and willed conflict, if necessary. (Kohl, 1994, p. 130)

Preferring to shy away from "planned and willed conflict," I have spent many years believing that creative maladjustments belonged to a few chosen superheroes of education whose practice is marked by social activism and a critical praxis, individuals who, through an unyielding spirit and against all odds, prioritize teaching for social change on behalf of and in solidarity with those less privilege or disenfranchised. Their circumference of activism often encompasses change beyond the school doors.

I think, for example, of community activist and educator for social justice Mary Cowhey (2022), who has devoted her life's work to giving back that which is most needed for families living in marginalized communities, and that which in a democracy such as ours is most certainly a given right: power and voice; I think of arts educator, researcher, and activist for social justice Patty Bode (Nieto & Bode, 2012), who understands the power art has to engage students and communities in willful self-determination, individual and collective healing, and as meaning makers able to transform their lives from the depths of their hearts to the very spaces within which they experience their worlds.

It never crossed my mind until recently that creative maladjustments can be manifested in quiet and calculated ways; in maintaining the belief that teaching that derives from the internal tools of creativity, imagination, critical thinking, and empathy can be very loud and hard to ignore.

I continue to this day, after so many years, to work on developing what Freire refers to as "armed love":

> Without it they [teachers] could not survive all the injustice or the government's contempt which is expressed in shameful wages and the arbitrary treatment of teachers, not coddling mothers, who take a stand, who participate in protest activities through their union, who are punished, and who yet remain devoted to their work with students. (Freire, 1998, pp. 40–41)

I am learning that this "armed love" does not need to look and sound like a heated march or boycott outside school doors, or a contentious debate in front of the board of education. It can instead look like the performance art projects that my students bring to life for the school community and for their families, projects coded in messaging that pushes through the limits of the status quo and that draws from the bicultural and bilingual experiences of my students, and from the literary genius of Americans of color, who through song, poetry, critique, novels, and children's literature awaken our hearts and imaginations to envision ourselves in a new America that makes a protagonist of the lost and the invisible. It can look and sound like the mentoring relationships I share with in-service teachers attending the courses I teach at the university that for me are a means of connecting myself to practitioners eager to learn and transcend the unshakable infrastructure of education. It can look and sound like this very piece of writing that wholly exposes my teaching heart, my alternative perspectives on mainstream education and the development of teachers and children, and that, even as I write, I wish was less coruscant and flowery.

Today after 3 decades in the field, I am proud to say I feel deeply that my life as a teacher and my creative maladjustments have led to constant attempts at reinventing myself, experiencing education in varied settings and roles and engaging with learners of all ages. I teach with as much joy and enthusiasm today as I did 30 years ago. And the things that made me cross and charged and simply mad then continue to elicit the same response from me today.

Through the years some things have been as consistent as this joy and pain, and while I understand I provide no grand scheme to be replicated, the following insights may encourage other teachers to consider exploring alternative and more humane means of teaching that can lead to their abilities to creatively maladjust and reinvent themselves and avoid burnout and disillusionment in the profession.

Practicing Empathy and Exercising Imagination Through Journaling

For many years I have kept a teacher journal, a habit that gained momentum during my years as a graduate student at the University of Massachusetts at Amherst. The program of study held rigorous expectations for ethnographic writing, encouraging the use of anecdotal data to closely examine the relationships between theory and practice as well as the sociocultural/sociopolitical contexts of teaching and learning. Once I left this ideal and elite setting and stepped onto the real world, I faced a rude awakening. Here is a reflection piece that encapsulates the 10 years of this professional transition from suburban to urban education:

> Part of learning the ways in which this new community did education depended on the ways in which language use factored into the "doing" of education. How teachers and administrators spoke of teaching and learning, of curriculum and assessment, and most dramatically of children was inherently embedded in a deep culture of institutional discursive practices that I was not accustomed to, and that I internally responded to as inappropriate, at times crass, or simply unprofessional and rude—or, worse yet, as biased and racist.

The struggle in this respect was real, dense, conflicting, and ultimately very alienating. Those first 10 years of teaching were harrowing and at times isolating; they pushed me to reflect on spaces within myself I didn't know existed. Except for the presence of the kids, these years were very lonely for me. Yet within this loneliness—perhaps because of it—I thrived. My teaching and creativity were ignited with a perseverance to hold onto the discourse of academia, to hold steadfast to those distant scholars whose work consoled me and kept me afloat, to view the classroom experience through an ethnographic lens and always within a sociocultural/sociopolitical frame.

Initially my journal writing resembled field notes rather than journal entries, but eventually the hectic pace of experience took shape in prose. At home, unable to shake the million little pieces of the day, I would glue together the joy and the pain, shaping it into poetry. Sometimes the poems were from the perspective of my students, giving them power and voice, their personalities flying off the page. At other times, the poems illustrated the joy and unbound energies of our little ESL classroom, located in the school basement. Some poems, such as the one below, spoke to the reproduction of injustice prevalent in traditional urban classrooms, the very spaces where my ESL immigrant children spent a great deal of the day. Some poems attempted to reconstruct the events of the day through the release of "armed love," without the fear of intimidation, finding the freedom to capture the wrongs to make them right.

Below is a poem I wrote in my journal during the years in which I taught in a basement closet classroom. It has a stammering rhythm, off-putting and disregarding; I heard it daily, on repeat, at the threshold of the door of a 4th-grade classroom as I went to pick up my ESL groups. For years I felt like a coward for not being able to do more to stop this refrain, but in retrospect it was this harsh dissonance that fueled my teaching heart into creating melodic, beautiful learning experiences free from fear, sarcasm, and abuses of power.

Carla

Turn around, be quiet, sit down,
Take out your homework,
Stop talking, stop walking, stop tapping,
Stop blinking, stop fidgeting,
Stop daydreaming, stop whining,
Stop complaining, stop making excuses,
Stop smirking; stop clicking your teeth,
Stop smacking your lips
Stop that attitude.

Put that away, open your backpack, pick that up,
Place your signed tests on my desk, what's that?
No signed tests? then lunch detention.
No homework? Then the red line for recess.
Take out your reading books, copy what's on the board,
Put your papers in your folder,
Raise your hands, put your hands down,
No you may not go to the bathroom,
No you may not get a drink of water,
No you may not borrow a pencil; bring your own,
Come to school prepared.

Mrs. Foster's words are hard and dusty
like the 100-year-old red bricks
that are stacked in the shape of a school
She is impenetrable—her words are
all commands "I said stop talking" she bellows
Her words a bitter wind slamming doors shut
blowing papers around the room

We stop talking but not because she tells us to
but because our words are turned inside out
shoved back down our throats
choking the life out of our ideas and

the stories of yesterday we were
eager to tell.

What kind of sentence is this?
Where's the punctuation?
Capital letter here, what's the main idea?
Read. Louder. Faster. Faster.
Slow down. Your reading makes no sense.
Fill in the blanks. Choose the right word.
Break up the word. Sound it out.
Read faster. Think. You're not thinking.
Now retell. Stop, that's not a retell,
That's a summary.

Kids sink into their collars and
disappear into their dirty, wrinkled
pretend white polo shirts, but not me.
My head sticks out further than a giraffe's and
her droning, sarcastic and tired inside her head
words find a comfortable place in my own head
and suddenly for a brief moment she and I are allies,
both bored, and both at the brink of death.

Fill in the blank, Choose the word that makes
Most sense. Wrong. Furnace and furnish have
Nothing to do with each other. Wrong. The word is
Fish not finish. Dive not drive. Self-correct when you read.
Self-correct. She repeats. Sticking to a decades old script.

What's the main idea? She hammers in
What's the author's purpose? She pounds.
What is the author leaving out in this passage? . . .
My hand goes up . . . and I say . . . That he doesn't know
we can't read?
The hammer gets mad! But
I think it's funny

We can't talk and can't say
"we don't understand the
chopped up version of the story,
The stop and go version of the story"
The "There's no time for discussion"
version of the story

Move on to Cause and Effect . . .
Easy answer . . .
Hatred of reading

disregard
for words.

Now for the finale . . . drum roll please . . .
How does this connect
to your personal experience?
You have ten minutes to write it down . . .
Our pencils don't move except to erase and erase
Timer goes off papers are collected
Our experiences nothing more than dirty smudges
on yellowing thin paper,
Where's your name she yells to the boy over there,
I raise my hand I feel so brave and say
I forgot my name.

In Mrs. Foster's room words in books die
And books on the outside suffer too
at the hands of angry students defiant
fighting humiliation

Because they know nothing of
what they should know
But they know for sure this one thing
They know
How much
They hate
Reading.

"Get in line to the bathroom" the command
    is sullen and each word an effort to say
    We race to the door pushing and shoving our way out
"Get back" in your seats. You act like animals.

How old are you anyway? How many years
have you been in school? Let's try that
again and we line up like robots.

We march out with our heads down
Grieving the death of so many words.
Girls to the girls' bathroom.
Boys to the boys' bathroom.
This is how we commemorate the death of words
In Mrs. Foster's classroom—with
A funeral procession to the bathroom.

When I read this poem, I am brought back to the exact space and
time where this classroom lived and I, their teacher, taught. I think more

specifically of my ESL students, what it meant for them to navigate a new language and new customs in a classroom setting that promoted silence and fear, a system that ignored the diverse cultures and languages that informed their experiences inside the classroom and out. Many of the ESL children were immigrants from Eastern European countries, Central and South America, and South Asia. While Carla did exist, and did have this teacher, the Carla of this poem is an amalgamation of voices and personalities representing the multiple children who endured an education that at its core kept them limited in their English language development, but that in the end failed to limit their ability to resist and assert themselves against the rigid and humiliating context within which they experienced learning.

The teaching described in the poem above is characterized by a pedantic series of instructional and behavioral commands and base questions, punctuated by sarcasm, power, and humiliation. Sonia Nieto in elaborating on Martin Haberman's work on "the pedagogy of poverty" states,

> In spite of its widespread use, this pedagogy has little success and students leave these classrooms with minimal life skills. Unsupported by theory, by research, and by best practices of successful urban teachers, "the pedagogy of poverty" is instead a set of negative attitudes and beliefs—in reality, a philosophical stance—based on a deficit perspective about urban students enacted through pedagogy. (Nieto, 2013, p 23)

Sadly, this harsh, rigid script continues to play out across urban classrooms throughout our nation, often in the most disenfranchised communities. Except today there is a more insidious manifestation of the deficit perspective of teaching in which orderliness, silence, stillness, and false attentiveness provide the illusion that learning is taking place. Safir and Dugan (2021) refer to this as a "pedagogy of compliance" that "rests on invisible norms of dominant culture (quiet, compliant, task oriented, individualistic)" (p. 109).

Keeping a journal fashioned after my own passions for literary and poetic texts allowed me to practice empathy as a teacher. It was my way of entering into the experiences of my students; a way of connecting to them through my inner child. I don't see how else I could have survived a devastatingly cruel example of how school itself was the biggest bully in the playground. No professional development attended in these years addressed Carla's classroom experience, nor the abhorrent deficit-driven teaching style that characterized more than just this one teacher's approach. Mind you, the years I am referring to were within the first decade into the millennium; classrooms such as Carla's were still thriving and very much alive having crossed into the 21st century unscathed and unchanged.

When I first became a teacher at the young age of 24, I had no experience or background in teaching; what I did have was a vibrant inner child.

That inner child remains a cherished friend even today; we often meet at the crossroads of reckless abandonment through imaginary play and the corner of empathy. I truly believe that in the service of children, it is best for one to consult their inner child for lessons in how to make teaching substantial, memorable, and culturally and socially just. Practicing empathy through journaling can connect teachers to two things: the child they were, and the adult they became.

AESTHETIC SPACES THAT FOSTER A PRACTICE OF IMAGINATION

Children love beautiful things. They love the whimsical and playful miniatures that suddenly represent the large world in minutia, yet that manage to make giants of their experience. They love jingly sounds, snapping their fingers, clapping, stomping and running, and discovering how to skip. They pretend they are trees and rocks, imagining how these sedentary natural wonders might behave if they came to life. They catch snowflakes on their tongues, and splash in puddles; they crawl into spaces smaller than themselves and find in the nooks and crannies of their world the infinite release of time and space, unbounded and with no structure. They love transforming objects that for us as adults have fixed purpose; a pencil into an airplane, a broken computer key board into a cash register. They are enthralled when a mushy blob of play dough is transformed into a person, a burger, a chair. With crayons our human skin can be blue or purple or green, and the sun always sports a grin larger than life.

I am not describing here a romanticized version of the child of yesteryear. Nor am I describing only the very young child. I currently work in a K–8 school and I teach students at all grade levels. It is impressive to watch how, given the opportunity and the right materials, children even at the middle school levels will engage in creative representations of experience and the inventive manipulation of objects and props.

Because I have worked in private, parochial, and suburban settings, I know what the classrooms of privileged children can look like: classrooms that present children with a wealth of cultural and natural artifacts that render discovery and creativity possible.

Working now for over 20 years in an urban setting, I have experienced teaching in hallways, utility closets, reading closets, and what are often dirty abandoned spaces. Seeing the futility in complaining, I have instead chosen to transform these spaces into the most beautiful classrooms, rich in materials, cultural and natural artifacts, books in every genre, costume boxes and props, and a myriad of other curiosities and novelties that inspire rich talk amongst students and even richer student writing. The message on my door today says "E.S.L.: Every Student Learns," and, in the years of the closet classroom located in the basement, a hand-drawn picture of the Statue of

Liberty crafted by Carla and signed by all the ESL students was our welcome sign into learning.

All children deserve to learn in a beautiful environment that makes them feel alive and worthy; that fosters a love for literacy and the development of a positive self-esteem; and that places the student as part of a larger community. This is at the heart of a pedagogy for social justice. I strongly believe that beautiful spaces carefully crafted to stir children's curiosities and stimulate their senses is not a personal preference; it is an educational obligation that fulfills the right of all children to experience an education as much concerned with promoting hope and aspirations in the young as it is with developing their minds. This objective must be included in conversations intended to encourage teachers to create a practice of empathy and imagination within the frame of racial equity and social justice.

A classroom designed to promote creativity and imagination will enrich the developmental and linguistic capacities of the bilingual and bicultural child, and all children, regardless of race and ethnicity, who experience life on the periphery of mainstream middle-class culture. There may be a great deal that teachers cannot do to improve the negative conditions of many urban schools, but they can use creativity and imagination to transcend their experiences and the experiences of their students. A practice shaped by the promise of racial equity and social justice must honor that even the makeshift classrooms in school basements across America can become spaces where children can thrive respectfully and with integrity.

CONNECTING PERSONAL NARRATIVE TO UNCOVER BIAS IN TEACHING PRACTICE

I came to the United States from Puerto Rico having just turned 6 years old. I lived in Brooklyn with my Tía Rosita, my mother's sister, and her husband, my Uncle Marty, a first-generation Italian American. We lived in a neighborhood that was predominantly comprised of Italian immigrants, and only five blocks away the sounds and smells of Poland permeated the air. The block we lived on was just beginning to awaken to the sounds of the Spanish language, thanks to the rhythms of newly arriving Puerto Ricans.

My uncle spoke fluent English, Italian, and Spanish; my aunt was fully bilingual in Spanish and English and could also navigate Italian with ease. Between my parents (who joined me in Brooklyn the following year), my uncle, and my aunt, it was decided I would attend the parochial school five blocks away, Our Lady of Czestochowa, a parochial school run by Polish immigrant nuns who had fled Poland during World War II. The largest percentage of the students were Polish immigrants or first-generation Polish Americans; a small number were first-generation Italian American or Irish American. I believe my sister and I, along with perhaps one other family that I knew of, may have been the only Puerto Rican students at the school. Most of the day unfolded in Polish, except for our lessons. Daily prayers, songs, and masses were in Polish; all discipline was handled in Polish, and recess was a combination of Polish and English. The influx of new students from Poland was routine. In our presence the nuns switched from Polish to English with ease, but Polish always seemed to punctuate the moment.

To this day, I say with confidence that I was experiencing an unplanned bilingual/bicultural education, even though it was not necessarily the design of this parochial school. At home, language flowed between Spanish, English, and Italian; at school language lived between Polish and English. Interestingly, I don't recall ever feeling lost or confused, but I do remember hearing the Spanish in the Italian and Polish languages, an intuition that later transferred into an ability to locate English/Spanish cognates in print. Within the year from my arrival to Brooklyn, I was reading in English, and moving successfully through school. This upbringing primed me to be a teacher of English to students who speak other languages. From a young age my world was marked by cultural heterogeneity and linguistic diversity.

Professional Development on racial equity and social justice centers around the examination of bias and privilege. Often the reflective activity is located in perceptions of our adult interactions with the world. However, of considerable importance is connecting to the relationship one had to education in their childhood. For example, reflecting on my story has helped me understand what language bias truly means. Having lived in a world of language differences, it never crossed my mind to view the use of languages other than English in public settings with suspicion. Yet once removed from the heterogeneous environment of New York City, I began to experience a less favorable reception of my bilingualism, specifically my use of Spanish. I began to learn how monolinguals in homogenous mainstream settings found the use of Spanish "rude," or interpreted it with suspicion, labeling it as "un-American." They had no problem letting me know their feelings.

Research on bilingualism has for years shown the positive neurological and cognitive effects of bilingualism, and bilingual education research (Garcia & Kleifgen, 2018) has proven that the use of bilingual strategies in the classroom promotes literacy and thought development. Yet so many teachers continue to feel uncomfortable allowing their students, especially those from low socioeconomic backgrounds, to engage in partner or group work that allows the use of a native language other than English. The primary reason given for this is that the teacher cannot regulate or assess if the students are on topic or if they are simply socializing, thus judging the use of bilingualism in the classroom as impacting classroom management more than literacy or knowledge development.

Similarly, in the younger years at the elementary level, it is not uncommon for the children of recently arrived immigrants or of families newly arrived from Puerto Rico to provide translation for their families as they navigate the complex bureaucracies of social institutions. Teachers typically respond through the deficit lens to the familial practice of children translating for the adults, usually responding with a "sympathetic" concern for the stress placed on the children by their very own families (recall the "poor, poor child'" form of empathy I mentioned earlier). More than once I have had to rectify this point of view, preferring instead to recognize the acuity of mind and creative instinct of the child present in using the social and cultural context of experience to accomplish an important task. Herein lies the power of the bilingual mind as it is nurtured in an educational setting shaped with empathy and social justice in mind.

The poem titled "Borofels," which appears in Sonia Nieto's memoir *Brooklyn Dreams* (2015) and was written by the renowned poet Martin Espada (Espada, 1993), captures beautifully the bilingual child's keen use of social context to problem solve real life challenges. It describes how a young Sonia accompanies her mother in search of the Board of Health. Navigating the subway transit system, young Sonia bravely approaches strangers asking "Where is Borofels?" and, not being understood, she instinctively knew to read the world in search of clues that would get someone to provide assistance:

> Sonia saw the uniform then,
> Blue coated trooper of U.S Mail
> And pleaded for Borofels. (p. 57)

Reflecting on personal narratives to uncover one's experiences of language, race, culture and class supports teachers as they encounter PDs that require them to transform their practice from the inside out. In dissecting their childhood experiences, they can discover how these early memories have shaped their willingness or resistance to grow within their teaching practice. PD that aims for racial equity and social justice must encourage critical reading and writing activity for teachers, starting from a depth of personal experience at the level of childhood in order to arrive at a practice that places the experiences of students of color as well as those learning English at the forefront of learning and teaching.

IN CLOSING

PD for racial equity and social justice must deliberately support teachers in the development of internal tools such as imagination, creativity, and empathy, the attributes of which must be rendered visible and tangible through classroom engagement and classroom design, as well as in social interactions with students, families, and colleagues. Teachers need to be able to walk away with the understanding that their participation in the mainstream culture positions them as experiencers of privilege; this privilege is what makes it possible to exercise unconscious power in the form of what Robin DiAngelo (2018) terms "aversive racism," a racism that is understated, yet present in lifestyle choices made by "well intentioned people who see themselves as educated and progressive" (p. 43). Very few of us are exempt from this category, which means our work as educators, and as citizens of a democratic society committed to racial equity and social justice, may be an ongoing project for the duration of our lives.

Teachers have the right to read the heavy books, the ones that inspire dialogue beyond opinion, the ones that encourage the risk-taking that comes with engaging in creative maladjustment. Intellectual and critical dialogue can happen only when teachers are equipped to elevate their thinking from "this is what I believe due to my experiences" to "these are the textual designers that support the instructional and curricular choices I make in practice."

Teachers should be encouraged to dialogue critically with the authors they read, comparing and contrasting their lived practice with the interests and goals characterized through alternative views of teaching and learning. Yet, the perspective taken by many educators is that teachers need less theory, and that more attention should be given to practice; this, too, needs to be re-evaluated.

The undermining of theory in practice has slipped into the danger zone, and it is time to reimagine a new relationship between ideas and actions. Walqui (2010) simply states, "In accomplished teaching, theory and practice are inseparable" (p. 25). Theory is the architectural foundation, the genius design that sets forth the image of human development. Educators are privileged to have the opportunity to sculpt teaching experiences that bring beauty and pleasure to the learning experiences of children, and to the teachers who teach them.

As so many teachers will admit to loving their students, so too that love must be understood as the emotion that ignites the joy and curiosity for the world of ideas. I am reminded of the question asked by the brilliant scholar and writer bell hooks, in the now classic text *Teaching to Transgress* (1994), who in challenging the objective, sterile traditions of academia, dared to address the role of emotion and feeling in the life of the classroom, by simply asking "If we are all emotionally shut down, how can there be any excitement about ideas?" (p. 155).

Practice void of "any excitement about ideas" is a practice shaped by routinization, and managerial attempts at controlling bodies and voices, and is the cause for why so many of our students and teachers flatline into boredom and complacency in the classroom. Loving our students must lead to our students loving to read, to learn, and most importantly, to loving themselves and each other in community. Yet another unexpected gift comes when they remember us, their teachers, and can love us back.

PD on racial equity and social justice must encourage teachers to read, to write, and to engage with the writings of scholars of education about alternative ways to view the complex traditions and conventions that persist in public education; and not only must teachers read, but they should do so with their whole self, in order to uncover their passions, fears, and vulnerabilities. This will support the development of a lovingness toward their craft and their teaching spaces, in addition to the love they feel for their students. It will set the path to "working toward equity" (Safir & Dugan, 2021, p. 29) with the understanding that the journey moves forward, but may never end. As teachers we must trust in the human capacity to develop, to imagine, to create change from within, and to form the social, cultural, and political experiences that create an individual's self-knowing and worldview.

REFERENCES

Brown, B. (2018). *Dare to lead: Brave work. Tough conversations. Whole hearts.* Random House.

Cowhey, M. (2022). *Families with power: Centering students by engaging with families and community.* Teachers College Press.

DiAngelo, R. J. (2018). *White fragility: Why it's so hard for white people to talk about racism.* Beacon Press.

Espada, M. (1993). *City of coughing and dead radiators.* W. W. Norton.

Freire, P. (1998). *Teachers as cultural workers: Letters to those who dare teach.* Westview Press.

García, O., & Kleifgen, J. A. (2018). *Educating emergent bilinguals: Policies, programs, and practices for English learners.* Teachers College Press.

González, N., Moll, L. C., & Amanti, C. (2005). *Funds of knowledge: Theorizing practice in households, communities, and classrooms.* L. Erlbaum Associates.

Greene, M. (1995). *Releasing the imagination: Essays on education, the arts, and social change.* Jossey-Bass.

hooks, b. (1994). *Teaching to transgress: Education as the practice of freedom.* Routledge.

Kohl, H. (1994). *"I won't learn from you" and other thoughts on creative maladjustment.* The New Press.

Nieto, S. (2010). *The light in their eyes: Creating multicultural learning communities.* Teachers College Press.

Nieto, S. (2013). *Finding joy in teaching students of diverse backgrounds: Culturally responsive and socially just practices in U.S. classrooms.* Heinemann.

Nieto, S. (2015). *Brooklyn dreams: My life in public education.* Harvard Education Press.

Nieto, S., & Bode, P. (2012). *Affirming diversity: The sociopolitical context of multicultural education* (4th ed.). Pearson Publishers.

Safir, S., & Dugan, J. (2021). *Street data: A next-generation model for equity, pedagogy, and school transformation.* Corwin.

Walqui, A. (2010, February 3). *Professional development scaffolding success: Five principles for succeeding with adolescent English learners: An interview with Aida Walqui.* https://www.languagemagazine.com/2010/02/03/february-2010/

CHAPTER 7

Journey Onward, Beloved Educators

Mary Jade Haney

I currently serve as a public school librarian during the school year and lead summer camps with a focus on professional development during the summer. As such, I challenge all educators to "Journey Onward" by taking small steps. I will forever be an educator because this journey is my way of *being the change I want to see in the world* (as Mahatma Gandhi advised). I believe that school is a microcosm of society, so I cannot imagine a world without "Beloved Educators" taking small steps to impact the greater good.

LEARNING FROM FIRST TEACHERS AND THE VILLAGE

Sustainability in the profession comes from intentionality. Every step taken, as a public school educator, must be intentional. Defining my educational journey and process is critical to remaining focused on the purpose of why I became an educator in the first place. Often as I am drinking my morning cup of coffee, I take time to think about my life as an educator. When I think of my first teachers, my parents come to mind before any other teachers. My parents focused on teaching us the importance of humanity. Both my mother and my father, as our first teachers, showed us what it truly means to be human in loving ways. Collectively and individually, they modeled the level of humanity they expected from their six children, a.k.a., the "Six

Pack." Since my parents are no longer on this earth with us, we aspire to carry on their legacy. Therefore, I am dedicating this chapter to my parents, *Katherleen "Howzell" McQueen-Haney* and *Samuel Haney Sr.,* our first *Beloved Educators.*

Before we entered kindergarten, my parents taught us invaluable lessons of love, joy, peace, patience, kindness, faithfulness, gentleness, self-control, integrity, respect, and responsibility. They taught us how to read and write, how to communicate, how to solve problems and think critically, how to lead, how to follow, when to speak up, and when to remain silent. Collectively, they taught us how to be human, to be ourselves while living in an uncertain, unpredictable, yet beautiful world.

Because of the intersectionality of my nontraditional and traditional learning spaces where I was celebrated as a learner, leader, and visionary, I am a teacher . . . being free to learn and create even while making mistakes along the way. There is an African proverb that states, "It takes a whole village to raise a child." My village was purposeful: Everyone around me was considered family. My village were those who loved me, valued me, and held high expectations for me. Through high levels of trust, we built strong and lasting relationships. My villagers were always with me, in my home, school, and community. Therefore, as an educator, I am constantly on a mission to be a member of a child's village, as suggested by Ladson-Billings (2009).

Each day I live, it is my mission to be the change I wish to see in public education.

If we want a change, we must constantly question ourselves and seek opportunities for change. Above all, we must never lose hope, knowing that the only thing constant is change. It is fitting to begin questioning how we are doing teaching, providing services, and maintaining our profession as educators within and beyond the context of a global pandemic in and out of school. I am not looking for correct or conclusive answers because there are none, but I am challenging all educators to think more critically about our profession and the services we provide to the most important people in the world, our students.

As educators, our focus must be on student learning rather than instructional compliance in isolation. I think of instructional compliance as "doing teaching" using scripted programs and resources vetted and adopted by individuals outside of schools and classrooms. Are we succumbing to the idea of instructional compliance more than student learning? Am I in the profession to impact student learning while engaging the whole child in humanistic ways? If instructional compliance is working, then I am all for it, but if it is not impacting student learning and achievement while also loving the whole child, then must I begin to lean in and change?

If we desire to responsively serve our students, we must use multiple data sources, both qualitative and quantitative. As we seek methods to improve the educational system, is this process solely focused on instructional compliance as a response to educating students within a global pandemic and beyond? Are we missing the beauty of teaching critical foundational skills in reading, writing, and arithmetic through social–emotional literacy? Are we using the knowledge of our students to plan and deliver focused instruction? Are we developing assessment tools that authentically reveal the brilliance in each child? Can a boxed curriculum, Multi-Tiered Systems of Support (MTSS), and Response to Interventions (RtI), and other educational services provided to children dehumanize them? Thinking about these questions can be heartbreaking for "Beloved Educators" who understand what it means to love the whole child in equitable ways. Until all teachers feel they have the choice to use their voice within their teaching and learning spaces, we will not experience true liberation in public education or in our world. Content and curriculum can collide when outside systems hinder teachers and their beliefs about teaching and learning. If that happens, teachers can become apprehensive and unsure about how to deliver truths that may not be comfortable and compliant. Liberation, in this context, is having the freedom to choose and use best practices and resources that will benefit students. Also, teachers should have the autonomy to change and adapt curriculum to meet the needs of all children. With this hope and vision, we will be on the path to equity for all.

Why are passionate teachers leaving and falling "out of love" with the educational profession? To be honest, I am not trying to provide answers to these questions. Instead I am challenging educators to be empowered by these questions as we continue to do the work of relationship building through love, trust, and service in humanistic ways.

Brian Camborne's Conditions for Learning (see Rushton et al., 2003), critical theory (Freire, 2000), and culturally relevant pedagogy (Ladson-Billings, 2009) provide the theoretical framework for the collaborative services I provide for teachers, students, parents, families, and community members. Each session begins with honoring the participants' "funds of knowledge" (González et al., 2005). Using this framework, I honor and build on strengths through multiple spaces (i.e., home, community, and school) of teaching and learning. During my formative years, most of my practical and most useful knowledge came from my parents, my first co-teachers, with instructional support from my village (i.e., aunts, uncles, cousins, friends, church members, teachers, and community members). They intervened by providing multiple opportunities to approximate by trying, retrying, and practice, with celebrations along the way. Are students the most important people in the learning process? If the answer is yes, then we must begin with the knowledge of our students and their families. We must build trusting relationships and motivational mindsets. Our aim should always be to support students in meeting their goals in challenging times beyond a global pandemic and spaces of injustices.

EARLY CAREER LEARNING AND LEADING AS
A CLASSROOM TEACHER

My journey to contribute to the educational life of children began as a 4th-grade classroom teacher in a rural community. While I believe that I had one of the best instructional leaders within our district, deficit perspectives were evident at times. In my initial years of working with her, she didn't expect success from some of the students because most came from low-income families. Her responses often reflected her beliefs.

During my second year, I developed more courage and confidence. As a result, we had many critical conversations about instructional resources, practices, and expectations. Through our journey together, we became a dyad, collaborating to focus on solutions to many of the challenges we faced. She was open to learning from me as I learned from her in the class-room community with students and family members. We grew together as literacy leaders.

Educators do not have to leave their classroom to enlarge their territory. They must know when it's time to journey on and find new spaces and places to learn, teach, lead, and grow. Above all, it's important to learn from every experience. The more I learned, the more I felt my classroom space more challenging as a teacher leader. It was time to embrace change, so I began to explore options to enlarge my territory. Educators can become advocates for students by engaging in action-research, collaborating with colleagues, writing articles, creating bulletin boards, engaging students in "Flash Mob" performances, presenting at conferences, joining professional organizations and so on. For me, leaving education, one of the most important professions in the world, is never an option, but I must always have joy and show love to my students, parents, families, colleagues, and community members. I will admit, sometimes with all the political noise that surrounds advocacy work for educators and students, our profession can be challenging. If you know being an educator is your passion and purpose, you must "breathe, but never leave." I've learned many important lessons in life, but one that has remained with me is that it is okay to walk away, to reflect, re-think, re-connect and re-create ourselves. The service work of educators could possibly lead us to different pathways that link us to classrooms directly or indirectly; therefore, I challenge teachers to find an educational path that keeps them physically, emotionally, and socially healthy in safe spaces.

VISUALIZING AND INTEGRATING CURRICULUM IN
THE ART ROOM

From 2001 through 2008, I taught visual arts (grades K–5) through an interdisciplinary lens with a focus on picture books and their illustrators.

During those years, I was able to focus on academic, creative, and cultural experiences, learning more about the importance of student engagement within the context of their funds of knowledge. Being in the art room was a wonderful space to explore curriculum through a multicultural lens while collaborating with students, parents, families, and community members. I collaborated with classroom teachers and provided support while conducting action research with teacher educators from a university that collaborated with a professional development school (PDS). The major goal was to improve literacy learning in grades pre-K–5 as students worked as authors and illustrators. Some of the other memorable learning experiences included "Sleeping Under the Stars," where teachers and students spent one Friday night at the school. We invited the astronomy club from our local university and students were able to view the night sky through powerful ground-based telescopes. These telescopes enabled students and teachers to see some of the planets in the solar system as well as the Seven Sisters. The principal engaged students by "cooking up a comet" using dry ice so that students could clearly identify the tail and other parts of a comet. We grew vegetable gardens and created rock sculptures, sketched on the patio, wrote poetry, enjoyed authors' celebrations, and published an anthology to include student writing and artwork. Additionally, I developed more programming ideas for our after-school curriculum by collaborating with teachers while in the art room. After 8 fulfilling years, it was time to *journey onward* as I assumed the roles of reading teacher, reading interventionist, literacy coach, and teacher educator.

EMPOWERING FUTURE EDUCATORS

Serving as a teacher educator is enlightening in many ways. Rewarding experiences have included multiple opportunities to assist in teacher preparation as an adjunct instructor who taught methods courses, led seminars, and supervised early childhood interns—a particularly empowering experience. My undergraduate students were passionate and determined to become teachers, and they did. This experience motivated and inspired me to keep moving forward in the profession while teaching and learning alongside future educators. It also informed my service as a reading teacher and reading interventionist before I became a literacy coach.

Serving as a literacy coach was a way to keep moving forward and learning alongside classroom teacher leaders. It also provided opportunities to co-teach in multiple classroom spaces, Pre-Kindergarten through 5th grade. Co-planning, co-teaching, and co-reflecting with educators with multiple grade levels opened a whole new world for me as a forever teacher leader. From these experiences, I never saw myself as an expert, but as a learner and leader. I learned that classroom teachers are so busy doing the work that they sometimes do not see themselves as teacher leaders. I began to encourage teachers to always see themselves as teacher leaders and take on a reflective stance. I also encouraged them to share with others through reflective conversations. I believe it is important to create your own professional learning plan while also accepting staff development to "breathe out" in the profession, that is, to deeply think about what needs to be done based on what you know is equitable for all students.

With these thoughts in mind, I returned to my first love, a classroom, teaching 3rd grade for 1 year. I immersed myself in all the work that I expected from 21st-century classroom teacher leaders. When I left the classroom, we had spiral-bound gradebooks with little squares for written lesson plans. Later, white boards were replaced with Smartboards. Each student was assigned a laptop. Years ago, my class had limited technology to support learning, and we were not serving 21st-century learners as teachers are expected to do in today's classrooms. Our students are digital citizens who are expected to use technology as a tool for learning and teachers are expected to access technology as a means, not an end, to improve student learning, thus increasing student achievement. Most of all, being a teacher was highly respected by parents, students, families, and community members. There were stronger beliefs in the community that classroom teachers could be trusted with delivering curriculum and instruction, and that they had the ability to critically link theory to practice. Has the teacher workload increased over the last decade? Have teachers' decision-making powers been limited? Are our classrooms becoming places where students feel validated and supported as individuals? Does teacher support look different? I have no answers for some of these questions. However, I believe in options. We have options; *the journey of a thousand miles begins with one step,* and the vision begins with a dream.

I am not declaring that good things are not happening; they are happening, but they may be superficial because of the workload and the limited power of teachers. Returning to the classroom felt different this time. Teacher support looked different, but there were professional learning opportunities. Unfortunately, these were pre-selected, and compliance was always expected with little to no voice.

SCHOOL LIBRARIANSHIP AND COLLABORATIONS

As a school librarian, my focus is to collaborate with students, parents, families, educators, and community members. My life as an educator has come full circle "in" and "out" of this public school library. Every day is a new day to serve in this profession as a school librarian.

INTERDISCIPLINARY SUMMER LITERACY CAMP

I collaborated with colleagues to create a joyful space in an after-school summer camp that fuels me and other teacher leaders while serving students in a collaborative space. As a school librarian, I advocate for collaboration with teacher leaders to create an interdisciplinary summer camp to enrich lives beyond the school walls. The camp is now 12 summers old and fully funded by a grant through the library program within our school district. Funding supports professional development stipends, hourly pay for educators when serving students in the camp, and instructional resources for literacy engagements within the structure of a STEAM perspective: Science (Social Justice), Technology (Plugged and Un-Plugged), Engineering (Economics), Arts with Humanities (Advocacy), and Mathematics (Mindfulness) structure.

On Wednesday, June 17, 2015, the camp moved toward social justice during an unthinkable tragedy that happened in Charleston, South Carolina. During bible study, nine parishioners were fatally shot by a White male in the basement of Mother Emanuel African Methodist Episcopal Church. Mother Emanuel is one of the oldest Black churches in the United States of America and a center for civil rights organizing. In honor and memory of the Emanuel Nine, we now begin the Literacy Live 365 "Flash mob" performance with a living memorial where we say their names.

Through a social justice lens, our camp intentionally provides time for teacher leaders to collaborate and reflect on theoretical frameworks integrated within their beliefs, experiences, and practices. They freely build curriculum around knowledge of students to learn new strategies, explore multiple resources, and approximate with instructional practices while exploring multiple pathways to learning alongside students, families, and community members in the camp, making these valuable resources in the service of students' "funds of knowledge" (González et al., 2005). Educators become free from political mandates and instructional compliances. In this space, I can serve as a librarian, professional developer, and literacy coach with a focus on critical theory and culturally relevant pedagogy. I am able to provide opportunities and resources to honor and value all cultures within our school, for example, by collaborating with parents to create family literacy nights, engagements with input on book selections, and community visits. At the summer literacy camp, we ask families to share their cultures through food, songs, stories, arts, and crafts. All resources come from families and community members. We have fathers who have a band, so they provide live entertainment during our Parent(s), Family, Community Day. Additionally, parents and community members provide refreshments for events based on their culture. The work that we collectively do at this interdisciplinary summer camp is extraordinary. It brings hope to the educational profession and it is making a difference. One summer, at the end of camp, the Camp Discovery STEAM Academy staff received the following email:

> *Ms. Haney and the entire staff of Camp Discovery STEAM Academy,*
> *I would like to thank you for the wonderful experiences that my children M_____ and A_____ were afforded in your Summer Program. M_____ is a special needs student who has struggled for years to retain any information. It brought tears to my eyes every day to see and hear about his day. He was able to tell me every day about the things he had learned in camp. He told me about Mary McLeod Bethune and how she opened a school for girls. He also told me that her great grandniece is the mayor of Mayesville. He sang different songs about strings, math, learned how to dance, and my favorite, he learned about courage. I've noticed major changes in both of my children and I am so happy that they went to your camp. I never once felt that they were not safe, and on the first day, you guys had it all together and so organized. I could tell when I first walked in that much thought was put into every detail of this program. I sincerely thank you for all that you have done for them. This program was blessed and successful. I hope it runs longer next summer.*
>
> > *Thank you.*
> > *K.M.*

There were no dry eyes in our circle because of the impact shared by this child's first teacher. I named this email "Impact Data Beyond a Test Score: We Made a Difference."

CONCLUDING THOUGHTS

You are an educator. You were born to make a difference in the lives of children. Believe in yourself, your students, and their families. As you journey onward, as an educator for life, I challenge you to stay healthy—not just physically, but also emotionally, spiritually, and mentally. Even after facing a global pandemic lasting about 3 years, we find ourselves still serving in the educational profession. You are gifted. Unwrap your gift. Impact our world.

As I serve in the most important profession in the world, my ultimate goal is to remain steadfast and intentional as I continue charting my journey while cultivating joy.

Without leaving the profession, you can continue to serve in different spaces. Educators have countless options beyond giving up. Journey onward, beloved educators! Don't miss the beauty of making a difference in the lives of students, parents, families, and your colleagues!

Eleven Ways to Journey Onward as Beloved Educators

1. Write reflective letters to yourself, reminding yourself "why" you chose the teaching profession.
2. Keep journals (i.e., personal, professional, gratitude).
3. Read children's books or Young Adult novels that reflect your beliefs.
4. Curate professional text sets based on your selected problem of practice.
5. Create a collaborative team of teaching professionals to go on fieldtrips, vacations, rest-and-relax days.
6. Stay connected to like-minded people through a circle of trust.
7. Conduct action research, write conference proposals, articles.
8. Collect jars of motivational quotes and words to pull from daily.
9. Keep portfolios and displays of letters, drawings, emails, Facebook posts, notes from students, parents, families, educators, and community members.
10. Honor your own time by being present with family and friends.
11. Celebrate YOU!

REFERENCES

Freire, P. (2000). *Pedagogy of the oppressed* (30th anniversary ed.). Continuum.

González, N., Moll, L. C., & Amanti, C. (Eds.). (2005). *Funds of knowledge.* Lawrence Erlbaum Associates Publishers.

Ladson-Billings, G. (2009). *The dreamkeepers: Successful teachers of African American children* (2nd ed.). Jossey-Bass.

Rushton, S. P., Eitelgeorge, J., and Zickafoose, R. (2003). Connecting Brian Cambourne's conditions of learning theory to brin/mind principles: Implications for early childhood educators. *Early Childhood Education Journal, 31*(1), 11–21.

Part III

THE MANY FACES OF SOCIAL JUSTICE

What does it mean to "do" social justice in education? Given the nature of this book, each of the authors describe some form of social justice in their vision and practice. Though some teachers may not define their pedagogy as social justice, we believe that most educators, from preschool to graduate school and in other educational and community settings, engage in social justice stances and activities every day. Otherwise, why become teachers?

Does "doing social justice" mean speaking on a megaphone at a rally? Gathering signatures on a petition to begin an ethnic studies program in a high school? Creating a curriculum on the Black Lives Matter movement? Does it have to be these "big things," or can it simply mean, for example, slowing down the curriculum to give students a much-needed break from a too-busy day to recuperate from the intense demands of school? Or acknowledging the value of all students by greeting them individually each morning as they enter the classroom? Can it mean reaching out to a family who may be going through a tough time, or insisting on the highest quality work from all students? Or even beginning a book company to fill an urgent need for Spanish-language books? We would argue that all these actions, as you'll see in the essays in this book, define different aspects of social justice. In this section, we meet educators who engage in varied activities that promote social justice, in the process redefining what it means in schools and out.

When Beth Wohlleb Adel became a middle-school social studies teacher 2 decades ago, she knew what kind of teacher she wanted to be. Because she had decided on being an educator for a long time, she had given this issue a great deal of thought. Although Beth had been a successful student, she also knew that her experiences did not always work for all students whose experiences and backgrounds might be quite different from hers. At the same time, she followed her instincts of what good pedagogy could be, and with an open heart and mind, she made it clear to her students that she wanted to learn from them.

In her honest and reflective essay, Beth describes some of the many lessons she has learned from her students, for example, to relax some of her rules and demands while continuing to set high expectations for them. She has become an even more thoughtful and sensitive teacher, understanding her students in more profound ways. As a result, students who might be described by other teachers as "difficult" have become her "canaries in the coal coal mine," so to speak, serving as some of her most trusted allies in the classroom. Beth has also learned to slow down the curriculum by allowing students to take a break from time to time, honoring their organic intelligence about what they need to become better learners.

Beginning her essay with a beautifully rendered land acknowledgment, Adi Martinez makes it clear from the outset the value she places on social justice in and out of the classroom. Adi has thought deeply about what it means to create a caring learning environment with and for her students. A high school English teacher, she describes how she became the teacher she wanted to be by learning from previous teachers who made a difference in her life, both in how she thinks about her relationships with students, and in her pedagogy. In her chapter, Adi recognizes that *what* and *how* she teaches reverberates not only in her classroom and in each of her students, but that it influences others in her school. Most important, Adi views education as a collaborative act, something that, given the competitive nature of learning in our society, happens in too few classrooms and schools Adi has found that the tremendous pressure on students and teachers in the past 2 decades to focus on standardized tests and accountability has led to unhappy students and classrooms. But she recognizes that teachers cannot take these challenges on by themselves. Instead, they need to count on others—colleagues, students, friends, and families—for help. Adi also shares some of the affirming practices she uses in her teaching, recognizing that it is not only the content that matters, but also the context in which it occurs. Abundant with empathy, caring, and thoughtfulness, her essay vividly demonstrates examples of social justice in action.

CHAPTER 8

Slowing Down, Learning from Canaries, and Listening to Resistance

Beth Wohlleb Adel

I remember climbing the enormous stairs into school as a kindergartner, my blue overalls boosting my courage, my pink sneakers weaving through the tables and chairs to find my seat. I silently studied the teacher and the culture of the classroom, desperately wanting to belong. From the back of the room, I discovered what behavior would win favor with each teacher, and I dutifully produced work that would help me win mostly top marks. As a cisgendered, White, middle-class girl, the rules were designed for me to succeed and to reinforce my privilege. So I bought in; I worked independently, in competition with other students, producing lots of work: long, illustrated and edited stories in 3rd grade, science fair projects in 6th grade, analytical essays in 10th grade, and mathematical proofs in 12th grade. I offered up these works as evidence that I was a good person, that I was worthy. I was praised by my family, by my teachers and, later, by potential employers. I had learned the game well, and I defined my worth according to the work I created. I was competent, I was productive, and therefore, I was good, and I belonged.

Most of my friends in school were also rule-followers who were rewarded with top grades. A different friend of mine, however, stands out in my memory: In the corner of the back row, where I was leaning forward and raising my hand, he tipped back in his chair and kept his hand down. He chatted with me, under the radar, throughout class discussions and asked me to give him the answer on tests. When I turned in my homework, he smiled, empty-handed. I honestly wondered how he was able to do this. How did he seem so happy? How was he able to hold onto self-worth and not produce much in class?

I loved working hard and feeling successful in school. My hard work taught me many valuable skills and facts. I cherish the learning that I accomplished. I gained entrance to college and I began a rewarding teaching career. At the same time, holding up independent production as the goal, and equating this production with my worth as a human being, did not lead me to truly connect with all of my students when I started teaching. If producing lots of high-level independent work means that one is worthy, how do I relate to the students who are not producing the type of work that I want them to? If certain students are not producing much, does that make them unworthy? These students frustrated me. I knew they could succeed. Why weren't they? I began to question what it means to be an effective teacher.

I have taught middle school social studies for more than 20 years. I have taught in urban, rural, and suburban schools, in traditional middle schools as well as start-up experimental schools. I now teach in a tiny K–8 school where I teach my students for 2 years and get to know them on a deeper level than is possible in larger settings. Throughout all of the places I have worked, I have reflected deeply on how the classroom can be a place where students and teachers can have the courage to be their most authentic selves, where we can become more aware of systems of inequity and address them in structural ways, and where we can support each other to speak up when something must be said to make the world a more just and hopeful place.

When I first started teaching, I knew I needed to hold all students to the highest standard. The key, I thought, was to work harder and produce more. I tried offering help, cheerleading, and teaching more creatively. I created arts-based, integrated units, with differentiated instruction and scaffolding for students who were learning English as a second language or students with disabilities. Despite my good lessons and passion for justice, I was failing to reach many students. I was missing a main point: Until I uncoupled the equation of *producing lots = worth*, for both myself and my students, I was reinforcing an educational system that is designed to benefit only the privileged members of society. Many of my students resisted this system. They disrupted class, they refused to do assignments, they didn't buy in.

I was accustomed to thinking that students who disrupted the lesson were a problem and needed to be "fixed." I continued to believe that I couldn't afford to slow down and listen to them; I felt I owed it to the group to keep moving fast. I would have a private, quick chat with a disruptive student in the hallway, and if that didn't convince them to "behave" I would send them to the counselor or the principal to convince them to be compliant and send them back to class so I could keep moving the curriculum along at a speedy pace. Rather than stopping to listen to the students, I pushed them to move even faster so I could get to the part of the Holocaust unit about how important it is to resist the rules, in order to move on to the unit about how industrialism is causing climate change and we all need to stop producing so much.

Since my early years of teaching, I have learned that our students need something very different in order to face our precarious future. I have sought an antiracist pedagogy that challenges the culture of production and prioritizes listening deeply to my students, especially when they resist. I am now learning to uncover the gifts that each child is bringing to the classroom, whether they are producing the essays or not.

SLOWING DOWN TO LEARN FROM RESISTANCE

Shawn Ginwright, professor of education and leader in youth development, describes moving "from hustle to flow" as one of the essential pivots to transform schools into places of justice and healing. He urges teachers to slow down to be fully present and transform relationships. He urges us to transform our teaching toward connection and belonging (Ginwright, 2022). How do I, a White woman who has bought into the culture of frenzied production, slow down to learn from students when they are resisting a classroom activity? I need time to increase my awareness of my privilege and the cultural conditioning I have received. Without awareness of my Whiteness, I unconsciously reinforce inequities in my teaching by simply doing what I was taught to do. I need to prioritize time to reflect, listen deeply without judgment, and admit that, as a White person, there is much that I don't know. I must learn and re-learn, as lifelong projects. I need to allow myself to make mistakes and learn from them. Fortunately, my students are always telling me what they need in all kinds of ways. I am sharpening my listening skills.

Sometimes students don't use words to communicate their most important messages. Through disrupting the lesson, students are communicating something, and it is usually important for me to listen. Rahid, a gregarious, compassionate, and thoughtful 7th-grader who had moved often, struggled to concentrate because he worried about his mother's chronic health condition. He had fallen behind in his writing skills and avoided any tasks that might reveal this. During a lesson on writing in my class, he threw his water bottle across the room and into the wall. He wasn't just engaging in an angry outburst, he was sending me a message. The way that I had structured the lesson, based on individual work, was reinforcing a system that was designed for privileged students to succeed, and resulted in students like Rahid feeling incompetent. While I needed to have a conversation with him about controlling his temper and hold him accountable, I also needed to rethink how I was teaching writing. Students learn collectively, through relationships. In particular, Rahid's social skills were gifts to the school and to his community. From the moment he set foot in school in the morning, he was talking with other students, playing games, and joking around. Although these skills are never recognized by standardized tests, they are essential skills that contribute to positive group dynamics, cooperative education, and a rewarding life. By insisting that each student produce their own work individually, I had been making his gifts invisible, instead prioritizing individual accountability over collectivity. My lessons were silently sending the message that the only work that counted was individual work.

Students like Rahid are like canaries in a coal mine, and if I slow down enough to listen, my lessons will transform. Coal miners knew the mine had too much carbon monoxide when the canary weakened and died, and they knew they needed fresh air. When I notice that students like Rahid aren't thriving, it means that everyone in the classroom needs more oxygen in the lesson. Shane Safir and Jamila Dugan (2021) explain the importance of centering the voices of the most disenfranchised members of our communities to guide our schools using antiracist methodologies. If I teach to the middle, and the struggling students stay on the margins, I will reproduce the inequities that led students to struggle. If I center the voices that are usually marginalized, the entire class will benefit. My next step was not to create an alternative lesson for Rahid, and go on with the rest of the class, and push him to the margins. My next step was to center *his* experience, and decide that the rest of the class needed more fresh air, too. This meant changing the nature of my writing lessons for the entire class.

Now students talk through their ideas in pairs or small groups, giving each other feedback throughout each stage of the writing process. I remind the students that our class goal is for 100% of the students to improve their writing skills, and we need to help each other through holding each other accountable and offering constructive feedback. I set aside more workshops for explicitly teaching students how to support each other as writers—how to recognize strong aspects of each other's work, and how to offer helpful, constructive feedback instead of a search-and-destroy method of finding each other's grammatical errors. My rubrics include recognition for students who are collaborative. And we take time to celebrate with each other after we collectively accomplish our goal.

SLOWING DOWN FOR SELF-CARE

Sometimes students take it easy on me and ask directly for what they need. If I only slow down enough to listen to their body language, and prioritize caring for ourselves, they will teach me how to teach them. One afternoon right after lunch in mid-September, my students came into the classroom slumped over and dragging their feet. I resisted my urge to cheerlead them into perking up, pushing through their exhaustion to produce more and faster. Instead, I slowed down enough to resonate with them.* I reflected back to them that they looked tired. Josh, a 7th-grader, responded, "It's not fair—when I was in kindergarten I had rest time and never appreciated it. Now we all need naptime!"

In the past, I probably would have given an empathetic smile and continued with the lesson, certain that we couldn't afford to "waste" any time by resting, breathing, or listening. This time, I realized that I needed to take my students seriously when they are expressing a need to care for themselves. Tricia Hersey, founder of The Nap Ministry (https://thenapministry .wordpress.com/), describes napping as the revolution that we need. She describes rest as "a disruption to grind culture" that "offers space for radical care and healing. Each person and each community gets to define what is enough rest for themselves" (Penniman et al., 2021). I reconsidered my lesson plan and decided I could make some slight adjustments so that we could afford to slow down enough for some rest. I also knew that, as adolescents, many students might be nervous to let their guard down to be able to really rest, and they would need me to keep watch for pranks.

"Okay," I responded, "let's have nap time. I will keep my eyes open and watch, so you don't need to worry that someone might sneak up behind you. You can rest your head on the desk if you want, and close your eyes." I turned down the lights. I had never done this before, and I didn't know if the students would actually allow themselves to rest, or whether this would make them nervous. To my surprise, most of the students closed their eyes. The room was completely silent until I turned up the lights again. The students were able to transition to the lesson with renewed focus, feeling cared for and heard. The feeling in the room shifted from being a place where I only pushed students to produce work to a place where we supported each other to be our best selves.

A few weeks later, when they entered the classroom on the day of a test, I could see anxiety on many of my students' faces. Again, I resisted the urge to cheerlead or push through. I decided to take a moment for the students to share with each other how to get through anxious moments. "Taking a deep breath helps me," offered Anya, an 8th-grader who holds herself to very high standards and can sometimes get overwhelmed.

"Let's try it," I suggested. "Let's take three deep breaths together and see if it helps us move through some of the anxiety." I led the class with a slow inhale. "Exhaling for longer than inhaling makes it even better," suggested Blake, who had courageously shared struggles with depression to the class. We exhaled very slowly. After three slow breaths, the feeling in the room changed—it wasn't just that the students felt less anxious about the test; it was that we were building capacity together, supporting each other, and sharing tools to get through the tough moments.

SLOWING DOWN TO BUILD EMPATHY

When we slow down enough to deeply listen to students and prioritize relationships over productivity, opportunities to reflect and build empathy open up. This may lead to opportunities for students to challenge each other to interrupt racism, bullying, and other antisocial behaviors. When we move so fast that we miss these opportunities, schools can perpetuate and reinforce discrimination in subtle and overt forms. As teachers, we are responsible for slowing down enough to become aware when our classrooms are reinforcing stereotypes or exacerbating unearned privilege, and we need to take the time to investigate, modeling for our students how to shift to an antiracist pedagogy.

In late September, the technology teacher at our mostly White K–8 school sent an email to the 7th- and 8th-grade teachers that a Korean American 2nd-grader had expressed frustration about how she was being seen. This student had overheard the older students calling her "cute" many times on the playground, and it made her feel like a baby or toy rather than a person.

I was grateful that this teacher had slowed down and was present to hear from a young child about her experience; that this student had trusted that she would be taken seriously and that this experience had not been dismissed or de-prioritized among the thousands of details teachers must handle each day. This was an opportunity to slow down, reflect on relationships and challenge each other to empathize and connect.

After meeting with the team of teachers, we came up with a plan to discuss this student's concern with the 7th- and 8th-grade students. In our next advisory meeting, we pushed the tables to the sides of the room and made a circle with the chairs. We reviewed the discussion guidelines: one speaker at a time; speak for yourself and no one else; if you disagree, do so respectfully.

I led with an easy question: "How is school going for you?" After easily going around the circle, we deepened the conversation with a harder question: "Has anyone ever called you something that made you feel bad, even if that wasn't the intention of the speaker?"

Then I shared more details: A younger student has been feeling uncomfortable when the older students call her cute. Right away, students understood that this was a problem: that even though there is nothing inherently wrong with the word "cute," when it's used to infantilize, or if it feels dismissive, it needs to be addressed.

Cara, an uncommonly empathetic 7th-grader, shared, "I remember being in 2nd grade. I felt old and I was proud of myself. When people called me cute, I felt like they weren't really seeing me."

As the students spoke from their own experience, they built a culture of trust, which allowed members to hold each other and themselves accountable. Toward the end of the circle, Cara bravely added, "I was one of the ones who called her cute. I'm definitely never going to say that again."

I asked the students if they thought that the gender and race of the student made a difference. "Yes, Asian girls can be seen as little toys in this culture!" Talia expressed. The students agreed that, without intending to, they had been operating on stereotypes and perpetuating them. It was a hard conversation, and it strengthened us as a community. We were building our capacity to listen deeply, empathize, and hold each other accountable in a culture of caring and trust. By slowing down enough to take this younger student's concern seriously, we prioritized relationships and sent the message that working toward racial justice takes time, and it is time well spent.

SLOWING DOWN TO CHANGE DIRECTION

When I consciously slow down to listen deeply, and shift my focus from productivity-at-all-costs to transforming relationships, I get better at recognizing when I have taken a wrong turn, and that I need to set a new course. This involves the willingness to be vulnerable in front of the class. Though not easy on my ego, it has the potential to transform a classroom into a place of deep connection and learning.

In October, I began an integrated unit that I had taught in previous years and that had become a tradition in my class. The unit involves imagining how the Constitutional Convention may have resulted in a different Constitution if the framers were a diverse group of people. In past years, I had assigned each student a historical figure to represent in a role play. The historical figures represented diverse races, genders, and social classes. The unit is a big deal; other teachers on my team have designed lessons to integrate with this unit across disciplines and it culminates in a big production. This year, after I assigned racially diverse historical figures to my mostly White students, I received the following note from Talia, a very courageous and insightful 7th-grader:

> I just wanted to say that I feel uncomfortable with some things happening in the role play. I understand that we are trying to give a voice to those who had none, but I feel that the way it is being done, is not just inappropriate, but what I feel is also cultural appropriation. Not just this, but we are playing culturally significant jobs like Native American healers or chiefs. In my opinion, if dressing up

as your character is problematic, then pretending to be them is almost worse. I also feel like privileged white kids playing people who are different races than them, is in a way also pretending to understand the racial oppression they went through, which for most of the students, is something that they will never go through themselves. I completely agree that people who didn't have the freedom of sharing their thoughts at that time should get the little justice we can give them, but I feel like there are different ways it could be done. I understand that the role play is not that far away, and there might not be a way to change it. But I feel like it could come across as cultural appropriation and in a way even racist.

When I received this note, I was struck by the courage it must have taken to write to a teacher with these thoughts. By slowing down, I was able to calm the defensiveness that began to cloud my thinking: (*I'm not leading them to cultural appropriation, I'm building empathy! I can't cancel this unit! Too much work went into it! Other teachers have built their lessons to support this role play!*). Instead of acting on my defensiveness, I sat down with other teachers who collaborated on the unit and shared Talia's objections. We talked about how doing antiracist work depends on the context. This unit may have been fine in the past, but in this moment, the pain of appropriation was so heightened that it felt wrong to continue the unit the way we had planned. We collaboratively reworked the unit so that my students researched diverse historical figures without pretending to represent them, and they used their research to develop their own analysis of the Constitution.

The following day, I stood in front of each class and faced my students with transparency and apologized for opening a door to potential cultural appropriation. I thanked Talia and acknowledged the courage that it must have taken to write the note. I also developed a follow-up lesson about cultural appropriation, timed just before Halloween, so that we all could understand it better, and students could avoid cultural appropriation when planning their Halloween costumes.

Logistically, it was a lot of work to rework this unit after it had already begun. I'm grateful to collaborate with colleagues who support listening to resistance. The music teacher and I supported the students to write songs based on their research of the characters, and developed an incredible musical that we performed for the entire school. In the end, the unit was better than I could have imagined. Even though it is more work, listening to students and shifting assignments based on their feedback creates an atmosphere where students feel seen and respected, and this creates the sort of classroom where people want to learn. I still have questions about when it's appropriate and healthy to engage in role plays as a teaching tool to develop empathy. I know that, in this moment, we made the right decision. After this unit, the culture of my classroom subtly changed. Instead of breaking the students' trust in me, their trust in me deepened. I had shown the students that honoring each other was more important than plowing forward for the sake of the end product. We became closer as a community of people learning from each other and willing to be vulnerable in the process.

OUR CHALLENGE AHEAD

The students we are teaching now have an incredible challenge in front of them. How will they lead a world with an uncertain future? They will need to use tools that are different from the tools we have used in previous generations. In the words of Audre Lorde (2018), "the master's tools will never dismantle the master's house." Our culture of individual, competitive work based on frenzied production is what has brought us to a breaking point, ecologically and socially. Our planet cannot withstand more endless production. We will not fix our planet by changing lightbulbs. We need to transform the way we live. Our society cannot withstand continuing to hold up the equation that *production* = *worth*. If I teach my students that they must produce and compete at all costs, I will be reinforcing the problem that got us here.

How do we identify the tools that will lead us to a better future? I have begun to listen deeply to resistance from my students in order to find these new tools. When students resist the system, they are intuitively pushing their teachers to find a better way. Instead of trying to "fix" them and convince them to go along with a competitive, individualist system, we need to pay attention and see these students as our teachers, offering clues toward transforming our classrooms to work collectively and to practice building networks of support. Slowing down to listen and re-evaluate our lessons will allow for deeper constructivist education, more effective antiracist pedagogy, and collective responsibility. Students will not only learn more this way, but they will uncover new ways to see the world. These are the tools that our students need to develop now.

The change I am suggesting starts with shifting our focus toward deepening our relationships with students. I can only do this if I can slow down enough to really hear and resonate with students' needs and strengths, admit that there is much I need to learn from them, and see their resistance as gifts to the classroom. It will lead us to prioritize self-care in order to build capacity for empathy, vulnerability, and new ways of caring for each other.

NOTE

* I am indebted to Romina Pacheco and Safire DeJong, who taught me skills in resonance practice, a transformative tool to listen deeply with one another, developed by Relational Uprising as part of their Relational Culture Framework.

REFERENCES

Ginwright, S. A. (2022). *The four pivots: Reimagining justice, reimagining ourselves*. North Atlantic Books.

Lorde, Audre. (2018). *The master's tools will never dismantle the master's house*. Penguin.

Penniman, L., Hersey, T., Brooks, C., Le Cunff, A.-L., Singleton, G. E., & Haynes Johnson, A. (2021, August 10). 5 meditations on what "enough" means, from food to rest to diversity.. *Yes! Magazine*. https://www.yesmagazine.org/issue/how-much-is-enough/2021/08/10/meditations-on-enough

Safir, S., & Dugan, J. (2021). *Street data: A next-generation model for equity, pedagogy, and school transformation*. Corwin.

CHAPTER 9

Running on Empty
Using Empathy and Kindness to Challenge Classroom Practices

Adriana Martinez

LAND ACKNOWLEDGMENT

I write from Nebraska, where I currently reside on the past, present, and future homelands of the Pawnee, Ponca, Oto-Missouria, Omaha, Dakota, Lakota, Arapaho, Cheyenne, and Kaw Peoples, as well as the relocated Ho Chunk (Winnebago), Iowa, and Sac and Fox Peoples. I am grateful for the ways Indigenous Peoples continue to be stewards of the land despite having their work disrupted through colonization, theft, and broken treaties. I strive to be in solidarity with Indigenous Peoples and maintain a respectful relationship with the land.

INTRODUCTION

I never intended to teach English at a Midwestern suburban high school, and yet that is what I am doing. I certainly never thought I would feel at home in the Midwest, and yet I do. I grew up on the East Coast and developed a sort of sense of ethical superiority over the rest of the country as a result of what I perceived as the East Coast's highly progressive politics. I was raised on my mom's stories about how terrible the Midwest is as a result of ideological homogeneity, which tends to result in discrimination toward minoritized peoples. As a child, she dreamt of moving to the East Coast and, in her twenties, that dream came true. When I moved to the Midwest for college, she was dumbfounded. How could I leave the promised land? Over a decade later, she has trouble comprehending why I've stayed.

The Midwest is by no means perfect, but I feel fortunate to be at the school where I am teaching. While my district, like many, has plenty of room to grow, I appreciate that teachers are repeatedly asked to be mindful of minoritized student experiences and we are asked to innovate to make education accessible to all our students. I appreciate that my administrators are willing to have difficult conversations about the ways our building needs to grow and, more importantly, are willing to hold themselves and others accountable in the effort to make our school more equitable. I appreciate that my colleagues are often quick to pitch in when they notice help is needed, whether it be covering a class, offering a kind word or curricular advice, or simply lending their ear so that another can vent. That said, the vast majority of staff in my building are running on empty.

While drafting this essay, I went through student letters and reflections I've collected over the years. One of my students wrote a thank you letter to me in which they quoted Mustafa Kemal Ataturk, who compared good teachers to candles in that the light they provide for others is dependent on burning pieces of themselves. While my student was trying to acknowledge that teachers give parts of themselves to their students, this quote feels especially poignant right now.

The pandemic has taken its toll nationally and internationally. I am fortunate in that my family and my immediate region has taken less of the brunt of the trauma than others. That said, I am exhausted. I feel incredibly guilty for how tired I am. My body is fatigued and it's often hard for me to pay attention to anything once I leave work. Nothing is egregiously wrong in any facet of my life, and yet the context in which my students and I exist is rife with trauma. Teachers are leaving the field in droves. I wonder how many teachers have had their hearts broken because they've left the field. We join the field because we believe in the power of what good teachers can do for students, their families, and the community.

Throughout this chapter, I reflect on what brought me to teaching, what I try to do with my practice, and what I see for the future.

NARRATIVES ON EDUCATION

Family

Growing up, I was struck by my family narratives about the way education was a tool to rob, undermine, and dispossess my parents of their dignity and hope. I was confused by the juxtaposition of my mother's commitment to education despite what she endured. And I was interested in the names of the teachers whose brief kind or supportive words were enough to sustain her academic motivation and eventually become part of our family mythology.

My mother is a phenomenal storyteller. I was raised hearing about the joys and sorrows of being the ninth of ten children, the complexity of being Mexican and having a Spanish home language in rural Nebraska, the pain and humiliation of racism and poverty, and the pride of being able to thrive despite countless hardships. One of the trends within her storytelling was the injustice of the schooling that she and her siblings received. The system she endured viewed our family, and our heritage, as deficient. Our culture, our language, and the space we occupied was seen as alien and thus unworthy of being treated with kindness, warmth, and empathy. I grew up on the stories of the counselors who dissuaded my mother and her siblings from pursuing college and who minimized their academic successes: the stories in which my *tías* were put in special education because of their accented, albeit fluent, English; the stories in which my grandparents were unable to advocate for their children's education because of the shame they felt about their own limited educations.

Unlike my mother's family, I didn't have many negative experiences in K–12 at the hands of teachers or staff, but I also had very few transformative ones. It was my perception that, for whatever reason, my teachers didn't make a significant effort to connect with their students.

Teachers

In college, for the first time I was around teachers who were excited by their work and excited to share it. When I first arrived at college, I had no idea what I wanted to do with my life, but I suspected I wanted to be an agent of change in the world. I liked the content I encountered within my English and Ethnic Studies coursework, but it was the teachers, as opposed to solely the content, that drew me into the academic conversations. I reflected on how I felt around my teachers and what I hoped to make others feel in the context of my future profession. As I continued taking classes that interested me, and worked with professors with whom I connected personally, all paths led me closer to teaching.

Frankie Condon. In the course of my undergraduate degree, I rarely met with my academic advisor, and yet I have her to thank for encouraging me to take a course in Writing Center Theory (the theoretical underpinnings of the writing center as a space in and of itself, its positionality in the university/collegiate setting, and the work consultants do with writers) and apply for a position as a consultant in the writing center. I can't remember what her pitch entailed, and to be honest, I'm surprised I took up the suggestion because, at the time, I didn't often take advice from anyone.

So, I found myself working for (she would say *with*) and learning from Dr. Frankie Condon. She was one of the first teachers I witnessed discussing aspects of what they were learning for their own purposes. In one class period, she referenced that she and her friend (the esteemed Dr. Vershawn Ashanti Young) had recently watched the movie *The Help*. She talked about bits of the conversation they had afterwards, specifically pertaining to the limitations and missed opportunities in the movie's portrayal of Black women. It was astounding to me to hear an adult, a teacher no less, talk openly about the ways they construct and deconstruct their lived experiences. From a teacher's perspective, I can understand that one of Dr. Condon's motives in sharing the anecdote could have been to model the way one might critically self-reflect on the stories they consume. In this sense, her anecdote was an invitation to her students to engage with their world in a similar manner.

By taking Dr. Condon's Writing Center Theory class, as well as working for her as a writing center consultant, I had the opportunity to begin analyzing the ways in which I occupied space and how it affected those around me. Under Dr. Condon's guidance, consultants (not tutors) analyzed power dynamics at play in the writing center as a space and possible power dynamics between the consultant and the writer, especially as it pertained to minoritized writers. At that time, despite working as a writing center consultant, I didn't see myself in the role of educator. I worked with writers to help them achieve their stated goals. I tried not to assert my own motives onto the writers with whom I worked, which, to some extent, is what I felt teachers did.

John Raible. At the same time I was learning from Dr. Condon, I also had the privilege of learning from Dr. John Raible. The university I attended offered alternative spring break trips that centered on service learning. There were several options the year I participated, but the one that stood out most to me was a trip to Pine Ridge reservation. The purpose of the trip was to bear witness as an ally and learn from the Lakota community about what our group, none of whom were South Dakota residents or part of the Lakota peoples, could do to support them. In order to go on the trip, students had to take a multicultural education course. While I still didn't envision my professional future to be in education, I wanted to go on the trip as a result of previous coursework in Indigenous American studies, so I enrolled in the class.

The class consisted of twice-a-week lectures in a large lecture hall, as well as a small group recitation once a week. It was during the recitation that I found Dr. Raible's passion compelling. In the context of lecture, he provided materials to juxtapose what public education could be with what it lacked. At the same time, he led participants through additional modules that pertained to the history of Indigenous Education in America and helped participants reflect on their own experiences in education. I became interested in the juxtaposition of the history, present, and possible future of education, especially as it pertained to making education more equitable for minoritized populations. I was intrigued that, despite having extensive knowledge in all the ways education had been used to dispossess, Dr. Raible still believed in its potential.

Eventually, the time came to go on the trip. Very quickly, the community that students and staff had spent months building deteriorated. Despite being well prepared, we interpreted differently what we experienced on Pine Ridge. With some exceptions, this occurred along racial and ethnic lines. Some White students didn't view specific school practices and policies as rooted in the legacies of systemic oppression, whereas the students of color saw and felt the legacy of educational inequity. White students saw the efforts to resist the history of cultural genocide as sufficiently moving toward equity, like language reclamation programs, whereas students of color grieved the need for such programs in the first place. Some participants quickly dismissed evidence of colonization, theft, and broken treaties as issues seen in non-Indigenous communities. Others became despondent at how we were supposed to witness and simultaneously understand the ways in which we were implicated in what we saw.

At the time, and in reflection afterwards, I thought about what Dr. Raible was trying to do, and what it might mean that the shared experience did not seem to result in the intended outcomes. I eventually focused on Dr. Raible's clear commitment to the power of education to disrupt the truths many students hold about the world and ask students to be uncomfortable, to grow in a way that becomes more community-centered and conscious. I became interested in the ways that he seemed unperturbed at the disconnect between what was, and what was *supposed to be* on the trip. He took the situation in stride and used it as a moment in which he learned and reassessed as the teacher so that he could reposition what he asked of students. It was the first time I had seen a teacher take failure in stride.

Brent Toalson. The principal with whom I started my teaching career retired in 2020. Before he left, I requested critical feedback from him. In my mind, this was going to be a prime opportunity to receive potentially tough to digest feedback on my time as a teacher. While he did not necessarily give me feedback about myself, he did share a story about himself as a young administrator at a different school in our district. In the story, he emphasized how one year he decided to stop lamenting what wasn't working and instead roll up his sleeves and get to work. He had a vision for how the school could better serve students and, instead of waiting for someone else with more power to do something about it, or being one more voice in the chorus of the ways the school system is failing, he decided it was up to him to do what he could. One notable initiative he began is collaborative teaming for freshmen and sophomores. This initiative allowed teachers of Social Studies, Science, English, and Math to find ways to overlap their content and discuss the students they shared so that they could better support student learning. In our district, most high schools have approximately 2,000 students. As a result, scheduling is challenging and most students change core teachers at semester. In the collaborative teaming model, this doesn't happen. Students retain the same core teachers across the school year and those teachers are able to plan together to support the wide variety of student needs. The changes he brought forth are still in effect decades later and should be used to serve as models for the rest of the district. Much can be said, perhaps, about why they are not.

His story led me to reflect on the ways I'd spent my career thus far. While I was proud of the work I'd done in my classroom and with individual students, I felt my commitment to the school was lacking. I feared that I had become a voice in the chorus and was absent from the spaces that generated change schoolwide.

As a result of Brent's example, I reframed what it meant to me to be a teacher. My job is not just between myself, my students, and their families, but is also in my commitment to the school. Every fall, students in one of my classes, AP Language and Composition, read an excerpt from the Puritan John Winthrop's speech "A Model of Christian Charity," more commonly referenced as "A City Upon a Hill." In his speech, my students observed that Winthrop repeatedly returned to the idea that the success and health of the individual is rooted in the success and health of the community writ large. Similarly, the work I do with students will have a finite amount of success unless the school community in which I teach is reflective and healthy. This realization was not a critique of my school, but rather an acknowledgment that my work and efforts cannot be limited to the walls of my classroom.

PRACTICES I USE TO CREATE AND SUSTAIN COMMUNITY

Greeting Students Every Day

Each day and each class period I strive to greet my students by name. It doesn't always happen, due to passing period student conversations, students walking into the room in groups, my running quick errands, etc. That said, it is a goal I have.

If I greet a student as they enter, but I don't use their name, there is a significant chance they won't respond to me. For some reason, be it their age, or the time of day, or the other things on their mind, I don't think my students register general salutations as intended for them specifically. So, if

I greet them when they enter but don't use their name, even if they're the only student entering at that moment, most of my students don't respond or acknowledge the salutation.

What's the point of greeting them by name then, if they're reluctant to acknowledge or return the greeting? The point of greeting them doesn't have to do with training them in basic courtesies, or making myself feel seen, but rather it is to make sure they know I see them individually. I want Khang to know that I know he is in class and I want him to suspect I will notice his absences. While many of my students rarely tell me that greeting them makes them feel comfortable or happy in my classroom, they do comment if I miss a day.

Many students don't feel seen at school, especially if they're in a large school. To spend such a large portion of their young lives in a place where they may not feel seen or heard or valued affects not only their ability to engage in content learning, but also their understanding of self in the context of the world.

Facilitating Discussion and Collaboration

A central aspect of my practice is small- and large-group discussion and collaboration. I emphasize to students that knowledge is rarely developed within a single individual. We talk about how every text they read is the product of collaboration—either multiple individuals collaborating over the text or collaboration through space and time. Thus, we talk about how it is a crucial skill to be able to approach learning situations from the perspective of knowledge development as a collective act.

It is my hope that by creating consistent opportunities to work together students will approach one another with the expectation that they will find something valuable in one another and in themselves. I provide students with sentence stems that help them position themselves compassionately around one another and make sure their critical engagement is always with a person's ideas and not with the individual themselves. Many of my former students have expressed stress and discomfort with being asked to share ideas with their peers—they fear being wrong, being ridiculed, and being found out as an academic fraud. Many of those same students have also expressed that by the end of the year, they were able to be comfortable in their discomfort and they were often more sure of the conclusions they drew because they expected to have to explain them to others and potentially defend them.

If learning is a collective act, then ideally students would feel responsible for one another in the learning space, and perhaps that sense of responsibility would translate beyond the classroom walls. Several of my colleagues have shared with me that my students sometimes discuss material from my class and invite their teachers to share input. While their other teachers don't always have all of the context for the conversations my students want to have, it has become clear my students enjoy sharing their knowledge with their teachers with the expectation that their teachers will be able to provide additional ideas with which to grapple. In this sense, the community created in my classroom expands to involve other people in my students' lives, reiterating the communal act of learning.

Modeling Curiosity

Some of my students encourage me to start a podcast because they allege they like hearing me talk about things that interest me. While it could be true that they like to listen, it is also likely true that they feel they've gotten away with something if they encourage me to talk for 10 minutes about the latest thing I read, watched, or heard. What they don't always understand is that I want them to hear adults be excited about learning that's driven by curiosity.

We know that one of the challenges of learning within a school system is homogenization of content and teaching styles. While some schools are fortunate in that they have alternative models that honor student choice and support inquiry and exploration, not all school systems allow for this. One small way I have found to try to promote curiosity and inquiry in my students is by modeling my own. For example, the other day in class students were listening to a podcast author interview about the nonfiction text *The Big Thirst*, by Charles Fishman. In the interview, Fishman explains that water is often used in unexpected ways. He explains that rocket launch platforms are often doused in water to dampen the sound of the rockets. Without this measure, the rockets would be blown apart by the sound emitted from their engines because the sound reverberates off the launch platform. I stopped the podcast and asked, "Does not that just blow your mind, pun intended! Did you ever imagine that sound was powerful enough to rip things apart? Who has seen the episode of *The Office* in which Dwight gets excited when fire trucks come to the office and he pumps his fist in the air? That is how I feel right now thinking about sound waves." While I was being honest and I do think that is wild, I wanted students to hear me say it. High school students are often in a constant state of mild embarrassment and I have noticed that some of that embarrassment stems from thinking learning is fun or interesting. Additionally, my students enjoy any opportunity to laugh at what they perceive to be my quirkiness or goofiness. It is my hope that if I model excitement then they may feel they have permission to follow in my lead, at least within my classroom. So, even when they laugh at me, even when they tease me, I listen and wait to hear them express interest in learning something new.

Fostering Accountability

I came across the term "warm demander" in Lisa Delpit's (2013) work. First coined by Judith Kleinfeld (1975), "warm demanders" are teachers who have high expectations for their students and approach those expectations from a place of compassion (see also Alexander, 2016). When I reflect on the teachers I have known, in school and out, those who have been most impactful have had this quality.

In a course reflection, my former student Hunter shared with me that they appreciated my consistent feedback to them. Hunter said that while they'd always done well in English classes, they had the suspicion that their teachers weren't actually reading their work. Though they received a grade, they rarely if ever received feedback, either corrective or affirming. They shared they were alarmed when they got their first essay back from me and saw that it was full of comments. After the alarm wore off, the student reported feeling hopeful that they could expect my attention and feedback. In fact, quite a few students from that class felt the same way. At first, they feared that what I expected of them was unachievable. As the year progressed, they were reassured when they discovered I was always willing to provide feedback, work one to one, and celebrate their growth. Many students said that for the first time, the combination of my expectations and support allowed them to stop worrying about their grade and focus more on their growth.

These anecdotes are not meant to call out Hunter's former teachers, especially given that I know little about the context of their courses and their lives, nor is it meant to celebrate my own efforts while disregarding the efforts and successes of others. Instead, the anecdote affirms that most students feel empowered when I can show them that I see them and their potential and push them to grow, even if the pathway to growth is uncomfortable.

Seeking Collegial Community

As we know, teaching requires not only our intellect but also our constant emotional presence. As a result, teaching can be exceptionally draining. Integral to my practice is the community I have gathered around me, a community consisting of various people within the school in which I teach—teachers, paraprofessionals, library staff, security personnel, and administrators. These are people with whom I can share my joy, grief, frustration, and hope. It is cathartic to know I am not alone in my successes, my failures, and everything in between. These are the people who support me and challenge me.

Reflecting and Providing Feedback

One of Dr. Frankie Condon's repeated phrases was "for whom is this a gift?" She encouraged her writing consultants to think about this especially during a writing consultation. She asked us to humble ourselves and critically self-reflect to make our work with writers as successful as it could be. She also encouraged us to remember that our voices were not the most important voices in the consultation, and that we needed to center writers and their work.

I still think about that phrase in the context of my classroom and school: For whom is this a gift? When I create my own curriculum or adapt the curriculum provided by the district, how do I know my choices are affecting students positively, both in the context of what I know they will need and also in the context of what they want from their schooling? How do I know my participation in the most recent staff meeting positively affected others? How do I know my emails home are providing opportunities for family engagement and not inadvertently shaming or superficially celebrating family support?

In each of my courses, I create a number of reflection assignments I ask students to complete. Some of these include a standardized form in which I ask them to provide me with anonymous feedback on specific instructional and curricular choices I've made, as well as on the classroom environment. I ask students to complete more open-ended reflections in which they have more room to direct the conversation. I work to use student feedback when revising my course in order to make sure their voices are as present as they can be. I rely on my administrators, with whom I have a trusting relationship, as well as my colleagues for additional instructional and professional feedback, with the hope that they may be able to raise questions I've not thought of and function as an additional set of eyes on the work I try to do with my students. I also work to incorporate all family feedback, both positive and negative, into my course revisions. While it can be easy to disregard and dismiss negative feedback, especially that which is particularly inflammatory, I push myself to honor it with some time and consideration and distill it into what I feel are the family's core concerns. I can then decide if those core concerns merit course revision or if they should be let go.

Building Confidence

In 2021, I began binging Netflix's *Queer Eye*. The reality show allows people to nominate loved ones who they feel are in some type of social–emotional rut and need support to move forward. The show is without question a feel-good experience: Each of the five hosts, also known as the Fab 5, spend the show getting to know the nominee, identify a root of the nominee's predicament (fear, insecurity, low self-esteem, etc.), and work to build the nominee up throughout the week they spend together.

One of the things that has struck me about the show is the way the Fab 5 make the nominees feel about themselves. When Tan takes nominees shopping, he always makes them feel that they deserve to feel good in their clothes and bodies. When Bobbi remakes nominees' living spaces, he makes them understand that their home or place of residence should be one that adds positively to their lives by providing an orderly sanctuary. By the end of the show, the nominees always have hope for the future and believe that their personal qualities have the potential to bring them future happiness and security. The Fab 5 aren't just sources of superficial positivity, though there is much exuberant positivity; they also provide wisdom and encourage introspection in order to help the nominees grow.

The more I watch the show, the more I hope that I am like the Fab 5. I hope that I am pushing when students need pushing, I hope I am comforting when students need comforting, and I hope I create an environment in which students feel comfortable in the discomfort of trying new things.

FINAL THOUGHTS

I question the future of teaching. I question what I'm doing in a system that doesn't align with my ideals of liberation and equity. I question what I'm doing when I prep my students for high-stakes testing and future high-stakes environments when I know those tests and environments are inherently inequitable and harmful. I question what I'm doing when the community I serve claims that teachers are paid too much, or teachers serve as an indoctrinating machine, or teachers don't do enough. I question how I will resist closing my classroom door to the cacophony and shut myself and my students away from our communities.

For now, I keep my door open. I keep inviting students, and colleagues, and families to the ideas I offer my students. One of my students shared with me that she talks with her mom about every book she reads in my class. A father told me that he reads each book we read in class with his son to help build his son's confidence so that he may be more willing to engage in class discussion. A mother told me her daughter hated the ending of a book so much that she required that her mom and grandmother both read the book so they could discuss it together. A student I didn't teach came into my room to ask what one of my classes was learning next so she could be prepared for when her friend wanted to discuss that with her. While this doesn't happen in every class, I do get this feedback at least a few times a year. Learning is a communal act. It is an act of love, compassion, and hope.

Each spring I teach Shakespeare's *The Taming of the Shrew* and I come back to this line that comments on the two adversarial protagonists: ". . . where two raging fires meet together, they do consume the thing that feeds their fury." It is my hope that this will be our future. It is my hope that the anger and frustration many in our community feel about the inadequacies of schooling will meet the frustration and anger schooling staff feel about the obstacles that prevent them from enacting their ideals. It has to. Teachers are leaving the field and we can't afford for the trend to continue.

Dr. Frankie Condon's words have been a recurrent theme throughout this text, and I'll leave you with a few more. About a decade ago, she told me that I should envision the work I do as planting seeds. Gardeners, like teachers, always have a little more work to do, and that's okay. We will do what we can, everything that we can, with the hope that those who come next have a little less to do. When we are tired, we take comfort in those doing the work beside us.

REFERENCES

Alexander, M. (2016). *The warm demander: An equity approach.* [blog]. Edutopia. Retrieved from: www.edutopia.org/blog/warm-demander-equity-approach-matt -alexander

Delpit, L. (2013). *Multiplication is for white people: Raising expectations for other people's children.* The New Press.

Kleinfeld, J. (1975). Effective teachers of Eskimo and Indian students. *The School Review, 83*(2), 301–344.

Part IV

TEACHING AND ACTIVISM IN THE CLASSROOM AND BEYOND

Teaching inevitably invokes advocacy. We never met anyone who became a teacher to make millions, although most of us expected to at least make a living wage—but even that has sometimes been elusive. Instead of seeking fame or fortune, most teachers enter the field because of less tangible and more noble goals: a commitment to young people, a dedication to the art of teaching and learning, a love of a particular subject matter or community, or even broader values such as doing some good in the world or working to safeguard democracy. Of course, there are people who simply stumble into the profession as something to do "in the meantime," while considering their options in marriage, starting a family, or finding that elusive glamorous job that many young people dream about.

Although many new teachers leave the field after just a few years, many others stay the course. But no matter their motivation or ideals, some people soon find that teaching is not for them. Sonia, although deciding at the age of 10 that she wanted to be a teacher, found the job so overwhelming and draining that she nearly left after just 2 years. Luckily, she returned the following year to begin what would turn out to be an incredibly rewarding life of over 50 years in public education, first in middle and elementary schools, and later in higher education, where she found her love for teacher education, research, and writing. Alicia, on the other hand, had decided early on that she would *never* become a teacher. Being the daughter of two educators, she accidentally fell into teaching a few years after completing her college degree. Without having taken even one course in education, she soon discovered that she had indeed found her place in life. Thirty years later, she's still at it.

Most educators consider themselves advocates; it comes with the territory. They may not demonstrate their advocacy in the same ways, but they would no doubt describe themselves as caring deeply for their students, their craft, the subject matter they teach, the community they serve, or all these combined. For some, activism is a natural extension of advocacy; for others, it's about believing in and standing up for the best interests of their students, becoming an active member of their union or other professional organization, or even running for town or city office.

Laurie García was a three-time advocate: classroom teacher in private and, later, public schools, school committee member (though she is no longer in this role), and activist in several political campaigns. Her story clearly reflects the connection between advocacy and activism. Besides grassroots volunteering in various political activities in Vermont, Laurie canvassed for Bernie Sanders when he first ran for mayor of Burlington, VT, in the 1980s. In that role, she learned and honed strategies in direct political action, many of which would serve her well years later when she ran for a seat on the school committee in the town in Massachusetts in which she and her family had moved. Although it's been a winding road, when you read her story, it will be obvious that Laurie García is a devoted teacher, advocate, and activist.

Jorge Lopez had been both advocate and activist for over 20 years, beginning as a high school student, when he finally found adult mentors who believed in him. In his essay, Jorge recounts a tale common to many children of immigrants and students of color: worn down by his teachers' dismissive treatment or outright racism, as a child he felt a deep embarrassment and even shame about his identity—a brown-skinned child with a working-class family who had little formal education. Jorge describes his years in elementary and middle school as "oppressive, dehumanizing, and disempowering." It was only in college that he was introduced to ethnic studies, the field that would eventually become the major passion and goal of his teaching and activism. The profound transformation he underwent in college led to his conviction that all marginalized students need to go through a similar process to learn to love themselves, their identities, and their families and communities.

It was when he put his love for ethnic studies in action through curriculum development that he truly found his forté. In Jorge's essay, we read about the results of his belief in ethnic studies and the impressive work he has done with colleagues and students who have benefited from his talents and his vision. Jorge writes about the tangible form of the curriculum that he could only have dreamed about as a young child.

Heather Robertson-Devine had wanted to be a teacher since childhood, but she was equally drawn to the bigger issues in what she describes as the *ecosystem* of education, that is, the larger context, including the systems and institutions around education. As a result, at first Heather did not study education *per se*, but rather decided to explore issues that focused on inequality, specifically by majoring in international relations and Latin American studies. After later studying education, Heather had multiple jobs in the field: She taught language arts, social studies, and science in the elementary grades and middle school. She has also been a teacher of Spanish as a foreign language (though it's hard to understand how Spanish can be called a foreign language in a nation where about 50 million speak it as a native or heritage language). Because she is a fluent speaker of Spanish, Heather has also been a bilingual teacher of several subject areas. Her love for the language and the people who speak it is evident to anyone who knows her, although her current role is less associated with direct teaching.

A self-defined *teacherpreneur,* Heather at first found it hard to describe herself as anything but a teacher. That's because she always *felt* like a teacher regardless of the specific job title she had. Fluent in Spanish and deeply aware of her privilege, she understood that many of the students she taught did not have the advantages she had, including having access to reading materials in their own language. It was after 2 decades as a teacher that she realigned and redefined her identity as a *teacherpreneur* to more closely reflect what she now realizes is her core identity. In effect, her company, *Books del Sur,* has become her classroom. It is where Heather, assisted by teachers and other education professionals, creates professional development experiences for teachers and librarians and helps educators and administrators understand the crucial need for Spanish language books for young people who might otherwise not have access to culturally relevant and linguistically accurate books. While most commercial book sites and stores might carry translations of English language books, Heather opted for something more authentic: books that reflected not just the Spanish language but also the various cultures of Spanish-speaking students and their communities, including literature, folk tales, histories, poetry, and more. When Heather's "big dream" took off, she knew she had found her place in the education ecosystem.

Read on to see how Laurie, Jorge, and Heather define their roles.

CHAPTER 10

The Winding Road to Educational Activism

Laurie García

I had never planned on being a teacher, and I have often questioned my decision made years ago to switch from the program in social work to human development. Forty years later, I still look for ways to do more than "just teach" language. The skills I learned while studying for my master's degree in intercultural relations have been very beneficial in my varied roles over the decades in teaching ESL, working as an international student coordinator, and especially now teaching Spanish in the district that is fourth highest in the country per capita for refugee resettlements. As I begin to count the years left to retire on one hand, I reflect on what has brought me the most professional and personal satisfaction. The relationships I have formed with countless students and other educators, as well as my role as an educational activist, have kept me in the fight to tackle many of the inequities often found in public education.

BEGINNING MY JOURNEY AS AN ACTIVIST AND INTERCULTURALIST

Among my collection of prized mementos, I still treasure my red *Bernie for Burlington* button. I proudly wore it while canvassing for the man that would become the first socialist mayor. It represents my formal entry into political activism, which began in the 1980s. I entered my freshman year as a social work major at the University of Vermont and continued to take courses in Spanish, for I felt I wanted to learn the language to be able to help the growing number of *hispanohablantes,* Spanish-speakers, I would strive to help as a social worker. Since I was unhappy with the course content, I switched to human development and family studies in my sophomore year. It was in the School of Education, but I had no intention then of becoming a teacher.

I surrounded myself with like-minded people and joined CISPES (Citizens in Solidarity with the People of El Salvador) and Ralph Nader's Vermont PIRG (Peoples Interest Research Group). I was excited to volunteer for my preferred political candidate in my first campaign. I had turned 18 only a few weeks before, so I was thrilled to be able to vote for the first time. When Bernie Sanders won by only 10 votes, I quickly realized how important it is to reach each potential voter. Later, I was fortunate to be granted an internship in the Mayor's Youth Office, directed by Jane Driscoll, who would eventually marry Bernie.

I had a professor and mentor whom I adored, Armin Grams. I can still hear him say not to call children *kids,* for kids are baby goats. In addition to teaching about the theories of Bronfenbrenner, Ericson, and Piaget, he convinced me about the merits of studying abroad. For my semester abroad, I chose the School for International Training's program in Granada, Spain. Their Experiment in International Living was the oldest study abroad program in the world. I was 22 years old and headed to Granada to live with a Spanish family, and my Spanish was at a low intermediate level, at best.

I became *Laura,* their *hija and hermana,* and we have remained close to this day. They truly are my *familia española,* and as I stated before, my semester abroad truly changed my life. I never experienced culture shock living with them. However, I had a dismal reentry shock when I had to return for my final semester at UVM. After graduation, I waited tables 7 days a week to return to *mi familia en Granada* and continue my quest to be bilingual. I got on a plane shortly after New Year's, but with a one-way ticket. I had plans to rent an apartment from *mi familia* in Granada for a few months and then travel Europe and visit Greece before going to Israel to volunteer on a kibbutz. Most of those travel plans changed when I met a Spanish man on the way to an outdoor festival, *Jóvenes por la Paz.* Eugenio became my international relation, and the reason I eventually chose to get my master's degree in intercultural relations. We have been happily married for over 30 years, with two bilingual children.

MY ENTRY INTO TEACHING

While living in Granada, I became a teacher out of necessity to make money in order to live. I learned how to tutor English from another American I knew who had done the same. Using *El País Semanal*, I cut pictures out that students had to describe using different adjectives. I traveled around the city on foot to different classes daily to work with students of varying ages and abilities, including a doctor. I found myself having to learn British English, with different vocabulary and grammar, for students taking the Cambridge Proficiency exam at that time. I looked for a master's program that would allow me to return to Spain for my internship and thesis, so I chose Intercultural Relations with a focus on International Education Exchange. I wanted to become a foreign student advisor and help students in their transition to the American educational system while promoting more educational exchange. My classes in Intercultural Communication and Intercultural Helping Skills have helped me in a myriad of situations, especially now, as I teach in a public school district that has numerous refugees and immigrants.

The World of Private School Teaching

After getting married and spending another year in Spain so my husband could complete his mandatory military service, we ended up in the world of private schools, beginning in Wellesley, Massachusetts. The world of preppy affluence was extremely foreign to me, as I was the product of public schools. Pregnant with our first child, I tried to hide my nausea and I interviewed to become a dorm head; soon after that I heard we could move into and run a small dorm of seven young women, five of whom were international students. The model at this school was to keep residential staff separate from teaching, not typical of the triple-threat model used by most independent schools (teaching, dorm parenting, and coaching).

On the other hand, my husband had always wanted to teach but was studying to teach Spanish in Spain (like a regular ELA teacher here) when I met him. His degree in *Filología Románica* did not prepare him to teach Spanish to elementary school students in a fancy day school in a suburb of Boston, but he seized the opportunity. The two of us also ended up becoming the whole Spanish department of another school, which specialized in the performing arts. I am unsure how we balanced three private schools' responsibilities at once while becoming new parents. In addition, neither of us had been formally trained in anything we were teaching. This, however, is how many teachers start in private schools—no formal teaching preparation but a passion for teaching an academic interest one had explored in college. Having experienced equal time in both private and public schools, I often compare the two models and wonder why parents opt to pay so much for classrooms taught by mostly uncertified teachers. There is something inherently wrong with our public education if parents, especially those not using the boarding model, feel their children can do better at private schools. This is not a criticism of the families opting for this, as we did the same for our own children.

Boarding schools have been filled with students from many walks of life, and there are a multitude of reasons for choosing this model. As an international student coordinator, I relished my role of serving as a mother for those far away from their native lands and parents. In addition to my advising role, I designed and taught ESL classes. The relationships I formed with my students more than filled my desire to counsel those in need of support. One such relationship was with a young lady who had escaped the unimaginable atrocities of the genocide in Rwanda. A Christian relief organization had funded the relocation of a group of students to boarding schools in the United States. Celeste had horrific PTSD, including debilitating migraines. She would only agree to attend sessions if I accompanied her. I found that the ESL skills I had learned were invaluable at that point, as the therapist conducted a visualization exercise with advanced language skills. This young woman looked to me as an emotional anchor, especially after she received news via my phone that her father had died in Rwanda.

After switching to another smaller, independent school nearby, I began teaching Spanish. Becoming the department chair, I oversaw the ESL department and began teaching courses on U.S. culture and overseeing the ESL department. The population differed at this school, but there were students there as well who benefitted from the close-knit model of an independent school, who needed added support that most regular public schools could not readily provide. I also formed very special relationships there, while my students were mainly from the surrounding area. My sweetest memory is of a group of four that became known as *mis niñas*, a group of girls I taught at multiple levels for successive years, ending in an Advanced Placement class. I could not imagine reading Allende's entire *Casa de Los Espiritus* with any other high school level class, but it is not often you can teach a small class of four! We are still in touch, and I relished the opportunity to have a reunion together over Zoom during the isolating times of the pandemic.

Parents and guardians choose independent schools for a variety of reasons, including smaller class sizes, more academic offerings, and additional classes in the arts. In the past decade, there has been a trend for parents of athletes to opt out of the public system, as they feel the level of competition will enable their athletes to reach the dream of playing at the college level. Some even enroll in a postgraduate year to give them the athletic lead after graduating from public high school. These cases do not take needed resources from the public schools as do the "public" charter schools, which were supposed to provide the benefits of private schools without the astronomical costs. Public funding continues to be drained by charter schools that were supposedly created to *help*, but that now do further harm to public education!

Finally Becoming a Public School Teacher

After many years of teaching at private schools as an ESL teacher, an international student coordinator, and a Spanish teacher, I decided to make the switch to public schools. My only public school district experience had been a part time position years before. This happened when "pothole funding" came about in a regional district right when a nonprofit based in Chicago, called Language Odyssey, decided to close; at the time I had after-school programs running throughout the state. The regional school had wanted me to stay when a full time position opened for September, but I opted to teach part time in the private school where we were living, for this provided an easy solution for childcare issues. Ten years later, I received a call from the chair of the department who was retiring, as they needed someone to teach the upper levels of Spanish. I then made the conscious decision to teach in public schools and try to offer the same benefits my language classes had at the three private schools where I had taught.

When I first returned to that regional district to teach various middle and high school classes, there were some students who were rushing to change classes, complaining that I was speaking too much Spanish! I had left a private school where we started the first day with our 7th-graders in immersion into all the languages. Why were students in this public school still being taught to memorize vocabulary lists in English and Spanish, the same way that did not work for me in high school?

In that district, it became my goal to excite students to use their Spanish. One of my favorite projects was to have students create fables using the two past tenses they had learned. They were creatively illustrated and laminated so that we could donate them to the children's waiting room at a local hospital. While I thoroughly enjoyed my classes, the fixed schedule was challenging; exhausted seniors shuffled in each morning, and I ended my days with 7th-graders with excess energy. I felt I had made the right move to teach in public education, and I was trying to jump through the hoops that the Department of Education put in my way to get licensed. After teaching there for 2 and a half years, I was told that due to budget problems, one Spanish teacher had to be cut. The old *last one in, first one out* policy applied, and it did not matter that the district had called me to leave my private school post 3 years before. These personal experiences ignited my fire to do what I could to promote world languages in public schools. In future speeches, I related these incidents to the lack of support for world languages in public schools, which often leads parents to seek alternatives, whether in charter schools or independent schools. I ended up teaching in another district that lost a lot of funding to students who opted to go to a local Chinese immersion charter school, but the district itself had to cut Chinese and other world languages when the funding was scarce. The irony was almost laughable. Language was termed an *aesthetic,* where students would choose among art, drama, and language. I tried to defend the necessity for students to take 2 full years of language in middle school, but unfortunately spoke up too much without having professional status. It was once again necessary to look for another job.

My most recent district happens to have the highest percentage of immigrants and refugees in Massachusetts and the fourth-highest in the whole country. After 8 years of teaching different Spanish levels, I will also be teaching three levels of ESL. I have been working with the district to fully support all languages by promoting the *Seal of Biliteracy*, which grants special recognition to high school graduates who demonstrate fluency in two or more languages. It is important to encourage all students to do more than the 2 years that are "just" required to get into a 4-year college, and to learn all four areas (reading, writing, listening, and speaking) of their home language in order to test so they can achieve the honor of having a Seal of Biliteracy on their diploma; it would help them for college entrance and for any profession they seek.

Now, my greatest satisfaction in teaching is when I can celebrate the variety of cultures in my district. For example, during online teaching, my students did a recipe project with my guidance. Together with their family members, students made popular dishes from their cultures and recorded them using Flipgrid. Iraqi mothers helped their children, as did *abuelos* and *abuelas* from Puerto Rico, and many were speaking in their own languages, and then in our class explained the recipes in Spanish. For Día de los Muertos, students brought in an artifact that represented a deceased loved one, and they wrote a description of the person. Even students who had experienced trauma found it healing to share their love for their dearly departed.

It is important to integrate heritage and native speakers into the classroom with culturally relevant pedagogy, when even students who have been schooled in Puerto Rico through middle school were being placed in Spanish One as recent arrivals, and had to to jump through degrading hoops to be in more advanced levels. Many school counselors say students need 2 years of a foreign language to be admitted into a 4-year college and do not understand that Spanish is their first language. It is extremely beneficial to promote the Seal of Biliteracy, and explain to students that speaking more than one language is a badge of honor.

As most teachers know, education often takes its greatest forms outside of the classroom. In my current district, I have looked for ways to celebrate the rich diversity of our student body schoolwide. As the advisor, I changed the title of the club from Foreign Language Club to World Language Club, which I had also done for our department title. Using the model from *Teaching Tolerance* (now renamed *Learning Justice*) from the Southern Poverty Law Project, I organized *Mix it Up* lunches. To entice students to break down barriers and sit with students they would not normally gravitate toward, we had contests based on the richness of the more than 50 language groups at our schools. We decorated tables with placards for birthday months, which we made in the multiple languages of the schools. Students were given entry cards where they had to learn how to say *happy birthday* in the various languages represented at their tables. They asked people to write down the ways they would say it in those languages. The cards were then entered into a raffle for gift cards provided by the administration.

As a club leader, I looked for other ways to celebrate our multiple cultures and languages, such as, before Thanksgiving, writing what students were thankful for in multiple languages on huge posters hung in the cafeteria. Similarly, for Valentine's Day, the students decorated heart lollipops, each with a heart tag in multiple languages as a fundraiser—white hearts for *peace,* pink for *friendship,* and red for *love.* Of course, there were multiple challenges to get hundreds ready, including making sure the Arabic and Mandarin messages were printed properly. Another fun activity to celebrate diversity is an oral language identification game that was played at the History and Heritage Fair, a yearly event sponsored by the History Department. Before the language club got involved, the fair revolved around international cuisine brought in by the students and posters made by students in history classes. The students loved coming in their regional attire, and they enjoyed dancing together to the rhythms of their many cultures. We asked students around the school who spoke a variety of languages to record the same sentence in their language. Attendees of the fair, including students, families, and staff, were able to use headsets connected to the file on a computer and check off which language they thought was being spoken to say "Welcome to the fair." Languages included those studied at our school, Spanish, Italian, and French, and those spoken by our multilinguals, including Arabic, Karen, Kurdish, Malay, Nepalese, Romanian and Russian, Somali, Ukrainian, Urdu, and Turkish. These languages represent the amazing diversity of our district, and the activities teach the students to celebrate multiculturalism and ethnic pride.

The activities promoted at my current school echo those I had created years before as an ESL teacher and international student coordinator at the independent school where we once lived, and where my husband still teaches 30 years later. There, the administration had to be convinced that an orientation for the new students arriving was beneficial, for the administration had said they did not want them to appear to be "different"; the students were expected to take placement tests, get settled into dorms, and learn the ropes only a weekend before classes started. The program I created to support the international students is still a mainstay more than 20 years later. In that role, I was humbled to receive an award for promoting intercultural understanding and peace after planning and implementing a campuswide international fair and assembly. The international students loved dressing in their regional attire, demonstrating their languages, and teaching the community about their customs. There is no reason why the diverse student bodies of public high schools should not be encouraged to do the same.

Bilingualism, often multilingualism (since many speak more than two languages), should be encouraged and celebrated. Dual language activists, including me, rejoiced when Massachusetts passed the Look Act, *Language Opportunity for Our Kids,* and abolished the archaic and detrimental English Language Only laws in 2017. California had preceded Massachusetts by one year, and the West Coast advocates also led the charge in the Seal of Biliteracy.

RETURNING TO ACTIVISM WHILE TEACHING

My road to activism was paved with a call from our local teacher's union to become a delegate at the state Democratic convention in 2013. At that time, I had no idea how to even become a delegate, so I researched the process of attending our local caucus. My husband went with me, and we were both nominated and elected to be delegates. In addition, we started to attend the monthly meeting of our local Democratic committee, becoming members 2 months later. One and a half years later, I was asked to meet with two longtime members. Our chair was moving out of town, and they asked me to run for that role, and I was elected.

As a Spanish teacher, I had seen over and over again the deleterious effects of budget cuts and high-stakes testing. The first subjects to go are those not "tested," and language departments across the nation have been whittled down as levels and languages are cut. As the new chair of our city's Democratic committee, I hosted a large event for our Distinguished Speaker Brunch, where I sat next to our guest of honor, Congressman Joe Kennedy. While eating, we had a conversation in Spanish as he told me about his experience in the Peace Corps, which was started by his great uncle, JFK. From 2004 to 2006, he volunteered in the Dominican Republic, and while helping the locals to improve the local economy and grow tourism he became very proficient in Spanish. It was gratifying to greet a room of more than 200, including some of Massachusetts's most influential political leaders. Politico reported on the event and observed that it was a showing of the Democratic *Who's Who* of Western Massachusetts. It provided a powerful platform to speak about public education, and my opening remarks included,

> As a public school teacher, I can't fathom how any of my colleagues could ever support the other party. We are in the trenches and know the negative ramifications of lifting the cap on charter schools, the detrimental effects of high-stakes testing, the exorbitant cost of college tuition, the impossibility of paying off loans, and most unfortunately, the necessity to practice shelter in place and lockdowns in our schools.

I then asked the guests to take a moment of silence in deference to the victims of the most recent school shooting, which at the time was in Oregon.

It was not hard to get support in a room full of Democrats, most of whom shared my values. Unfortunately, we all learned what would transpire in the upcoming presidential elections. Even though I had once worked for Bernie Sanders, and I was very torn about whom I would offer my allegiance to, it became evident to me one afternoon that fall that I would support Hillary Clinton. As chair of our local Democratic Committee, I was lucky to be invited to a small gathering at a local restaurant to meet the candidate. I was captivated when Hillary began to speak about the necessity to support public education and give more credit to the teachers who deserved it. As we could pass through a receiving line and have our pictures taken individually with her, I was able to thank her for her much-needed support of public education.

I jumped onto Team Hillary and prayed we would finally see the glass ceiling shattered at the same time as quieting the Trump supporters. It is truly dumbfounding that educators could support anyone who would eventually name Betsy DeVos to be Secretary of Education, but I have often clashed with Trump-supporting teachers in my district.

Even though the Massachusetts Teachers Association (MTA) had originally suggested going to the Democratic convention, it wasn't always smooth sailing to get all Democrats to agree on an agenda that would be best for public education. Money was pouring in to increase the number of charter schools. I proposed to my committee that we run a forum to educate people about why it was important to fight against the expansion of charter schools to the detriment of public education. Some of the long-standing committee members spoke up and said that it was not our mandate to do things other than getting Democratic candidates elected. In a strong teacher voice, I quoted the platform of our party that stated our demands for *free, high-quality public education from preschool through college . . .*

After my lengthy speech explaining what could happen if more money was siphoned from our school budgets, the committee voted to host a forum to educate the voters. At that time, in April of 2016, we did not even know that the bill would be called Question 2 on the ballot that fall. However, we organized Our Public Schools, a Forum to Celebrate Public Education, and our event fliers stated, "Learn how charter, choice and possible changes to these policies impact funding. Take action to protect, preserve and improve our public schools."

On the day of the event, I welcomed a packed room of those interested in the fight, including people from many neighboring towns. Our featured speaker was Barbara Madeloni, then the president of the Massachusetts Teachers Association. It was the MTA that had spurred my initial interest in becoming a delegate at the convention 3 years before. Another speaker that night was a member of Easthampton's School Committee, a person with whom I had taught at the one independent school in town. He shared the specifics about the detrimental effects of charter schools and the drain on the school budget.

That same spring, I also traveled to the State House to testify in opposition to Bill H3928. At one point in my formative years, I had been afraid even to make phone calls, but I found myself standing at a lectern in front of the packed room and Senate committee giving a speech where I stated,

> In my city alone, $783,142 was siphoned to charter schools during the last fiscal year, the same year that 18 positions had to be cut throughout the district due to lack of funding. Teaching in the city where I live is not an option, as language is at the bare minimum, beginning in high school. Students should be practicing and refining their fluency that they garnered throughout the years of language study highlighted in the Massachusetts Framework, not beginning from scratch in the ninth grade . . . *I ended by saying*, "our students deserve more, but the answer is not in creating more schools and a two-tiered system . . . Keep the Cap: Public Funds for Public Schools."

The ruling on the cap still proves to be quite detrimental to public school districts.

Running for Public Office

A year after the forum and after testifying on Beacon Hill in support of public education, I decided it was time to run for public office myself. I determined to put my experience where needed most, on the school committee. It was a contested race, with nine vying for six spots. My platform focused on my experience in education and my proven leadership. I was elected to three terms, and nobody could have foreseen what we faced in my second term during the height of the pandemic and the shutdown.

Being a teacher on a school committee is both empowering and belittling, and I felt it most during the crucial decisions of 2020. Little did I know that unfathomable circumstances would arise as we all faced the horrific COVID pandemic. As school committee officials, we faced the most daunting decisions anyone could ever have imagined when deciding to run for public office. As a teacher, I knew firsthand what it was like to face a screen of students who were often disengaged and didn't have their cameras on.

Teachers are rarely thanked sufficiently for the work they do. At one point at the beginning of lockdown, it seemed that parents around the country finally recognized us with comments such as, "How do they do it? I can't stand being with my own children day after day, never mind someone else's." Unfortunately, the praise soon turned to venom against teachers who expressed fears about returning to the classroom and putting their lives or the lives of family members at risk. Countless parents attended our meetings and sent us emails, all offering their opinions on both sides of the debate.

A Teacher on the School Committee

In this role, I often had a unique perspective of the situation. Our decisions were being made about our schools, but I had the insight as to what was going on with my students, colleagues, and myself, a teacher at risk because of my high blood pressure, not to mention the transient ischaemic attack (TIA, or ministroke) I had the year before in my classroom, in front of my students. The summer of 2020 is a blur. We held two meetings a week—an open work session on Monday evenings followed by an open school committee meeting the next night. Hundreds of people attended on Zoom. Instead of picket signs, people posted messages of hatred on the Zoom screens. Social media became ignited with parents spewing their feelings. Anti-mask campaigns began, and one was even started in my teaching district by a member of the counseling department.

I consistently made decisions based on science, as I sat on the COVID Response Team, where we were fortunate to have input from an epidemiologist. I offered to share the data from our COVID Response Team, which was first welcomed by my teaching district. However, as politics got involved and the divide deepened, I was told my input was not welcome, as I was only a teacher there.

For months, I was the school committee person on the COVID Response Team and reported back to the committee when important votes had to be taken. Unfortunately, this incurred the wrath of various parents who just wanted their children back in school, on the playing fields and the basketball courts. They never considered the rising cases that put us in the red danger zone. To complicate matters even more, we were negotiating with the union for a contract. The teachers on the union side were using many of the fears of COVID and tried to add stipulations into the Memorandum of Agreement. I had to constantly weigh what was best for the district against listening to the teachers' fears.

Over the years, my political activism and connections to policymakers paved inroads to help promote policy that would benefit public education. Three years after the forum to keep the cap on charter schools, I again helped the MTA with a forum to "Fund our Future." This time, we were focused on the antiquated formula of the Foundation Budget, which determines funding for public school districts. It proved extremely beneficial to have personal contact with multiple state legislators, as I could send them a personal invitation to attend, and one state representative from a neighboring district, Aaron Vega, even agreed to present. He was a leading sponsor of the Promise Act, bill S.238/H.1416, An Act Providing Rightful Opportunities and Meaningful Investment for Successful and Equitable

Education. That forum was also enormously successful in bringing together educational activists from Western Massachusetts, including multiple legislators, who agreed to attend.

The landmark Student Opportunity Act was signed into law in November 2019, and commits the state to achieving equitably funded public schools over a 7-year span, promising $1.5 billion in additional annual state aid once the law is fully phased in. Unfortunately, districts that are not considered one of the "gateway cities" have received fewer financial benefits, and even those with the greatest problems are still fighting to receive the necessary funds to provide for all of our students in a just and equitable fashion.

The personal contacts I had for a variety of legislators also came in handy when teachers in Massachusetts were fighting to get vaccinated before being forced back into the classrooms. It was absolutely ludicrous that teachers were pushed down on the list of those eligible to receive the first vaccines, and another neighboring State Representative, Lindsay Sabadosa, quickly jumped onto the cause and cosponsored a bill. Similarly, I had been able to communicate with Senator John Velis about the proposed Early Retirement Act that he sponsored but was unable to see passed.

In my serving district, I had been determined to uphold one of my campaign promises when I first ran 6 years ago, to start a dual-language program in our district. After being detained by the pandemic, we began to visit other districts that are running dual-language programs. Our local newspaper ran a front-page story about the conflict between the superintendent and me, since she had not included the program in her current vision for the district. The article included my quotes from a school committee meeting, wherein I shared that "multiple scientific studies have proven that children best learn another language before the age of 10, so our English speakers will benefit tremendously in a program that also provides formal education in English and Spanish for our heritage speakers in town." In a follow-up interview, I added that the creation of a dual-language program fosters a greater appreciation of other cultures in the global community. I also shared that continued participation has yielded increased cognitive abilities and improved test scores for students with dual languages.

COMING FULL CIRCLE

Professionally, I often reflect on my initial goal to become a social worker when I first entered college. I even looked at programs in recent years to see if it could still be a reality, and if I could be an adjustment counselor. The number of study hours without a guarantee of a job made it unrealistic at this stage of my life. Nevertheless, the same reasons that originally led me into an undergraduate program for social worker—to fight for the underdog, to give everyone a voice, and let young people know that their social-emotional well-being is always more important than a grade—can be done in the classroom and can be done as an educational activist.

Forging everlasting relationships with students and making a difference in their lives is what truly keeps me going, even when I question why I still do what I never planned to do. I save the notes, photographs, and tokens of affection I've received over the years. One of the most significant relationships I have ever formed occurred with a Muslim Kurdish refugee in my latest district. I was probably the first Jewish person she ever got to know, so the bond is even more meaningful. After teaching her Spanish, her fourth language, for 2 years, I received a thank-you email before her graduation:

> I know I have never told you this before, but I always considered you as my mom who didn't give birth to me, but treated me as if she really did. If I'm succeeding today, it is because of you, my source of support, inspiration, and motivation. I must be so lucky that I met you. And I thank God who placed you in my life.

Five years later, when I was considering switching to a SLIFE (Students with Limited or Interrupted Formal Education) position, Ayat, (who exemplified the remarkable success of such a student) wrote a letter of recommendation for me. In it, she provided the highest compliment:

> She had so much influence on me that I said to myself, "I've got to be like her." I loved teaching because of her. I loved a whole new language because of her. I wanted to be a teacher and not an engineer like I always wanted to be because of her.

I believe influencing students to become future teachers is one of our most necessary and important roles, especially as this nation faces a debilitating teacher shortage. Ayat is one meaningful example of the now *thousands* of students I have taught. I cannot say that all the relationships have been positive, nor stress-free; however, a plethora of students have given me reason to continue on this winding, often bumpy road.

CHAPTER 11

Write to the City

Practicing Humanizing Pedagogy and Ethnic Studies in Boyle Heights, Los Angeles

Jorge Lopez

In 4th grade, my teacher, Mrs. Miller, drew a circle on the chalkboard and ordered me to place my nose in it as a punishment for "talking" in class. Nervously, I stood up from my seat, walked up to the front of the class, and looked at my peers. Mrs. Miller, a tall, White elderly woman, stared down at me with furrowed eyebrows. I placed my nose on the dusty green chalkboard, making sure that it was inside the circle Mrs. Miller had drawn. I stood there until the bell rang at the end of the period. By the 4th grade, I had already experienced numerous dehumanizing school experiences from my teachers. My kindergarten teacher once washed my mouth with a bar of soap while another teacher held my arms back. She made my sister—who was in the 2nd grade at the time—witness the punishment. Another time, this same teacher summoned me to her desk and swatted me on the top of my hand with her ruler multiple times; I was only 5 years old.

MY EARLY SCHOOLING EXPERIENCES

I hated elementary school. I hated having to sit in unloving classrooms, where I struggled to understand English as well as other children. Most of my White teachers could not pronounce my Spanish name correctly, and soon I began going by George. In 5th grade, I had a difficult time with math, probably because my 3rd-grade teacher would often pinch into my skin with her long nails as she walked down the desk rows. I grew afraid to ask her for help. Rather than help me make sense of math, Mr. Kay, my 5th-grade teacher, sat me on a table next to his desk and had me copy the answers to the math problems he assigned from his teacher edition textbook. I felt isolated, unimportant, out of place. That feeling of not belonging structured my kindergarten-to-8th-grade school experience.

By middle school, I learned to be ashamed of my field-laboring parents for not speaking English and for having a job that was looked down upon by the dominant society. I can recall lying during a 6th-grade class activity where students had to stand up one by one and tell the class what their parents did for a living. Many of the kids in the class, most of whom were White, came from military families or worked on the local navy base. Most of the Mexican kids' parents worked in the fields as farmworkers. As my turn to share approached, I felt anxious and embarrassed to say that my parents picked tomatoes and lettuce for a living. When I stood up, I said, "My dad is a supervisor of the field workers," and sat down quickly, feeling ashamed for being untruthful. I knew I was different from the White kids. I could also see the difference among Latino students whose parents had better-paying jobs and could afford to buy them expensive Nike shoes and clothing.

With neither an understanding of social injustice, class, and ethnicity nor a classroom community that embraced my experiences and material conditions, I developed an internalized identity of a subordinate being. I felt as if everything about me was defined as less than the middle-class White teachers and students. Attached to this difference were my name, my home language, and my brown skin. In middle school, my peers began to call me *Indio* (Indian) because of my dark brown skin and Mexican Indigenous features. Their condescending usage of *Indio* further disempowered my sense of self, especially given that schools never celebrated the experiences and history of Indigenous people. Everything about me felt subordinate and foreign at school, from my physical appearance to my home culture, social class, and my intellect. I never felt smart enough throughout my entire K–8 schooling: not smart enough to speak English, not smart enough in literacy, not smart enough in math.

In my K–8 schooling, I learned to not embrace my brown skin, my name, and my existence while on school grounds. I learned that my Mexican culture and ways of being impeded my assimilation into White American culture. Gilbert Gonzalez (1990) describes similar patterns that viewed Mexican culture as a problem and emphasized acculturation into the dominant White American culture (Gonzalez, 1990). My elementary and middle school years, from the mid-1980s to early 1990s, are defined by memories of racism, classism, and dehumanizing, emotionally painful realities. American schooling denied me the space to learn about my Indigenous roots and the Mexican experience in the United States. These educational erasures have been our shared historical experiences through settler colonialism, and they have continued through various de-indianization colonial projects to exterminate and culturally kill Indigenous identities and ways of knowing (Bonfil Batalla, 1996). I can recall my middle-school self, denying with shame my Indigenous appearance and the label *Indio* that my peers placed on me. Even though my grandparents spoke some of our ancestral P'urépecha language, I never made the connection that I too was Indigenous. On the contrary, I yearned to be more what White middle-class America looked like—and my school was the teaching grounds for it, particularly for Mexican kids.

My years in high school were marked by a need to fit in. In my search for belonging and identity, I joined a tagging crew and hung out with youth who were part of cliques and gangs in my school. In my later high school years, I was fortunate to find adult mentors, including a college counselor and an immigrant rights attorney whom I met through a youth employment program at my high school. They both guided me on the college track and began to encourage me to reflect on my cultural identity—to think about who I was and where I came from. However, it was not until I made it to college that I really experienced a transformational and empowering shift of my identity and where I was given the tools to critically make sense of my entire schooling experience.

WHY I TEACH ETHNIC STUDIES

I teach ethnic studies in part as a revolt against the kind of schooling I received as well as to engage in an alternative humanizing pedagogical project. Schooling should not be what I experienced; rather, its purpose should be to empower students by placing their culture, lived experiences, and stories at the center of the curriculum. The role of the educator should not be to marginalize and disempower students, particularly students of color who have a shared history marked by genocide, slavery, colonization, and economic exploitation (Darder, 2015). Antonia Darder (2015) asserts that hegemonic schooling tends to eliminate differences within schools and society, while denying or erasing communal histories, cultural knowledge, and political self-determination. Rather than deny the daily human lived realities of students, teachers can instead embrace them through a humanizing approach that nurtures self-reflection, relationships, and the knowledge that students bring to the classroom. Schools should develop in students a critical lens of systems of oppression and dominant narratives and equip them with tools for emancipation and agency to create a more just world. Exposing students to knowledge of self, ethnic studies, and critical scholarship has the potential to transform their school experience, as it did for me when I went to college. Schools can guide students in exploring their identities deeply through a personal and collective process. And teachers can help students make sense of the world by identifying social narratives and "rewriting narratives of identity, nationalism, ethnicity, race, class, gender, sexuality, and aesthetics" (Anzaldúa, 2015, p. 7). I teach with these goals in mind.

Before entering the classroom as an ethnic studies teacher, I needed to form my political and pedagogical lenses. I had to experience my own transformation before facilitating the transformation of young people in the classroom. Having experienced oppressive schooling, disempowerment, and dehumanization from kindergarten through high school helped me better understand students with similar experiences. In the spirit of the Mayan greeting *In Lak'ech* ("you are my other me"), living my realities as a Mexican student from a poor immigrant family, going through the American schooling system and transforming through college and now standing before my students as a teacher, I have the ability to see my Chicanx/Latinx students as my other me. Having this insight and understanding positions me in a place where I can best meet the needs of my students.

I often think back to my own experience in schools and wonder: What were my needs? What were the harms that teachers and the schooling system inflicted on me? What kinds of education, classroom community, and teachers might have empowered me and healed the dehumanization that comes with inhabiting America as a poor person of color? Through critical reflection and thinking about the younger me, I can see myself in the eyes of my students, and I hope to be the teacher that I never had. Through *In Lak'ech,* a concept grounded in an Indigenous worldview, I am addressing my students' humanity, their identities, ancestors, and existence. America's schools and social narrative have historically erased or distorted our stories and existence as a people, and through my deep commitment as an educator serving my people, my hope is to challenge and disrupt dehumanizing and racist practices of schools. My students hear my story and we collectively hear each other's stories, which have resulted in enriching community relationships, and the powerful human feeling of visibility and being heard. I also hope that my students can see themselves in me if it helps with their adult envisioning and thinking of themselves as college graduates working for social justice, or even future ethnic studies teachers as some of my students have been inspired to pursue.

I chose to teach ethnic studies because it works to undo the historical erasure of our voices and experiences as people of color and it challenges racist, White-centric curriculum. Through ethnic studies, I can place our personal experiences, dreams, realities, fears, and voices at the center of the curriculum to address the holistic selves of my students. Empowering classroom spaces have the potential to undo many of the harms that schools have historically created. Ethnic studies and similar spaces of empowerment allowed me to love myself, embrace my brown skin and culture, and find knowledge of self by way of my ancestors.

Taking ethnic studies classes in college and engaging in activism developed in me a desire to continue to work toward the liberation of my people and continue the work of historical social justice activists who inspired me. As an ethnic studies teacher, I feel a deep commitment to my students and the community that I serve. My work is not only teaching; instead, I view it as movement work—that is, continuing the legacy of leaders who paved the way and fought to create a more socially just world.

Ethnic Studies at Eastside High School

Boyle Heights today is one of the largest working-class Mexican American and Latinx immigrant communities in the United States (Villa & Sanchez, 2005). The neighborhood is a vibrant cultural hub close to downtown Los Angeles. However, community members are facing many economic challenges because of the increasing cost of living, gentrification, and poverty. At Eastside High School, students in our classes share stories of their experiences growing up as young people of color in Los Angeles. The current expansion of the ethnic studies program at Eastside High School and across the state of California comes at a time when students of color constitute a majority in many public schools. In the near future, high school students will live in a country that will have no racial majority group. Public schools in the United States are at a historical crossroads that will require dramatic change to address educational inequities and uneven policy outcomes that persist. Ethnic studies classes and educators who engage in humanizing pedagogy have an enormous potential to pave the way for that kind of change.

Creating the Program

In what follows, I describe Eastside High School's ethnic studies program and the specific ethnic studies curriculum in place there. Notably, Eastside High School teachers incorporated stories, conversations, and *testimonios**

---

* Drawing on the broad scholarship on *testimonio* as a critical race methodology (Pérez Huber, 2009), I refer to *testimonio* here and in the classroom as the process of sharing personal experiences as a way to create knowledge and theory.

into our ethnic studies classes, and through a sustained engagement and belief in the transformative power of stories, we built trust, encouraged dialogue, and developed critical literacy in our classrooms. In the tradition and legacy of ethnic studies, we centered students' lives and experiences.

Understanding any discussion of ethnic studies and Eastside High School requires understanding the long tradition of ethnic studies. For me, teaching ethnic studies at our school site at Eastside High School and demanding its implementation at the school district level was, and continues to be, charged by the movement that was sparked by students, educators, and communities of color of the 1960s.

Without the solid foundation of ethnic studies courses I took as an undergraduate student, perhaps I would not have had the empowering and personal transformation that I experienced during my college years. Ethnic studies set the foundation toward my career as a social justice teacher with a critical pedagogical lens. It strengthened my commitment to work alongside students in the struggle for liberation, assuring that our voices are heard in school. At the core of ethnic studies is providing a "liberating educational process" (Hu-DeHart, 1993, p. 52) that challenges Eurocentric curricula and recovers histories of peoples whose stories have been neglected. Teaching ethnic studies at Eastside High School has opened up a space for young people to have their voices heard and affirmed. What makes this movement particularly powerful is that this is happening at an educational institution that has historically done the opposite with students of color and Mexican/Chicanx youth in particular. Engaging with a curriculum that recovers instead of erases the histories of people of color at a school institution not only reaffirms students and their experiences but also empowers them to see themselves as people who hold valuable knowledge.

The teaching of Mexican American Studies began at Eastside High School in the decades that followed the 1968 student walkouts that demanded classes that taught the Mexican American experience, history, and culture. When I began teaching there in 2001, the course was not being taught yet. In the early 2000s, United Students, an educational justice club based in several East Los Angeles high schools, led a campaign for ethnic studies that convinced the school principal at my school to offer elective courses. United Students recommended that I teach the course, and I continued offering various types of ethnic studies courses over the years.

Teaching elective courses in my early career gave me the opportunity to grow creatively, create curriculum, and teach about the experiences of urban youth of color using narratives, poetry, research, critical theory, popular culture, music, and media. These skills and teaching experiences influenced the work that I do today in my ethnic studies classes. Although ethnic studies course offerings at Eastside High School were not consistent from year to year, by 2014 we had established a robust program with broad student reach. Two of my colleagues and I felt that this was an opportunity to design a two-semester ethnic studies course centered on the stories of our students and their Boyle Heights community. We were also motivated by the movement that was building in response to the 2010 attacks on ethnic studies from Arizona's House Bill 2281, which banned Mexican American Studies, ethnic studies curriculum, and related books.

Ethnic Studies Courses

The ethnic studies courses at Eastside High School are part of the long tradition of ethnic studies that includes the 1968 student walkouts. When we (as teachers) began designing the curriculum for our ethnic studies program at Eastside High School we wanted to center the voices and stories of our students. We wanted to design a curriculum that honored students' histories and cultures by creating a curriculum that captured narratives often left out in traditional schooling. Our hope was to create an engaging course where young people could explore their identities, engage in collective knowledge building and learning as a community, and feel empowered by the histories of communities of color. We understood then, and still do today, that many of these hopes are tied to what educators and students were seeking to create in the social movements of the late 1960s.

Ethnic studies courses have a long history and what is taught looks very different within its various disciplines. Having taken most of our college courses in the field of Chicana/o studies, we entered teaching with prior knowledge that helped us design the curriculum with a similar vision. For me, having taught numerous electives during my first 10 years of teaching influenced what I believed was important for my students to learn. We agreed that the course should be centered on the stories of our students and the culture of the community in which we teach. The name "Boyle Heights and Me" surfaced in our initial planning conversations, and we rolled out the course with this place-based title on our first syllabus design.

Scaffolding Humanizing Pedagogy: Themes and Questions From the Course Syllabus

Knowing that we would be engaging students in an educational journey of transformation and critical awareness that might be painful, joyful, and at times uncomfortable, we felt it necessary to begin the first semester with a unit titled "Building Community, Identity, and Knowledge of Self." This unit is designed to define community, facilitate strong relationships, and create a united community of learners. It is during this unit that I introduce students to the Indigenous roots of restorative justice and engage them in conversations through the circle process, particularly community building circles. Other activities include icebreakers, games, and getting-to-know lessons and questions. Within this unit we begin to delve into the definition of identity and begin to explore the layers of identity while having students explore their intersectional identities. Students explore what knowledge is and learn that they are both carriers and creators of knowledge. They analyze "official" historical narratives from traditional schooling and textbooks and learn about the importance of ethnic studies in sharing minoritized narratives. We engage students in readings, share-outs, and activities, such as crafting a timeline, to reflect on their lived experiences, realities, dreams, goals, and future envisioning. We encourage students to continuously think, write, and share their lives with one another, so that they can get a deeper understanding of themselves and the other students in the class. During this theme we typically end with a poetry unit, where students have an opportunity to write poetic spoken word pieces and read them to each other.

Boyle Heights and Me: Our Course Syllabus

The course "Boyle Heights and Me" puts young people at the forefront of conversations. Through this course, students participate in dialogues about their lives, communities, and historical moments of injustice, change, and liberation. Though we did not use the term *humanizing pedagogy* to describe it when we designed the curriculum, I argue that we pursued a set of teaching approaches, philosophies, and goals that together form the basis of what I refer to as humanizing pedagogy (Camangian, 2010; Darder, 2015; Paris & Winn, 2013; Paris & Alim, 2017). This humanizing pedagogy had a three-part vision: (1) to build *trust* and strengthen relationships with and among students so they felt open enough to participate; (2) to facilitate *dialogue* among students as they participated in a collective learning and teaching process; and (3) to encourage students to adopt a *critical literacy* framework and to understand their communities and lives as sites of critique and resistance. As we sought to make our ethnic studies classrooms relevant to our students, we were taking up a long tradition of resistant, humanizing teaching—and militating against a similarly long tradition of oppressive, dehumanizing "teaching" that had targeted students of color like us in the public schooling system.

Inspired by the work of Paulo Freire (1970) and Antonia Darder (2017), as ethnic studies educators we recognize that learning is continual and collective, and that as human beings we learn by participating "actively in producing meaning" through a revolutionary educational practice where students become literate "about their cultural histories and lived experiences" (Darder, 2017, p. 117). We believe that education should be transformative and serve to develop our humanity. This conceptualization of education as a liberatory practice and project pushed us continually to seek ways to engage, develop, and tap into the imaginations of our students. We take an asset-based approach in our curriculum, recognizing that our students bring and create knowledge, and reside in a community filled with cultural wealth, and continue to exist in resilient ways (Yosso, 2005). In summary, we conceptualized teaching as a humanizing project. We did not reduce or dismiss the humanity of our students; instead, we embraced it. We saw them. We listened to them. We engaged them with care. Without building these relationships or trust with students, we would have had no dialogue or critical literacy in the classroom. First, students needed to know that we cared deeply for them. Consequently, we sought out ways to build meaningful relationships and trust with students, so that they would reciprocate that care and compassion in their dialogues and textual readings of the material conditions around them.

With the principles of this humanizing pedagogical project in mind, we found that our course can be encompassed and anchored in the three major themes of *resistance, resilience,* and *reimagination.* Within these major themes are various units and day-to-day activities and guiding questions that encourage students to investigate, dialogue with, and reflect on to facilitate the process of developing their critical awareness. Some of the day-to-day lessons vary every year, as they are responsive and adapt to the existing political climate and socially relevant events. The sub-themes of resistance, resilience, and reimagination have changed slightly; however, they stretch across an academic year and are divided into five to six themes; within each theme we have essential questions that guide lessons for each thematic unit.

We initially created the theme of "Mapping Memories" to include some components of cultural geography. The way we designed this theme was by having students think about the power of place and its impact on our identities and lived experiences. We had students look at neighborhood maps, including redlining maps drawn during the neighborhood's early period, to speak about housing segregation in Los Angeles. Mapping areas in the community where they spend their time, they shared memories of those spaces. We wanted them to learn that geographic spaces are not static. These spaces are always changing, and many of those changes are a result of oppressive, discriminatory, or racist policies. Moreover, these spaces have manifested differently throughout history and continue to do so to this day, through the wave of gentrification that families are still confronting in Los Angeles today. Students spend time learning about the community of Boyle Heights to track its history, identify neighborhood assets, and begin to examine root causes of community problems.

Themes and Essential Questions From our Course Syllabus

I. Building Community, Identity, and Knowledge of Self

Where do I come from?
Who am I?
What memories capture the problems and struggles in my life and community?

II. My Roots, My Culture, My Dreams

What are the root causes of my struggles?
What cultural wealth do I possess and how does it support me?
Where do I hope to be? (emotionally, physically, mentally)

We were able to integrate different teachings that incorporate collective art making to think about root causes of struggles that youth and their community members undergo. Under the theme, "My Roots, My Culture, My Dreams," we do an art analysis project titled, "The Rose that Grew from the Concrete," a name inspired by the work of hip hop artist Tupac Shakur. In small teams, students use various art mediums, such as drawing, painting, collaging, to create a large collective art piece that illustrates a rose growing from the concrete, representing resiliency and dreams amongst social toxins, struggles, and lived experiences. This art project is healing, and it allows for students to be in communion during the process of creating and sharing their experiences and future hopes. Building up toward this project, students learn about Yosso's (2005) concept of *community cultural wealth* to help identify their strengths and have a language to speak about the wealth and assets of their community, families, and culture. Many students point to the roots of the rose, and write about the support, teachings, and motivation from family.

III. Indigenous People, Colonization, and Me

What do I know about my Indigenous roots?
What are Native values and practices?
What are the seven pillars of colonization?
Who is responsible for Native American genocide(s)?

In the third theme, "Indigenous People, Colonization, and Me," we were intentional in having students learn more about Indigenous people before delving into colonization. Teaching Indigenous people's ways of life and knowing is especially important to me because when I was going through this learning process as an undergraduate student it was transformational and central to my identity formation. I felt that it was most appropriate to spend more time on this theme because most of our students are of Mexican and Central American heritage, having historical roots to Mesoamerican Indigenous peoples. It is during this unit when students for the first time begin to make sense and understand their own family connections to Indigenous cultures and languages, such as Zapotec, Mixtec, or K'iche' Mayan people. Students engage in oral history, tracking the oldest family members alive and asking questions about their homeland, stories, traditions, and Indigenous roots (if family members can track them). Students learn that because of conquest and colonization, Indigenous languages and their cultural identities have been erased from family histories. However, through the process of this project, students identify Indigenous groups from the regions that their eldest family members are from and begin to research their history, traditions, and culture. There are always students who come back to class excited to share that their grandparents, aunts and uncles, and other family members still speak an Indigenous language. Students share interviews and stories, too. For example, one student, Jimmy, included a video interview in his slides of his uncle speaking Zapotec from his Indigenous roots and people of Oaxaca, Mexico. I find it beautiful to see students craft slides of their homelands, their Indigenous roots, and tell oral histories to each other in American classroom spaces that have historically erased Indigenous culture and ways of being. Through the process, students are teaching each other of Mesoamerican Indigenous people and culture, and showing that they are connected to its resilient people. By engaging students in lessons like these that draw on knowledge from their family and personal lives, and by finding ways to make learning relevant to students, I am engaging in what Camangian (2010) has referred to as "literacy teaching frameworks that maximize students' abilities to read, write, think, and communicate in their own interests" (p. 182). As Camangian (2010) notes:

> Teachers must draw from young people's "robust" literacies to connect their curricula to the needs of students struggling to navigate culturally alienating schooling institutions and the harsh conditions of everyday life. Applying sociocritical literacy in the context of autoethnographies requires that students read and write counter-stories (Solórzano & Yosso, 2002) as an empowering means "toward critical social thought" (Gutierrez, 2008, pp. 149, 182).

In our class, students learned to read their lives critically and, in doing so, created counter-stories—that is, stories that highlight minoritized experiences, militate against dominant narratives, and do the work of "exposing, analyzing, and challenging the majoritarian stories of racial privilege" (Solórzano & Yosso, 2002, p. 32)—to narrate their humanity against a public schooling system that otherwise dehumanized them.

Students also learn about North American Indigenous peoples' history and culture in the United States. They read about Native American values and practices through a document centered around the Navajo Diné ways. Students then create artistic illustrations using color pencils highlighting a Native American value or practice that they believe needs to be manifested more in America. Students often select "respect for nature," "group harmony," or "generosity." We felt that by having students become familiar with Indigenous ways of life they can begin to draw distinctions to Western values, compare them to American values or values that they live by. Having a foundational understanding of Indigenous history and culture is critical for student's own identities and important to learn before introducing colonization. We want our students to understand what was destroyed through conquest, theft, and colonization. We also want them to recognize that Indigenous history did not begin with, but rather preceded, the arrival of Europeans. We teach colonization using the "seven pillars of colonization" found in *Rethinking Schools* publications. Students learn to identify the system of colonization and draw critiques to the legacy of colonialism and colonizers. It is in this unit that students learn about colonial hierarchies of power, class, and race, including land theft, enslavement, genocide, White supremacy, and the origins of capitalism. Using this learned knowledge, we engage students in a Socratic seminar simulation on Christopher Columbus from *Rethinking Columbus* (Bigelow & Peterson, 1998). Students put Christopher Columbus on trial and hold the system of empire, colonizers, and monarchs of Spain accountable for the genocide of the Indigenous Taino people. By the end of this unit, students learn a truthful history of Columbus and the toxic legacy of European colonialism that they have never been exposed to in school, and they also realize that history textbooks erase histories of oppressed people.

IV. Colonization, Castas, Colorism, and Beyond

What are the consequences of colonization, past and present?
How do hierarchies maintain colorism, racism, sexism, and other forms of oppression and discrimination?
How do we begin to decolonize?

The fourth theme, "Colonization, Castas, Colorism, and Beyond," is covered during the spring semester. We continue to discuss colonization but focus more on the colonial era. In this theme, we examine European racism and the institutionalization of the caste system in Mexico that resulted in a stratified society that placed Indigenous and African descendants at the bottom of the hierarchy and European descendants in a place of privilege and power. This theme becomes a historical bridge to discuss the origins of colorism, racism, sexism, anti-Blackness, and other forms of oppression and discrimination. Students engage in collective dialogue as a class and share their experiences of the different "isms." As we continue to interrogate why the different forms of discrimination, privilege, and power exist, we introduce students to the "four Is" of oppression: (1) ideological oppression, (2) institutional oppression, (3) interpersonal oppression, and (4) internalized oppression (Bell, 2013). This framework often resonates with students as we define and provide examples of these oppressions, which they then use to make sense of the oppression in the world around them. Oftentimes, this new lens allows students to name internalized perceptions of themselves, such as beauty standards, or the connections between racism, White privilege, and internalized oppression to how students perceive their own brown skin, and its proximity to Whiteness. Students learn that the origins of the many systems of oppression are not ahistorical. Instead, they are rooted historically and manifest differently across time. Given the long histories of colonization that people of color have experienced, we end the unit by challenging students to think about one question: How do we begin to decolonize? Through a self-analysis art activity, "Colonization and Me," students visually depict aspects of their life that they believe are colonized and consider how they might decolonize those areas. For example, in Sandra's illustration, she points to her stomach and writes, "I am colonized in the area of eating junk food, like chips and soda, and I can decolonize my diet by trying to eat more natural like my indigenous ancestors." Students begin to think more deeply about how they have been impacted by colonization, and they imagine how they can change themselves and the dehumanizing conditions around them.

V. Resistance as Resilience and Liberation

How and why do communities resist?
How do I resist?
What is transformational resistance and why does it matter?

The fifth theme of the course, "Resistance as Resilience and Liberation," focuses on challenging systemic oppression and collective resistance for community change. During this unit, students learn about historical liberation movements, such as the Chicana/o and Black Power movements of the 1960s, and also contemporary movements to stop gentrification; resistance to anti-immigrant attacks; or Black Lives Matter. Students learn how youth during the 1968 East L. A. Walkouts engaged in resistance and how Indigenous youth today advocate for Native land and environmental rights. We believe that if we want students to understand the ongoing resilience of marginalized groups, they must learn from models of resistance and liberation both past and present. That is why, earlier in the semester, it was key to learn how Indigenous communities viewed the world and lived before European contact. We typically have students read and analyze the works of liberation movement activists to learn the freedom dreams and alternative worlds they imagined and fought for. It is in this unit where students learn about different strategies that social justice movements have used to create social change. Throughout the school year, students get exposed to various forms of injustices and its consequences on marginalized communities. Our hope is to end the course with optimistic, empowered students who feel confident that they can transform their oppressive conditions. Students learn they are descendants of ancestors who have survived land theft, enslavement, genocide, and colonialism. We want our students to know that their existence is a form of resistance, that they come from people who have resisted injustice across time, and that they will continue to survive and thrive.

Under "Resistance as Resilience and Liberation," we introduce students to Solorzano & Delgado Bernal's (2001) idea of transformational resistance. As students see their own resiliency, we make sure they have the language and tools to resist and transform conditions in their lives and communities. As such, students learn the difference between reactionary behavior, self-defeating resistance, conformist resistance, and transformational resistance. Using this framework helps students reflect on where they are at and where they want to be in terms of their oppositional behaviors and development as agents of change. We express to students that we want them to be transformational resistors and invite them to engage in social change as the activists they learned about in the course. We have a series of social justice student clubs on campus that students can get involved in, and also have guest speakers throughout the school year, including members of organizations, artists, or leaders who were involved in the 1968 walkouts.

VI. Reimagining as Decolonization

How can we reimagine our realities to transform ourselves, our communities, our world?
How do I begin to heal? How do we begin to heal collectively?
In what ways can I transform myself and my community?

Under the sixth and last theme, "Reimagining as Decolonization," we engage all students in our ethnic studies courses in youth participatory action research (YPAR). In teams, we take students through a process of identifying issues or problems that they feel need change in their school or community. Students learn how to engage in qualitative and quantitative research methods and develop powerful research projects to get to the root causes of problems through inquiry and investigation. For example, a student team focused on how school police make students feel unsafe and also like criminals; a different team looked at the impact of gentrification on family stress levels. After conducting surveys and interviews across campus and throughout the community, students generate their findings and call for actionable solutions through presentations to the school community, including administrators, teachers, and counselors. Selected teams present in a poster session at our annual Eastside Stories conference, which brings together students from various Los Angeles schools. We communicate to students that engaging in YPAR inquiry is itself an act of transformational resistance. By selecting a topic they care about, looking at it critically, and finding possible solutions to transform unjust conditions that are impacting school and community members, students are doing research as a practice of both resistance and reimagination. This project, which engages about 500 9th-graders and a school community, puts the power and voice in the hands of our young scholars who are addressing the consequences of colonialism and systemic oppression while sharing their visions of a new world that they dreamed together.

Our *Testimonio* Student Book Project

Following this project, we end the school year with our *testimonio* student narrative book project, in which students tell their stories and practice reimagination. To honor the voices of our students we have them spend time imagining and writing into existence the way they want their lives and communities to exist beyond oppression. The notion of reimagination is inspired by Paulo Freire (1970) who teaches us that critical pedagogy helps us move beyond fatalistic and fixed ideas about the conditions of our lives. This final writing piece is academically and emotionally rigorous, given that we are asking students to imagine liberating solutions, and a humanizing existence to many of the problems that have personally harmed them.

Our ethnic studies student book series originated in an existing relationship I developed with 826LA, a nonprofit writing organization that works with schools to engage and support students in many forms of writing. Prior to our ethnic studies book series, I collaborated with the organization through world history and food justice courses. For our first ethnic studies book project, *This Is My Revolution: Thoughts on Resistance, Resilience, and Reimagination in Boyle Heights*, we were deeply inspired by (1) an open letter from James Baldwin (1970) to Angela Davis and (2) the book *Between the World and Me*, written by Ta-Nehisi Coates (2015) as a letter to his son. Mirroring this letter-writing approach, my two partner ethnic studies teachers and I begin the book introduction with a letter dedicated to our student scholars that tells our journey in crafting our ethnic studies course, "Boyle Heights and Me." In this book introduction, we wrote the following:

> The book project was meant to serve as a counter-narrative to the very hegemonic structures we critiqued and challenged in our classes. Our course curriculum and this project were deliberately created to place you, our youth, our critical scholars, and our future at the forefront of the conversations that will undoubtedly shape our communities and our world.

Although these words were written over 6 years ago, it remains evident that when we center student knowledge as "legitimate" knowledge in our classrooms, it reveals experiences of oppression and injustice, and holds space for their *testimonios* to speak in schools that have traditionally been Eurocentric and marginalizing (Pérez Huber 2009).

In our book project, *This Is My Revolution*, students wrote letters to their future selves, to the school district, to revolutionaries, and to family. Other students wrote poems and reflections on sociopolitical topics and on issues of injustice and oppression. Their letters are filled with hope, faith, and visions of liberation. As in the tradition of written *testimonios,* students have a desire to document and tell their experiences of struggle, survival, and resistance (Pérez Huber, 2009). In the years after their 9th-grade experiences in class, students returned to our class to tell their stories to the new 9th-graders. It was transformational to witness my former 9th-grade students engage in storytelling and dialogue, and offer support and guidance on youth survival. Students engaged in *pláticas* on how to navigate through their adolescence or through challenges and obstacles created by systemic injustice. These ethnic studies peer relationships allowed for 9th-grade students to see themselves in their older counterparts, ask questions on navigating life as teens, and build a sense of hope for their future, particularly if 9th-grade students are experiencing heavy struggles.

At the end of our letter in *This is My Revolution*, we write, "Ultimately, the work we created with you was driven from a place of love, love for Boyle Heights, the school community, the families, and most importantly the love we have for each and every one of you." I believe that we are all grounded in a teacherly love that Freire characterizes as a "a loving commitment to our students and our political dreams" (Darder, 2017).

During each school year, students and I engage in the student narrative book project, transformed together in this yearlong process. We begin to get to know each other at the beginning of the school year by sharing parts of ourselves and our lives. We continue to get to know each other and build relationships through the conversations and stories we tell throughout the year. Former students often visit the class to share stories that they had written and shared in previous classes. By the end of the school year, when we have established a strong sense of connection, trust, and faith in our classroom community, the students write as I guide them through the process. When the book comes out, typically toward the end of the first semester of their 10th-grade year, we gather again at a book release celebration to retell their stories in community with Boyle Heights.

While the writing prompts change every year, they encompass the three larger themes of *resilience, resistance, and reimagination* that are interwoven throughout the course. Students often write about how they see themselves resisting or overcoming oppressive conditions they have survived, or they write about people that inspire them to be resilient. They also write about what they imagine their lives and world to be beyond oppression in a more humanizing and liberated world. Our hope is that publishing their writing can contribute to their healing and transformation journey.

In our second ethnic studies student narrative book—*You Are My Roots: Letters on Resistance, Resilience, and Reimagination*—we drew on inspiration from Freire, Tupac Shakur, and Jeff Duncan-Andrade. Duncan-Andrade cites the work of Tupac in his analysis of youth growing up in toxic environments, citing the metaphor of "the rose that grew from concrete" to capture young people's resiliency and tenacity to live, dream, and hope. Building on the work of Freire, Shakur, and Duncan-Andrade, we write in the book's introduction that we view ourselves as political gardeners who plant seeds of liberation and tend a rose garden, in so doing supporting the blooming of our students' critical consciousness, and the healing of their damaged petals. This quotation from our introduction captures the spirit of our school year, our pedagogy, and this book:

> Our hope for our students is rooted in heart. It is a revolutionary love birthed from a hunger for justice and change, propelled by emancipatory dreams of an unshackled world and absent from suffering of the soul and void of savage oppression. It is a political hope that inspires action and a persistent critical reflection on our liberatory educational practice. We teach hope so that the hopeless can trust that they too can daydream beyond our classroom walls and rethink the landscape of L.A. transformed as a healing environment. We want to instill in our students that change is a collective action that begins with deep reflection of their minds and the exchange of words through voice and paper.

Darder (2015) writes that Freire's politics of love must serve as a force in any political project and as a motivation for struggle. In many ways these teachings guided our work, which is grounded in love and hope for liberation in the lives of our students. We want our students to have a deep and critical understanding of oppression and also have a space to hope, dream, and develop their agency, which can unfold in transformative ways throughout their lives.

In the book, we continued with the same style of letter writing; it is divided into sections of letters to historical leaders, to themselves, to important people in their lives, and to future ethnic studies teachers. Students wrote letters to Tupac, Cesar Chavez, Sal Castro, Malcolm X, their community, and their family members. In a letter to future ethnic studies teachers, one student wrote:

> I must admit Ethnic Studies has improved my self-esteem in my personal as well as my academic life . . . Students such as I have also learned more about ourselves and that we have the power to change not only ourselves but society as well.

Throughout the book, students discuss topics that involve their personal lives, their transformation, and what they learned that led to that transformation; many students point to historical events and leaders of color. With this newfound knowledge and way of seeing the world, students discuss how they envision and hope to transform their futures.

Our third ethnic studies student narratives book is titled *We Are What They Envisioned: Expressions of Resistance, Resilience, and ReImagination.* The book is organized with letters and reflections dedicated to ancestors. In the introduction we, as teachers, write personal letters to our ancestors. For me this book volume is especially important, as I was able to honor and thank my grandmother and P'urépecha ancestors, who left with me a yearning to learn about my indigenous roots, ways of knowing, and love for history. The theme was born out of a unit we titled "Resistance in My DNA," inspired by Kendrick Lamar's song "DNA." In the song, Lamar speaks about his African roots, what he has inherited throughout the course of history, including all the trauma that came as a result of oppression. In this unit, students engaged with two community artists to develop poster art, a shirt design for ethnic studies students, and a mural we painted on our school wall on the theme of our ancestral knowledge. Many students chose to write letters to their ancestors, imagining their past lives, sharing what they have achieved, while envisioning their own futures. In a letter written as a poem by a Chicana student, in the following excerpt she writes:

> To My Dearest Ancestors,
>   . . . I hope I'm your wildest dream.
>   You never would've imagined that despite all the pain and struggle, we'd come out on the other side. I say *we* because without you there is no me. And with me I hope I've become everything you wished I could be. Because of you I know we're going to succeed.
>   In the end I know I Am Your Wildest Dream.
>   As crazy as it seems.
>   So thank you for being everything you can be.
>   In my heart, through my veins, it's going to forever be you and me.
>   With the deepest love, Sam

In this excerpt, Sam's writing reflects feelings that other students similarly expressed, which is an intimate connection to their ancestral roots, and an authentic curiosity and reflection on what their ancestors experience and dream of for their future generations. In this spirit, our hope is that our students dream and create a future they imagine for their own future generations. We find that in this publication, student writers show their appreciation for the struggles of their *abuelos* and *abuelas*, their ancestors, and find deeper purpose in their present moment. Freire (1970) discusses that we as people create history and are also historical-social beings. In many ways this book project and unit on "resistance in our DNA" allowed for students to see their connection to history and how they have been shaped by historical events, and also realized their power to rewrite their future, while leaving their histories behind.

In our fourth book, *La Vida Es Un Regalo Sagrado: Expressions of Resistance, Resilience, and Reimagination,* students wrote letters, *testimonios*, and reflections on issues impacting their lives and their community. In a *testimonio* letter to her mother, student Tonantzin writes, "The journey to America wasn't easy but she made it. They traveled through the desert and had no food . . . Mama, you worked a dead-end-job and slept in a motel. Your fingers got tired from pushing the buttons of the machine. Your eyes got tired from inserting the threads into the needle everyday. But I'm proud of you, mama." Another student, Javier, writes that the way to not have our culture erased is by "telling stories about our past and teaching it in school. We can preserve the history of Boyle Heights by making books about Boyle

Cover art for our fourth ethnic studies book project, *La Vida Es Un Regalo Sagrado.*

Art by Kalli Arte.

Heights, resisting against gentrification, or trying to save the murals in Boyle Heights."

In the student book, Tonantzin takes the opportunity to tell and pass on her family's story of migration using her writing, voice, and oral history. Students are aware of the power of placing the words they write on student books that will become ethnic studies curriculum, classroom book sets, read by community youth and beyond. Tonantzin experienced the empowerment of the action of telling her mother's journey through the process of interviewing, writing, and publishing it. Both Tonantzin and her mother developed a stronger relationship of dialogue, as Tonantzin shared. Reyes and Curry Rodriguez (2012) write that *testimonios* offer empowerment to the narrators who experienced the event by voicing the experience. In this case, although Tonantzin did not experience firsthand migrating to the United States, she found empowerment in telling the story on behalf of her mother, thus empowering both of them with pride, voice, and love. Tonantzin was emotionally excited and proud to hold in her hands her copy of the published and beautifully bound book, designed with cultural images by community artists. As Javier asserts, "making books about Boyle Heights" resists historical erasure and preserves their culture and history. Reyes and Curry Rodriguez (2012) explain that *testimonio* empowers the speakers or narrator to transform the oral into its written representation not as an act of oppression and ignorance but rather as an acknowledgment of the revolutionary aspect of literacy" (p. 527). The written narratives, poems, letters, and various forms of *testimonios* in our book publications are both empowering and revolutionary for all involved in their creation process—students, teachers, readers, and community. In the process we are all transformed by reflecting on what we tell and write about, while creating amongst us all a collective consciousness (Espino et al., 2017).

Espino et al. (2017) contend that one way to resist marginalities, such as racism, sexism, and classism, "involves drawing upon and (re)telling one's lived experience to expose oppression and systemic violence" (p. 81). For our students, they tell stories of their families living through oppressive experiences as immigrants, or Latina students who face sexism in their school or neighborhood, or stories of living in poverty and other struggles. Our students find empowerment through the telling, and (re)telling: Some students continue to (re)tell their stories in the classroom and throughout their high school years, as students return as guests to share their stories to their 9th-grade peers. The experience of telling their experiences of oppression by engaging with the book volumes and the writing process is not only empowering; it also nurtures the feeling of collectivity where students do not feel alone. Students express feeling connected or as Prieto and Villenas (2012) describe in their research on testimonios with students, feeling intertwined with each other's stories and interdependent. In this way, students "bear witness" to their collective experiences and *sobrevivencia* (survival and beyond), which nurtures their resistance, resilience, and re-imagination (Prieto & Villenas, 2012, p. 416).

In a sense, these book projects we produce remind us of the critical literacies of care and critique that we adopt in the ethnic studies classroom. They embody the humanizing teaching practices that are at the core of humanizing pedagogy: critical trust, critical dialogue, and critical literacy. These modes of *testimonio* and *pláticas* have proven to be so powerful for students in my classes, which is why we center their stories and voices in our ethnic studies program and curriculum.

HUMANIZING PEDAGOGY AND BROADER IMPLICATIONS

The ethnic studies curriculum at Eastside High School centers literacy development through extensive writing in culturally relevant topics. Students learn literacy skills that transfer over to other subjects and overall academic achievement in high school and beyond. Also, through critical literacy development, and the use of youth participatory action research and other forms of agency development, our hope is that our students will develop the skills, confidence, and navigational clarity to pursue their academic goals and dreams.

When crafting ethnic studies curriculum and courses through a humanizing approach, the classroom community and curriculum can contribute to improving the emotional well-being of students. It can improve student self-esteem and give students tools to address their social–emotional well-being through integrated restorative justice practices. Humanizing pedagogy can not only live in ethnic studies courses; it can be implemented in other subjects, and has the potential to improve student relationships with the broader school community, students, and teachers. When students feel cared for, connected, uplifted, and engaged in their classrooms, they improve in school attendance and academic achievement (Dee & Penner, 2017). By learning their histories and cultures through ethnic studies, students gain confidence in their identities and acknowledge their communities and lives as valuable sources of knowledge. In other words, they become organic intellectuals who study the world and write their lives in relation to it.

REFERENCES

Anzaldúa, G. (2015). *Light in the dark/Luz en lo oscuro: Rewriting identity, spirituality, reality.* (A. Keating, Ed.) Duke University Press.
Baldwin, J. (1970, November 19). An open letter to my sister, Angela Davis. In A. Davis (Ed.), *If they come in the morning: Voices of resistance* (pp. 11–19). Third World Press.

Bell, L. A. (2013). Theoretical foundations. In M. Adams, W. J. Blumenfield, C. Castañeda, H. Hackman, M. Peters, & X. Zuñiga (Eds.), *Reading for diversity and social justice* (3rd ed; pp. 21–35). Routledge.

Bigelow, B., & Peterson, B. (Eds.). (1998). *Rethinking Columbus: the next 500 years.* Rethinking Schools.

Bonfil Batalla, G. (1996). *México profundo: Reclaiming a civilization.* University of Texas Press.

Camangian, P. (2010). Starting with self: Teaching autoethnography to foster critically caring literacies. *Research in the Teaching of English, 45*(2), 179–204.

Coates, T. (2015). *Between the world and me.* Spiegel & Grau.

Darder, A. (2015). *Freire and education.* Routledge.

Darder, A. (2017). *Reinventing Paulo Freire: A pedagogy of love* (2nd ed.). Routledge.

Dee, T. S., & Penner, E. K. (2017). The causal effects of cultural relevance: Evidence from an ethnic studies curriculum. *American Educational Research Journal, 54*(1), 127–166.

Espino, M. M., Vega, I. I., Rendón, L. I., Ranero, J. J., & Muñiz, M. M. (2017). The process of *reflexión* in bridging *testimonios* across lived experience. *Equity & Excellence in Education, 45*(3), 444–459.

Freire, P. (1970/2012). *Pedagogy of the oppressed* (30th anniversary ed.). Bloomsbury.

Gonzalez, G. (1990). *Chicano education in the era of segregation.* Balch Institute Press.

Gutierrez, K. (2008). Developing a socio-critical literacy in the third space. Reading Research Quarterly, 43, 148–164.

Hu-DeHart, E. (1993). Rethinking America: The practice and politics of multiculturalism in higher education. In B. W. Thompson & S. Tyagi (Eds.), *Beyond a dream deferred: Multicultural education and the politics of excellence* (pp. 3–17). University of Minnesota Press.

Paris, D., & Alim, H. S. (Eds.). (2017). *Culturally Sustaining Pedagogies: Teaching and Learning for Justice in a Changing World.* Teacher's College Press.

Paris, D., & Winn, M. (Eds.). (2013). *Humanizing Research: Decolonizing Qualitative Inquiry with Youth and Communities.* Sage.

Pérez Huber, L. (2009). Disrupting apartheid of knowledge: *Testimonio* as methodology in Latina/o critical race research and education. *International Journal of Qualitative Studies in Education, 22*(6), 639–654.

Prieto, L., & Villenas, S. A. (2012). Pedagogies from Nepantla: Testimonio, Chicana/Latina feminisms and teacher education classrooms. *Equity & Excellence in Education, 45*(3), 411–429.

Reyes, K. B., & Curry Rodríguez, J. E. (2012). Testimonio: Origins, terms, and resources. *Equity & Excellence in Education, 45*(3), 525–538.

Solórzano, D. G., & Bernal, D. D. (2001). Examining transformational resistance through a critical race and LatCrit theory framework: Chicana and Chicano students in an urban context. *Urban Education, 36*(3), 308–342.

Solórzano, D. G., & Yosso, T. J. (2002). Critical race methodology: Counter storytelling as an analytical framework for educational research. *Qualitative Inquiry, 8*(1), 23–44.

Villa, R., & Sanchez, G. (2005). *Los Angeles and the future of urban cultures*. John Hopkins University Press.

Yosso, T. J. (2005). Whose culture has capital? A critical race theory discussion of community cultural wealth. *Race Ethnicity and Education*, 8(1), 69–91.

CHAPTER 12

Finding My Place in the Education Ecosystem

From Classroom Teacher to *Teacherpreneur*

Heather Robertson-Devine

The last time I was a classroom teacher was in 2016. It feels uncomfortable to say that because I am a teacher. It is my core identity. Teachers are the professionals I admire most. They are my parents, they are my best friends, and they are my intellectual peers. Teachers are also the most important part of the education ecosystem. At the end of my classroom teaching career, I realized that the dual language ecosystem was missing a critical piece that I could provide. Since 2016, I have been a consultant and run a business that supports a critical piece of the dual language ecosystem: Spanish language literature. I did not make this shift lightly. In fact, I tried to avoid it for over 5 years. During those 5 years I explored many different facets of the education ecosystem. That time and exploration broadened my understanding of the ecosystem and how I could better support it.

My framework for looking at education as an ecosystem was influenced by my undergraduate degree. I studied international relations and Latin American studies. I loved learning about how our economic, social, political, and environmental systems impacted how the world works. More than anything, I was fascinated by how these systems perpetuated the division between the "haves" and the "have-nots" in our world. After reading *Kaffir Boy* (Mathabane, 1998) in 7th grade, I was acutely aware that I was one of the "haves" in society. I was aware that I had privileges many others did not because of the color of my skin and the family I was born into. Since then, I have had a burning desire to disrupt this inequity. During my undergraduate studies and for 2 years after, I explored how economic systems, legal systems, and social systems can disrupt the inequity between the "haves" and "have nots." My love of learning ultimately landed me in the classroom.

I started teaching 6th-grade bilingual science and language arts in a middle school in Milwaukee, WI. After that, I was a 6th-grade English language arts and social studies teacher, and then I taught Spanish as a foreign language in a middle school in Glendale, CA; following that, I had a stint as a 3rd-, 4th-, and 5th-grade bilingual teacher and instructional coach in an elementary school in Madison, WI; and finally, I was a prekindergarten–5th-grade English language learner support teacher in Lake Geneva, WI. In each of these places and roles, I encountered challenges that had an influence on my work. With each challenge, I relied on my colleagues, school and district leaders, and social structures outside of the classroom to work toward solutions. I have been fortunate to work with some of the most talented teachers, principals, and district administrators anyone could hope for. I am grateful for all these people and experiences because they have led me to my place in the education ecosystem: I have found where I feel the most confident, most satisfied, and most hopeful. I hope that my experiences help readers to find your place in the education ecosystem.

YEARS 1, 2—CULTURAL BIAS, RACISM, AND WHITE PRIVILEGE IN THE CLASSROOM

As I said, my undergraduate degree was not in education. I decided that I wanted to teach in a classroom while I worked in a Migrant Even Start Program. For my entire life, I had seen my parents make an impact in our small community through the classroom, but it wasn't until I was working in one that I really understood the systemic implications of being a classroom teacher. In order to make a sustainable impact, I needed to get a teaching license, so I moved back to my home state of Wisconsin and participated in the Milwaukee Teacher Education Center program. This was a program sponsored by AmeriCorps of Wisconsin where we would get a teaching license after one year of coursework and teaching.

While working in Milwaukee, I was met by an unexpected culture shock. I had lived in Wisconsin all my life, but in a small town outside of Madison and in Madison itself. Milwaukee is a much more industrial city, more culturally diverse than my small town, and one of the most segregated cities in the United States. I worked in a neighborhood where most people were Spanish speaking and had recently moved from Puerto Rico or Mexico. There were some serious cultural tensions between the two populations and gang activity was frequent. When I first wrote this, I stated, "the cultural differences between my students and me made it very difficult for us to have a relationship." However, it is more accurate to say that my White privilege prohibited me from having a relationship with my students. For example, I thought my Puerto Rican students were disrespectful when they called me "Missy," rather than that they were being respectful. Equally, I thought the same of my Mexican students when they called me "Maestra." In my culture, learning someone's name is respectful, but I quickly learned this was how my Spanish-speaking students were being respectful to me. I thought students were "bad" because they did not have the proper materials, such as a pencil, for class. These are just some of the many racist, ignorant, and misguided thoughts that I had about my students. Also, I did not consider the stress nor the trauma of my students' lives. So, when they fell asleep in class, I assumed they didn't care rather than consider why they were so tired. I had this one student who was 14 years old in 6th grade, which is 2 years older than the average age, and he would fall asleep frequently. I was relieved when he did because he was so disruptive when he was awake. When he did not return to school the next year for 7th grade, I learned he had pledged a gang and was expecting his first child. I was so surprised to learn all of this about him. However, the fact that I was surprised demonstrated how much White privilege I had and how deep my racism and bias ran. This combination was toxic to my classroom learning environment.

Not only was my White privilege, my racism, and bias a problem for my classroom management, but they also made it very difficult for teaching and learning. This became clear to me when I was teaching science and discussing pollution in large bodies of water. I clearly remember being so proud of myself that instead of just using the information in the 15-year-old text book, I printed out an article about Lake Michigan. Our school was just over 2 miles to the west of the lake. Therefore, I assumed all of my students had been there and knew it well. I assumed wrong. After about 10 minutes of discussion, I learned that many students had been there, but they didn't know what it was called. I also assumed my students and their families talked about the trash all over the beach, and the fact that it was often closed because of blue-green algae. I assumed this because that's what my family did. My erroneous assumptions inhibited teaching and learning. At the time, I knew that there was a problem but it wasn't until years later when I worked at Lincoln Elementary School that I gained the language and understanding to identify that the real problem was my White privilege.

In addition to the toxicity within my classroom, it also existed throughout the school. At the end of my first year of teaching, unionized staff in my school voted our principal out of the building by a vote of no confidence.

At that time, I also learned that our staff wrote more than 1,000 behavior referrals. Without a doubt, I contributed to that number of referrals. I was instructed that it was the third step that I was to take when a student was disruptive or defiant in class. I was to write a referral and send them to the assistant principal's office. I don't remember what most of my referrals were for; however, I clearly remember a student asking me in the middle of my lesson, "Ms. Robertson, do you swallow?" I was beyond humiliated. I sent the student out of the room with a referral. He returned before the class period ended with a note that said, "counseled," which meant that the administration spoke to him about his behavior and it was resolved. When I followed up with the administration, I was told that they did not call the parents, I would need to do that myself. I did ask the assistant principal to call them with me and she refused. The parents were Spanish speakers and I remember looking up the word "swallow" in the dictionary to call them. I felt completely humiliated and unsupported. When I talked with the parents and the child, they were all remorseful for the behavior and my relationship with the student somewhat improved. I realize that the number of referrals I'd written in the past is one of the reasons this situation was dismissed. However, the end of the year no confidence vote by the teaching staff gave me hope that a different administration and serious changes in my approach to teaching would lead to a better classroom ecosystem.

During the second semester, our licensing program required us to involve our students in a community service project. My partner teacher and I wanted to address the cultural differences between our students that identified as Mexican and Puerto Rican. We designed a 6-week unit about cultural identity that culminated with a mural in the hallway outside of our classrooms. The students collectively designed the mural. They selected flags from the United States, Puerto Rico, and Mexico. They selected cultural symbols including a *coquí*, a tree frog native to Puerto Rico, a snake, and a bald eagle. The flags and symbols were surrounded by the words "Raza Unidos." It was an incredible experience for me to see how texts, discussion topics, and studying mural art inspired learning in our classrooms. My ignorance began to give way to some small steps in understanding and knowledge.

I entered year two, motivated to be more responsive to my students and less judgmental. However, I did not have the curricular freedom I had in the previous year with our community service project because we were sanctioned by the No Child Left Behind (NCLB) law and requirements. As a result, we had mandated professional development. It was focused on how to use a software program that graded student writing. The professional development was very disconnected to what I needed to become a better teacher. I needed instructional resources that related to my class. My classroom had science lab tables, but no science equipment. Our science textbooks were more than 15 years old. There were very few books for my English and Spanish Language Arts classes in the book room. I needed support to improve my culturally responsive teaching strategies. I needed resources to be able to teach.

At the end of my second year, I decided that Milwaukee was not the best fit for me. I did not see how I could improve as a teacher with the resources available. More importantly, I knew that the school and children needed a teacher who understood them, was committed to them, and was willing to fight for them. So, I packed up my White privilege and moved to Los Angeles, CA.

YEARS 3, 4, 5, 6—SCHOOL LEADERSHIP: INSTRUCTIONAL RESOURCES AND PRACTICES

I taught 6th-grade English language arts and social studies, and Level 1 Spanish as a foreign language at a middle school in Glendale, CA. The teaching staff was clear and focused on instructional practices that supported differentiated and rigorous instruction for English language learners. Nearly all of our students were immigrants or children of immigrants and they were bilingual, if not multilingual. We had resources to teach and appropriate strategies to meet the learning objectives we had for our students and our assessments and instruction aligned to the standards. We posted our objectives and standards daily. The entire school was very clear on the academic expectations and curriculum. As a result, our data and test scores showed student growth and achievement.

I was enthusiastic about leadership and administration, so I started my master's in education leadership and policy. Classes were taught by administrators from the area and from our district. There were a few of us from my school in the cohort. The district administration gave us opportunities to be school leaders at the district level. I was selected to be the school representative on the social studies textbook adoption committee. Unlike the science textbook in Wisconsin, the social studies textbooks were written specifically for the state of California. During the process of reviewing textbooks, one of the textbook companies offered us free laptops and projectors if we purchased their books. Because we were public school teachers and our resources were limited, we went with that company. This was not an easy decision; it was a moral dilemma. All of us making the decision knew that offering the projectors and laptops was no different than a bribe. However, the content was not very different from textbook to textbook, so we went with the company that offered us more resources for our classrooms.

Reflecting on this experience, I realize how teachers' desperation for resources makes us an easy sell. The product doesn't have to be exceptional as educators are a vulnerable group with limited resources. I also realized how much resources mattered and how much they improved my success in the classroom. I did not have the same quality nor quantity of resources in Milwaukee as I did in Glendale and those resources definitely contributed to my students' success. However, when I was selected to be part of the district instructional initiative committee, I learned how instruction and resources combined are what really make an impact in classrooms.

In addition, I was one of two school leaders for the district-wide instructional initiative on summative writing. The goal was to teach all students to write short essays that summed up content. All instructional teams were engaged in this initiative. As a school leader, I led staff meetings that shared the district's vision. Each department in our school determined how to collect data, display data, and display student work samples. It was an incredible collaboration and effort put forth by all the departments. District wide the departments identified and created assessments and looked at data together. Across departments and schools, teachers and administrators conducted classroom walk-throughs to observe the evidence of summative writing. This was organized by a leadership team of teachers and every staff member participated. It was a powerful experience. This initiative was 2 years long and coincided with my master's degree. From this experience I learned the impact and power of district-wide initiatives that build on, and build up, teacher capacity.

Before teaching, I was a community organizer for environmental and human rights issues. This work showed me that small groups of focused and determined people can make a great impact. Therefore, working in a district that supported teacher capacity was the type of leadership I could really support. I valued teachers because it was my parents' career. I valued grassroots movements and the voices of people on the ground doing the work from my environmental and economic justice campaign work. My experience as an educational leader and a student of educational leadership and administration helped me understand the critical role of school and district administration in a healthy education ecosystem.

YEAR 7—THE CLASSROOM: THE HEART OF TEACHING AND LEARNING

Upon completion of my master's degree, I returned home to Madison, WI. I was determined to lay down some roots in my community and lead a school in a more formal way than I had in Glendale, CA. I took a bilingual teaching position in an elementary school because I knew that I wanted elementary teaching experience so that I could deepen my understanding of teaching and learning. I wanted to understand the process of reading and literacy development. I was incredibly fortunate to land in the community of Lincoln School. My principal was finishing her PhD in Leadership and Policy at the University of Wisconsin–Madison. She was very engaged in leadership beyond her school and understood the value of supporting educators like me who aspired to a leadership role. She is also one of the strongest instructional leaders I have ever worked with because she built strong school and classroom communities. She recognized my lack of experience in the elementary grades and paired me with an instructional coach.

My instructional coach and team were experts in literacy and instructional development. They knew how to run the workshop model so that students were always engaged, challenged, and valued. A workshop model includes whole-group, small-group and independent learning. Our school implemented the workshop model for both math and language arts. As a team we were constantly evaluating and reforming our instructional literacy groups. With my coach and a University of Wisconsin–Madison course on math instruction, I learned how to flexibly group my math students daily. I loved teaching because I fully understood Lev Vygotsky's Zone of Proximal Development (McLeod, 2019). Vygotsky's theory refers to the student's independent ability and how instruction can support them. This theory came to life for me after teaching math for a few months in my split 3rd- and 4th-grade classroom. For the first few months of the school year, I would teach math on one side of the classroom to the 3rd-grade students and then move my whiteboard to the other side of the classroom to teach the 4th grade. One day, I was struggling with my 4th-graders' lesson when one of the 3rd-graders who always quickly finished his work spoke up and explained how to solve the problem. It was then I realized that dividing students by grade level was meaningless. Through my work with my coach I was learning how students develop math and literacy skills and I learned how to identify where students were on the learning continuum. With this knowledge and ongoing support, I started teaching students by their skills. It was revolutionary.

It was the missing piece to my teaching. I had learned with my peers in California about the value of cooperative learning, checking for understanding, and formative assessments. However, it was not until I understood the continuum of literacy and mathematical skill development that I was able to plan lessons that engaged my students, challenged them, and advanced their learning. It was challenging, and it was also magical. My definition of teaching and learning became this sacred space where a teacher connects with a child and nurtures their mind and heart.

In addition to the conversations around students' abilities and skills, we often discussed White privilege and anti-racism. My principal was a social justice leader. Her PhD focused on school structures that supported inclusion. In the school she worked at prior to Lincoln she maximized her budget and teaching staff to push services into the classroom. That is, English language learners were not pulled out for instruction, nor were special education students. Instead, two teachers with different licenses were paired together to service all students. For example, in some classrooms there was a special education teacher and a general education teacher. She also partnered with the University of Wisconsin–Madison to hold classes at the school so that general education teachers could get another endorsement in English as a Second Language instruction. My first-year teaching there was also her first year as a principal. That year, she identified some problematic spaces in the school. For instance, students with special needs, mostly Black boys, were instructed in an old locker room with no windows, students of color were pulled out of their classrooms for Title I reading in the room above the library, English language learners, mostly Hmong, were pulled out of the classroom and given English as a Second Language support near the book room; Latino students who could not pass the English proficiency exam were instructed in three different bilingual classrooms. The school community called these classrooms the "Spanish kids' classes." As our principal looked ahead to her second year she was ready to make some serious changes to make Lincoln more inclusive. She would begin by dismantling these spaces and creating teams by pairing teachers with different teaching licenses: special education or English as a Second Language with a general education certified teacher. However, this did not solve the issue of the "Spanish kids' classes." However, due to some changes in district leadership and community support, our district agreed to end the early exit bilingual program and implement a two-way dual language program. This created an opportunity for my principal to hire me as a bilingual school instructional coach; I would lead our school's two-way dual language program. This was my first step out of the classroom and I was determined to support the educational ecosystem by supporting teachers and a program that would no longer segregate bilingual children.

YEARS 8, 9—SCHOOL CULTURE AND INSTRUCTION: DISMANTLING SPACES AND CREATING INCLUSION

Before the previous school year ended, the principal had drafted class placements and established teacher teams. During the summer she and I dismantled the segregated spaces she'd identified during the school year. We converted the special education "room" into the teachers' lounge. We painted the floor, hung some pictures, created a lending library, installed microwaves, a refrigerator, and furniture. We converted the Title I room into a space for special education teachers to have a desk and hold meetings. We moved the book room out of a classroom with beautiful windows and put all the books in the small rooms and closets where English language learners were receiving services. We had all of the storage spaces filled, so that students could fill classrooms. My first year as an instructional coach I was basically training to be an assistant principal. I was my principal's right hand. I supported a lot of behavioral interventions and I was exposed to the ins and outs of running a school.

In order to support the inclusion and dismantle segregated spaces, we hired another coach (me), paired classrooms so that there were two teachers, and we reduced class sizes to no more than 18 students on each teacher's roster, or 30 if they were paired. As the less experienced instructional coach, I supported the principal with the same 5–10 students with daily behavioral issues. Dealing with these behavior issues daily brought back many of the frustrations I had as a teacher in Milwaukee. We had very limited resources to help students. The students who frequented the office were traumatized. Quite honestly, I did not have the "stomach" to work with these issues. Some of the students were so traumatized that they would scream, cry, yell, and throw things for 30–60 minutes at a time, sometimes multiple times a day. While I could provide students a safe space, food, and warmth at school, I had no control over what happened to them outside of school and this made me feel hopeless. I didn't have the perspective of years of teaching to give me hope that students would exit. If you recall from my first year in Milwaukee, my most challenging student did not exit the cycle of poverty. Learning that being a principal meant that I would have to deal with a lot of behavioral issues helped me decide that it was not the job for me. I needed to work in a place where I could see hope. I knew that place was in teaching and learning. While there are principals who are instructional leaders, I knew that I was not capable of balancing the two roles well.

Therefore, I focused my energy on being an instructional coach and supporting our two-way dual language programming and classroom instruction. There was a lot of hope in a two-way dual language program because of the pairing of students from English-speaking homes and students from Spanish-speaking homes. Not having been a victim of systemic racism, I was praised and rewarded for my ability to speak, read, and write Spanish. It wasn't until I was supporting Spanish-speaking families in the U.S. education system that I realized how privileged I really am in the United States, in addition to the world. The most common sentiment in the United States is the notion that it's so great that White people like me are able to learn Spanish, yet immigrants don't learn English. However, the reality is that my students' English was usually more proficient than my Spanish. That double standard is a flagrant example of racism and I am hopeful that dual language programs will lessen such ignorance. We have already seen great progress. There are still issues that require attention such as the diversity of programs, the further segregation of African American students, and the achievement discrepancy tied to the socioeconomic status of children within the program. These challenges can be addressed through community education, school structures, and instructional structures. They are challenges that I believe my work as an instructional leader could positively impact.

As a leader of the dual language program, I was responsible for curriculum and resources to support teaching and learning. We had lots of resources in our school in English, but we severely lacked Spanish resources. As a school we allocated money to purchase more Spanish books, but our options were limited. I started my company Books del Sur during my second year as a school instructional coach. Many of my colleagues were selected for a Fulbright Scholarship to Chile to study children's literature. I had applied, but I was not awarded the scholarship. When I was making purchases for our school book room, they all requested books they had learned about from the program. I was unable to purchase them because they were not distributed in the United States and we could not make international purchases. So that summer, I traveled to Chile and with the help of my Chilean exchange brother (I had lived with him and his family when I studied in Chile during my junior year of college), we met with publishers and purchased some of the books my colleagues learned about. At the time, I did not consider Books del Sur a long-term solution to the dual language resource shortages in Spanish Language Arts. What was really needed was an equitable collection of books and curricular materials in Spanish like those available for English Language Arts.

YEAR 10—DISTRICT LEADERSHIP: CORE RESOURCES

After 2 years as a school instructional coach, my favorite district coach convinced me to take a position in the district office. There, I would be able to support dual language programs across the district and, even more importantly, participate in the English Language Arts curriculum adoption. I saw this as an opportunity to advocate for equitable resources for Spanish Language Arts. Early in the adoption, I learned that the products we were reviewing were not available in Spanish, making my role doubly difficult. Furthermore, the other teacher leaders on the committee and I believed that books were the best curricular resource. Books that represented the windows, mirrors, and sliding glass doors that Rudine Sims Bishop describes (Bishop, 1990). Books made flexible and dynamic grouping easier because they offer so many possibilities. As a district, we had been successfully implementing this literacy model for years but we lacked a critical mass of high-quality books in English, and even more so in Spanish. However, the administration determined that books and our literacy framework were not enough—the books needed lesson plans and student activities in order to best support teachers. The teachers on the committee, especially me, felt defeated and unheard. Our defeat was further exacerbated by the state legislature when they passed Act 10, a law which no longer allowed teachers to organize and negotiate as a union. At the end of the school year and the adoption cycle, the other teachers and I left the district office for other districts or returned to the schools in which we had worked. I returned to the classroom. I had the opportunity to teach the last 5th-grade class before our school completely transitioned to two-way dual language, and I took it! That year I learned that the district office was not a part of the education ecosystem that I was interested in working in because the rate of change was slow. Furthermore, it was too far away from the real reason I loved education, teaching and learning. I missed the joyful experience of engaging another human being in discovering something new that often happens when you read a story together or solve a problem.

YEARS 11, 12—THE CLASSROOM: BOOKS AND STUDENTS

The following fall our classrooms were filled with boxes of contrived English texts or books with lesson plans published specifically for the classroom. As we unpacked the books, we discovered stories about grandpa bathing with his grandkids and blackface illustrations in nonfiction texts about African Americans in the United States. We were told to use the lesson plans with fidelity, but quickly discovered that they all ended with "then adjust for your student needs." While this is appropriate pedagogy, it did not match the district rhetoric rationalizing why we purchased them. Furthermore, all the materials were in English. It was not until the end of the next year that the district office adopted a core resource for our Spanish language arts. The district allocated a huge amount of funding to the classroom yet it did not make positive shifts in the classroom ecosystem because it did not meet the needs of the students. It was better than nothing, but I began to wonder if it was possible to have classroom resources that did not perpetuate the oppressive narrative of children of color?

My hopeful heart led me to the University of Wisconsin–Madison. There I found two outstanding resources, one of which was the Cooperative Children's Book Center. I attended a presentation of their report about the books published that year. They review newly published books that are submitted to them and include the number of books written by people of color with people of color as characters. Their report showed that children's books do not reflect the populations of our classrooms. I was frustrated to learn that there were not many alternatives available. In spite of the district's decision to not purchase books, our school administration and leaders were committed to acquiring the books we knew we needed. We had an incredible school librarian and library assistant who managed our book room and they engaged the staff in collection mapping. As a school we spent our funds on books. As our school transitioned to dual language instruction, our Spanish book collection grew to support it. The work I had set in motion 3 years earlier continued and now, as a classroom teacher, I had more books and my students had more books to engage in the love of reading.

I continued to struggle a bit to engage my students with books because they really loved video games. They wrote about them and talked about them all the time. Knowing that changes in book publishing were slow moving, I began to explore the possibility of technology and how technology resources could disrupt the weak educational resources we had in our classrooms. This was 2011, so conversations around digital literacy access and one-to-one devices were hot topics in education. I was fortunate that the other outstanding resource at the University of Wisconsin–Madison was the Discovery Center, and within it was a group called Playful Learning. I took a class on Leadership and Technology and submersed myself within the gaming world. The possibilities for creative, interactive, investigative learning were exciting. I spent the next few years engaged with this group of creative people and the conversation around technology and digital literacy. I opened my classroom to graduate student research, my students played educational games, practiced online safety, and some were even coding. It was really great because my students were engaged and motivated.

During these years, my students and I read the Spanish literature from Books del Sur during Spanish Language Arts class. I struggled with reading comprehension and not surprisingly my cultural bias got in the way of connecting with some of the books. The Spanish I learned was "à la English," that is, I spoke and wrote Spanish the way that I spoke and wrote English. Books del Sur titles are not translations; they are written in Spanish and represent the diversity of the Spanish language from country to country. I did not have the knowledge of Spanish regionalisms and linguistic structures to deeply comprehend many of the books. Initially, I just thought the books were weird. Specifically, there was one series that is the most popular series in Chile. The main character is a boy who is always getting in trouble because of his adventurous spirit. Each book was a series of events. There was not a clear problem, climax, and solution. I found this incredibly weird and contrary to the language arts standards we were teaching. However, one day during Spanish language arts, a student who had recently moved to the United States from Colombia was reading one of these books and he started laughing aloud. He came over to me and shared the part of the book that made him laugh. When he read it back to me, I didn't understand why it was so funny. When I asked him to explain, he shared with me the nuance of the Spanish linguistic structure. He then told me how much he loved the book, the characters, the adventures, and how excited he was to read the other books in the series. This was a life-changing moment for me. It was then that I clearly understood a few critical things about literacy structures, resources, and teaching and learning. I learned that as a White woman and a Spanish language learner, I was a gatekeeper of resources. If I had not had that experience with my student, I would likely not share the book with my classroom, and therefore I would not have continued to buy it and sell it for Books del Sur. I would have closed the gate on this resource because I thought it was "weird." It was at that moment that I committed to being open to the complexities of language in Spanish language literature. I also learned firsthand how the linguistic structures of authentic Spanish language literature (not literature translated into Spanish) engage native Spanish speakers. I learned that I had more to learn about authentic Spanish language literature. I wanted to understand why the book did not have the features I was accustomed to seeing in literature, that is, a problem, climax, and solution.

My experience returning to the classroom was different from before because I was able to access resources that I did not previously know about. It was there, in Room 26, that I found my place in the educational ecosystem: It was working with students with rich digital and print resources. Not to give away the end of my story, but I no longer work in Room 26. However, as I will share, the time in that space and place continues to guide me today.

YEARS 13, 14—FAMILY: PRIVILEGING SPANISH AND PARENTING

The following year, it was time for me to focus on my own family, which forced me to leave Madison for Illinois. I was offered a teaching position in a district where the superintendent was my parents' former principal and their all-time favorite principal. I was offered a position to support English language learners and teach Spanish to 4th- and 5th-graders. The Spanish classes were new and were an initiative to replace the bilingual program required by law. In the previous years, the district struggled with their bilingual program. Student achievement was low and the district was constantly looking for teachers. Their solution was to offer Spanish to *all* students starting in 4th and 5th grade. While I preferred a two-way dual language program, I saw the opportunity for the Spanish classes to evolve into it. The superintendent was open to the possibility. As in other years, I started full of hope and excitement to build something in a school and in my home.

After 6 months of working and building the Spanish program, it was time for me to submit my budget request for the next year. I had very few Spanish-language books in my classroom, so I filled out the request with a long list of books that fit my unit plans. Within a day I received a phone call from the district curriculum director. She had a stack of questions about my order. After extensive questioning and defending myself, she said, "Spanish is supposed to be fun. We do not teach children to read in Spanish." I was dumbfounded, heartbroken, and unsure what to do next. For the most part, she and I saw eye to eye on literacy and literacy practices. I did not understand why she was so against them for Spanish class.

A few weeks following the conversation, the principal let me know that I was reassigned to only support English language learners and would no longer teach Spanish. When I questioned why, she stated that the district office needed to reallocate the Spanish teacher at the other school. I then shared with my principal the conversation I had with the district curriculum director and she connected the dots for me. The district's past history was not just due to staffing issues; it became a staffing issue after the district did not support the staff and isolated and chastised them for their students' low performance. I attempted to rally other teachers for the good of our students, but they had already lost that battle and were unwilling to engage.

I was heartbroken by the district's myopic vision and racist structures. I continued to work the next year, hopeful that the change was temporary and that I would be able to support our families despite the marginalizing structures. Part of my work was to support our families during parent-teacher conferences with interpreting. After one of the conferences, the conversation with one mom continued. She was asking me why I was no longer teaching Spanish to her daughter. I explained she had a new teacher and she was doing well. The parent expressed her disappointment because she had seen her daughter learning Spanish so well the year before. Then came an outpouring of her frustration with being a parent to a child who does not speak her language. She said they barely communicated, and when they did, her daughter responded in English. She shared how frustrating it was because she was unsure if they really understood each other. I was 8 months pregnant with my son and I empathized with the parent more than I ever have in my teaching career. I always wondered why teachers would say, "You will see it differently once you have a child." It was a very true statement for me. I could not imagine being unable to communicate with my own son in my native language. And once again I questioned if I was really able to make an impact or if I was just perpetuating the racist structures of our school system. I saw the grave impact of an unhealthy ecosystem. The leadership's racist beliefs that children should not learn to read in Spanish was toxic and I doubted my ability to overcome it.

Soon after parent–teacher conferences, my son was born and I began my 3-month-long maternity leave. I quickly realized how soon the 3 months would end and the dread of leaving him all day to work in a place that did not align with my values was nearly unbearable. While caring for my son, I had a lot of time alone to reflect and consider my other options.

I thought of myself as a *teacherpreneur*. I had adopted that identity the year before when I attended the Wisconsin State Reading Association Conference. There, I attended a panel of some of my favorite literacy leaders; Dr. Sonia Nieto, an editor of this book, was on one of the panels. One of the topics we discussed was testing. The state had just adopted a test and the same company was a sponsor of the conference. So, there we are in a large ballroom complaining about a test that continues to marginalize our already marginalized population and yet each one of us has a bag with the testing company's name on it. It was at that moment that I was struck by the contradiction. I shouted out something like, "Yeah, we need to ditch the bags!" This comment stirred the audience and the panel ended. I approached a professor I worked with at the University of Wisconsin–Madison to apologize for the disruption and she encouraged it and introduced me to Dr. Nieto as not only a teacher but as the founder of Books del Sur. Dr. Nieto was very interested in my work and asked me to share it in her book, *Why We Teach Now*. After writing it, I still didn't think much of it. I still saw myself as a teacher with a side hustle as a *teacherpreneur*.

During the second month of maternity leave, I contacted two bilingual program directors with whom I had previous contact through mutual friends. I made appointments with them to pitch my products and they were both incredibly supportive and made substantial purchases for their schools. Their support and the support of my colleagues in my former school district opened my eyes to the possibility of running a business and being more than *a teacherpreneur*.

Then in my second to last week of maternity leave something I could have never imagined happened. I was depressed and upset about returning to work and then in the middle of the day I got a Facebook message from Dr. Tim Boals, the founder and director of WIDA Consortium, an organization that provides tools and resources for multilingual learners. I thought, "Well, this is odd," but I had met him many times and we bonded over the fact that his daughter was a tennis player, as I had been, at the same high school. But his message was not about high school tennis. It was something like, "Heather, I'm at the International TESOL conference in Canada and your picture is up on the main screen. The keynote speaker, Dr. Sonia Nieto, is talking about you." I was confused, shocked, and convinced I was hallucinating from lack of sleep. I mean two really influential people in the multilingual education space are talking about me and one of them directly to me. Then ping, another friend messaged me on Facebook with a photo of Dr. Nieto and a huge slide with my name and Books del Sur in the background. This is when I realized that Books del Sur could really be a change agent. I learned that while I loved teaching, I was not in a place where I could support bilingual education and there was an opportunity right in front of me. The combination of Dr. Nieto recognizing my work, the desire of school leaders to purchase books from me, my desire to support bilingual families, and quite frankly, every other experience I've shared up to this point in my life all gave me the vision and clarity that growing Books del Sur was the best way for me to support the dual language educational ecosystem. It provided resources that were equitable, culturally relevant, and cultivated the love of reading in Spanish.

YEAR 15 AND BEYOND—BOOKS DEL SUR:
A BUSINESS LED BY A TEACHER

The first 2 years of growing Books del Sur beyond our small collection of books and sales was possible because I drove to my old school district. It was a 1 hour and 45-minute drive each way, and it was worth it so that I could be surrounded by peers who encouraged me to grow, supported dual language programs, and loved books. I was able to increase my sales and my book collection. Toward the end of my second year, a school district in Illinois that I worked with asked me to consult with them to develop their middle school bilingual curriculum. I was perfectly qualified for the work, but never thought of myself as a consultant, again, because I was a teacher. However, when I did the math, I would be able to make the same amount of money working one day a month as I did four Mondays a month. Also, my son was getting older and the 4 hours in the car was getting to be more difficult.

My first year out of the classroom was miserable. I was incredibly lonely and lost. I didn't know how to answer people's questions, "What do you do?" I just wanted to shout, "I have this big dream!" but I had no idea how to achieve it. I listened to lots of podcasts about business and eventually hired a business coach. It made a world of difference in my teaching, and I was hopeful it would do the same for my business. My coach was just what I needed. She helped me create structures and routines, she understood what it was like being a new mom and she surrounded me with a small group of women who were also passionate about their work and sharing it with others. The best advice she gave me was, "Take all the skills you learned in managing your classroom and use them to run your business." If you recall, I had terrible classroom management. The same is true for managing Books del Sur, but each year after that, my skills have slowly improved.

Like a good classroom teacher, I first identified my objectives. The primary objective of Books del Sur is to increase the quantity and quality of Spanish-language books available in the United States. A secondary objective is to reach as many schools as possible. We have been successful in partnering with product representatives across the United States. Nearly all of them are teams of mostly former teachers dedicated to literacy. They are not just salespeople, but rather people who are interested in relationships with school leaders and supporting classroom teachers with high-quality resources. In order to work with educators and get them the products they need, it is critical that we relate to them and understand their experiences. Therefore, having teachers on my team has made my products better and capable of reaching more classrooms.

My third objective is to expose dual-language students to the world of literature beyond the United States. We are so fortunate to work with publishers from Latin America and Spain. They lift up the classic authors of their countries such as Rafael Pombo, Ruben Darío, Gabriela Mistral, and so many more. They are also highlighting and growing an amazing new group of authors and illustrators who bring humor, culture, and regional narratives to students in the United States. This objective is very personal to me. While I was an exchange student during my junior year of college,

I learned so much about myself by learning from others. I also learned that there are so many ways to live in this world and that one is not better or worse than another—it's just different. My deep understanding of difference allowed me to look at my 20-something self in Milwaukee and understand that my struggle was because of my racism. It was *not* because there was something wrong with my students. Rather I was able to identify that there was something wrong with how I was looking at them. I was looking at them through my bias, ignorance, and inexperience. Books are a space in which the reader can experience the world through characters created by the author they may identify with, or not. However, the more experiences we can expose students to, the more our efforts may result in a more tolerant community. I believe that the more tolerant we are, the happier we will all be. I don't have a utopian world in mind; however, if I can contribute to the betterment of a few people's lives, then I have accomplished my goal.

I stated earlier that I am uncomfortable no longer identifying as a teacher. However, it is now more important to me to support teachers, students, and classrooms through the work of Books del Sur than having the title "teacher." I had been lacking the resources I needed in all my teaching experiences. This distracted me from the work I needed to do. I spent a lot of time looking for resources. Many of you know the drill: You go to your school book room, school library, public library, and often, to Amazon. This took away time and energy from my students. Often, I was up late or spent the weekend planning; therefore, I was exhausted when I reached the classroom. As a result, I was not effective at the one thing I could not delegate to someone else—teaching. In my final years in the classroom, I was able to see that regardless of how well I managed all the tasks in the classroom, the ecosystem surrounding my classroom was full of too many pollutants and it distracted me from teaching the students in my classroom. Teaching means observing students' behaviors and responding to them. There is no script for teaching. It requires a teacher to have knowledge of how the skill develops, identify where the students are on the continuum of development, and then determine how to support them to get to the next level. My goal at Books del Sur is to add to a healthy ecosystem. It is to ensure that teachers have the quantity and quality of resources to teach Spanish literacy.

To be clear, books are not the answer. They are part of a larger ecosystem with layers of culture, families, resources, school districts, schools, classrooms, teachers, and students. The impact of the whole educational ecosystem and our small part in it became clear to me when we rolled out our largest collection yet of 100 different titles of books for teachers to use for read-alouds to their whole class. Our sales team insisted that we needed lesson plans for this product because all the other products had them. Rather than hire a team of consultants who have written every other company's lesson plans, I wanted to tap into the experts—classroom teachers. We organized around 50 teachers from across the United States. They reviewed the books with a partner and wrote lesson plans. We shared the lesson plans with the teachers and staff of the schools that purchased the collections and we quickly realized that we had just created another pollutant in the classroom environment. It seemed so harmless and helpful at first, but what happened was that teachers felt frustrated that the lesson was too long, or didn't fit with their unit, or wasn't what their students needed.

We realized that we tried to do the one thing that only teachers can do, teach. We tried to create a product that replaces teaching. I recognize that some products with Artificial Intelligence can support learning, but I'm not talking about learning. I'm talking about the symbiotic relationship between teaching and learning. Teaching and learning include an interaction among humans. It means an emotional exchange between two or more people. It is what I defined in year seven of teaching as, "teaching and learning . . . this sacred space where a teacher connects with a child and nurtures their mind and heart." No corporation or lesson plan written by a corporation could have recreated the moment in my classroom when my student explained to me why he loved the Books del Sur book. This exchange is not unique—it is what teaching and learning looks like.

My work at Books del Sur is to provide resources to cultivate the joy of reading in Spanish, to cultivate the joy of teaching and learning in Spanish. It is simple yet very complex, which is the essence of ecosystems because of their multiple layers. However, I am hopeful that the more we learn from each other and respect each other, the better our ecosystems will become. As educators and participants in the education ecosystem, we must do our part and share with others how they can best interact with us by identifying our boundaries, how our interactions impact our micro-ecosystems, and by continuing to learn.

I have hope. I have found my place in the ecosystem and I hope you do too. I hope that my story encourages you to reflect on what your part is in the ecosystem. Where and how can you most positively impact the education ecosystem?

REFERENCES

Bishop, R. S. (1990). Mirrors, windows, and sliding glass doors. *Perspectives: Choosing and Using Books for the Classroom, 6*(3), ix–xi.

Mathabane, M. (1998). *Kaffir boy: The true story of a Black youth's coming of age in Apartheid South Africa.* Free Press.

McLeod, S. A. (2019). Vygotsky's zone of proximal development and scaffolding theory. *Simply Psychology.* www.simplypsychology.org/zone-of-proximal-development.html

Part V

TEACHING, HEARTBREAK, AND REDEMPTION

While most people can agree that teaching is hard work—something that became abundantly clear to families and the public at the start of the pandemic in early 2020 but was largely forgotten after children returned to school—teaching has now become something very different from what it was even a decade or two ago. Teachers, of course, know this; they often lament the conditions of teaching, sometimes wondering if it's the career for them even after more than a decade or two. And it's generally not their students who are the problem, but a combination of poor leadership, deranged thinking about how schools should be organized or how students and teachers should be held to account, dehumanizing policies and practices, little time to perfect their craft, or a pitiful lack of resources and respect. Together these factors make for sad schools and broken dreams. Many teachers end up looking elsewhere for professional fulfillment, or leaving the field altogether, often disillusioned and heartbroken. As a result, we lose the potential of what education could become for our students, schools, and society.

It's not only new teachers who leave, but also seasoned teachers, especially in times of crisis and stress. The three chapters in this section, all written by veteran teachers, are poignant reminders of the toll that the past several years has taken on educators. In Chapter 13, Yahaira D Márquez recounts her life as a teacher in the past 2 decades, reflecting on where she has been and where she is now as an educator. Like the other chapters in this section, hers includes both the angst and the wonder of teaching. A high school English teacher, Yahaira loves everything having to do with language, especially literature. A Puerto Rican (or, as some would say, "Nuyorican," combining Puerto Rican with New Yorker), she was raised in Brooklyn and excelled in the city's public schools. Yahaira is still in awe

189

that she is a teacher—despite all the hurdles and obstacles, the misgivings and questions—and that she now faces students every day who are reminiscent of her before she became a teacher.

Still with a trace of the discomfort of not quite fitting in, Yahaira understands her students who also don't feel "seen" in the natural way that more mainstream students feel they belong. But unlike her perceptions of not fitting in when she began her college years, she insists on her students being "emboldened," ready to take on the world, and she has designed a curriculum and pedagogy to make sure that happens.

In Chapter 14, we meet Seth Peterson, who is himself shocked that he can now count himself a veteran teacher, having taught in the Boston Public Schools for over 2 decades since he began his career. But rather than count his service in years, he does so in governors—six in all since he entered the profession. Seth laments the many ghosts who appear and reappear in both his waking and sleeping hours. An English teacher at a large urban comprehensive high school, he is haunted by the memories of colleagues, students, and administrators who have left their imprint on his life and his teaching. While ruminating on the past, Seth worries about the present and the future of education. He recalls colleagues who are now gone and from whom he learned so much. He is guilt-ridden as well by what he feels is the neglect of his own family.

If only because of the idea and promise of teaching, or because of the "ghostbusters" he writes about, Seth has stayed the course, with the knowledge that despite how incredibly draining and relentless teaching can be, it also brings redemption when, for example, he sees a student "get it," or when another student, years after he was in Seth's class, writes him a letter or a poem, or when despite all the gloom, he still sees the beauty and the magic in teaching.

Kerrita K. Mayfield, a veteran of over 30 years in the classroom, has managed to remain steadfast through a combination of audacity, faith, and hard work. Despite the mayhem in the profession, Kerrita's essay uses inspiring and poetic language to describe the "sticky promises of hope" teaching affords. A shrewd observer of education writ large and of the pandemic specifically, Kerrita bemoans some of the policies and practices that make teaching in public schools more difficult every day. Nevertheless, she is firmly dedicated to creating what she calls Humane Pedagogy in her classroom and beyond. For example, despite her frustration concerning the conditions in which she teaches, Kerrita is committed to the humanizing pedagogy she describes in her chapter.

The physical and psychic barriers created by the pandemic are the tangible effects that Kerrita's students experience every day. Yet despite the conditions in which she teaches, she insists on "doing theory" with her students and having incredibly high expectations for them regardless of their identities or socioeconomic backgrounds. While creating safe and loving spaces for their learning, she also expects them to engage in demanding curricula because, as she rightly declares, "public education is the only democratic promise this country has ever consistently kept to its people." In her essay, Kerrita describes some of the specific practices she has created to keep her students—and herself—afloat.

CHAPTER 13

Why Are We Here?
The Power of Being Seen and of Belonging

Yahaira D. Márquez

That's What She Said
Why are their eyes
those of shock—
heads cocked,
squinty eyes—
an investigation?
The words flow out
of my mouth within
this brick and mortar
of "knowledge":
understandings,
elaborations,
thoughts,
inquiries
about the texts—
passion within me
that I needed to share.

But their eyes
made me feel like
I should stop.
Was I wrong?
Not just about the texts,
but about being here?

I had come from a
cultural microcosm of support—
where others were like me,
I, like them—
we all had
the same struggle
the same dreams
the same *cojones*
and a family that seemed
impossible,
because that's exactly what
they didn't want us to view
life as.
At every corner
I'd hear the melodic sounds
of the islands
from which we'd come,
take in the amalgamation
of smells seeping out of windows,
and be in awe of the vibrant colors
spewing from people's tongues.
Though I had to learn
the rules of what to do
and where I could and could not go
(as Desperation and Hopelessness
had a tendency to rear their ugly heads),
it was home
and where I felt safe,
yet encouraged to go
and do more.

And so, I did.
But here it suddenly
feels grey and flat.
They had previously viewed
the hoops and tan skin
as a silent accessory
of the room.

But I was taught to think,
and to speak only
when something important
needed to be said.
And so they now stare
with an awe
that almost paralyzes me.

Almost—
because I come from
a long line of Boricua warriors,
because Mami didn't raise
una callaíta,
and because I now want
to show them,
to correct their ignorance,
and for them
to be in awe of the vibrant colors
spewing from my tongue—
the colors that were so clearly lacking
from their worlds.

—Y. Márquez

Over the last few years, and especially the last several months, these questions have permeated my thoughts while on my way to work, while speaking to colleagues, while prepping for a class, and sometimes even while teaching one—both virtually and in person. Don't get me wrong; I'm in my 20th year as a classroom educator, and I still feel as passionately about what I do as I did on day one (perhaps this is currently rare in the profession), but in more recent times I do find myself often greatly challenged and wondering about my purpose, digging deeper for those answers as the challenges and requests we face as educators seem to incessantly mount in our current climate. *Now if only the respect we receive within the profession would mirror that trajectory!* The clarity in my own mind and the idealistic perception of the classroom that I long for tend to get muddled while I'm hyperaware of students' struggles to get to school due to the responsibilities thrust upon them as a way of helping to keep their families afloat; students' anger and questions regarding their place in a world where injustices are recorded and replayed on various media platforms—injustices of which they see themselves on the receiving end; students' attempts at navigating illness, loss, and grief amidst a health crisis for which there seems to be no direct guidelines or path to "safety"; as well as students' personal struggles as they navigate their own identities, coming into their own as young adults. How do we go on as planned within the classroom (and, boy, am I a planner!), when we're all barely able to get a firm grasp on what our daily lives bring? How is this content even important right now?

FINDING MY PURPOSE

But, alas, we're teachers, on the front line of education, and so we must do something. We are civil servants and can't possibly stand in front of the room and throw up our hands (though we may be tested, making it feel enticing). And so, in these tumultuous, unpredictable, and emotionally charged times, I choose to fuel my own uncertainties, anguish, and frustrations into what I believe to be my calling; I've aimed to use my time in the classroom to make it all as relevant as possible—for both me and the students, to connect real life with the content (which for me is English language arts), and to help empower my students in a way that helps them recognize the importance of their experiences and their voices as propellers of change and growth.

At an earlier point in my own postsecondary educational journey, as a student who was navigating her lived experiences alongside newer opportunities, I felt a bit like an outsider. I knew that I appreciated discussing texts, analyzing authors' choices, and loved exploring those printed worlds in which I hadn't lived or about which I was not familiar, but what I didn't feel was a sense of belonging in many of those classes. I didn't feel wholly seen. It was as if I was there solely to receive knowledge and theories imparted by others, viewed mainly as a vessel to be filled, and not one that could help carry the conversation to a richer plain. As referenced in my opening poem, I had been raised in a Latin community in which everyone had a colorful story that only rivaled the fashion choices one would see walking up and down the Avenida. Though it was riddled with challenges and uncertainty, it was also a community in which I felt supported—and my elementary and intermediate schools, in particular, allowed all of their students from various backgrounds to celebrate and share who they were with others. I felt our voices, better yet—our identities—were respected and valued (retrospectively, for that time period) through decisions within the classrooms and schools as a whole. Additionally, there was a sense of camaraderie and an unspoken encouragement among peers.

I hadn't experienced this direct sense of otherness, of separation, of feeling that I was in the shadows (*and within a school*, at that) until I was 18 and had left what I had known as home. I did eagerly welcome the opportunity to sit in these undergraduate classes, as I wanted to expand my world to these new ideas, challenges, and experiences, but I also knew I had lots to offer with the differences I brought to the room: poignant insight brought on by a varied perspective. I just wish others also recognized that fact and had invited me in. I'd always been the kind of person and student who quietly studies, observes, and formulates and revises my thoughts before verbally sharing them, and I distinctly remember the moment in a literature course where the discussion ping-ponged between approximately four students and the professor. I had ideas to share and patiently waited for a moment to squeeze them into the dialogue, but that had started to feel impossible. Finally, I ignored the lack of invitation and burst through the door—I spoke up, sharing my interpretation and questions pertaining to the text. Though I no longer remember the book's title nor the associated discussion, what I clearly recall are the faces that stared back at me, which initially made me question myself. But their surprise soon washed away as they listened and realized I, too, had valuable contributions they may not have considered. And I was just getting started!

The last several years—and the heightened sense of imbalance, uncertainty, and injustice they have highlighted—have taken me back to that place. I do not wish for any of my students, who are mostly 15–17 years old, to feel disconnected within the classroom or feel like an undervalued outsider, and not all students will kick down that door sans invitation! I don't want my students to feel as if they are on the periphery of my class or wonder what any of *this* has to do with them or with their lives. *Who cares about this text? Why should I vary my sentence structure and writing style? How will this ever help me with my real challenges outside of this place?* No. I need them to understand the "why." I want them to feel that my classroom can be an extension of their lives outside of the building, and that the classroom is where they can share their thoughts and build their proverbial armor—for many of our students, that's what they'll need when engaging with our ever-changing world—so they can feel prepared on their individual journeys toward success. As an educator, I want to help expand their worlds and offer my expertise as a way of building upon their skills and understandings, but I want them to come into my class each day feeling emboldened. Primarily, I need them to know that I see them, respect them, recognize their different experiences, and welcome all that they bring to our community as a way of elevating our collective learning.

Being cognizant of all the individuals and the varied identities and experiences that walk through my door each period and year, and dutifully working to invite as much of it as I can into my instruction and classroom environment has challenged me as an educator—and even more so when paired with the physical and mental exhaustion of the times, along with a lack of resources, understanding, and meaningful support from many of "the powers that be" within education. And though all of that is true, I find that I cannot remain in a space where I'm focused on what is disheartening or lacking (and yes, there is a lot, and pushing that all aside is sometimes extremely difficult); instead, I need to hone in on what I can do myself and within my classroom to affect the kind of change within my students that pulled me toward this profession in the first place. And this begins with taking a keener and more invested look at my students each year, beyond names on a roster.

DISCOVERING MY STUDENTS

I thought I had always taken the time to get to know my students, but during these last several years of my career, I have had to dig deeper and make the practice even more meaningful: Who are they *really*? What are their lives like outside of school? What have their experiences been? Where else have they lived? What challenges have they faced, or are they facing? What are their likes and hobbies? And that's only step one . . . and it starts on day one. On that first day, this could be taking a simple inventory of who the students sitting in front of you are. This last year, being the first year fully back in person after a year and a half of virtual learning, I started with the use of technology in the classroom and had students select a pre-made Google Slide template or create one of their own that would serve as their introduction to the class. The templates were visually appealing and fun (remember, I do teach teenagers, so this can be important!), and with simply titled sections such as "About Me," "Fun Facts," "Pet Peeves," and a designated area for photos, students started creating. This one move, before jumping into the curriculum and discussions of ELA content, let the students know that, above all, I care about knowing who they are. Through this focus on the first day, I discovered family dynamics, various cultures represented in the class, birthdays, favorite pastimes, places they have vacationed or wish to vacation, family pets, topics that are important to them, languages spoken. I also presented my own to them as a model, which they appreciated. Hence, a classroom community was on its way . . . and a Class Google Introductions slide show was created! Yes, this was a first day, seemingly basic activity, but the information I gathered on that day was invaluable as a first step and provided me with a basis for my planning and interactions with my students. Furthermore, I referred to much of their introduction slide information throughout the year.

The collection of personal student data (and yes, I used the "d" word; I know, the hyper-focus on numeric data can be exhausting, but this is different) continues throughout the entire year and in various forms, not all of which need to be time consuming: standing at the door at the start of class to welcome each student and ask how their day is going; asking students to share what they've done over the weekend or what plans they have for vacation (even if it's watching a favorite TV series); having students participate in quick free-writes addressing various prompts; using anticipation guides at the start of a unit/text that asks them to respond to a set of real-world statements or scenarios connecting with the unit/text. One major component to this is being just as willing to share with the students as you're asking them to be when they share with you (within reason, of course). These are the practices that build the trust and openness required to help me understand who my students are on a deeper level.

But it doesn't stop there. I also have to ensure that I'm up to date with current events (including pop culture—*is it still ok to say something is "lit"? Or is it now "fire"? And what is "wi-rizz?"*) to know what is happening in our country and in the world, and to know what is permeating our students' lives. I then have to bring that right back to my students—which can be fun and is always surprising in terms of how much they know or don't know.

ENRICHING MY PRACTICE

One way to get my students to share their voices and knowledge while also building their confidence and understanding of the world around them is through a quick strategy I devised: Informed Citizens Cards (ICC). Essentially, I write a name, topic, issue, or news story on the board without providing any context. During the very start of the #MeToo movement, for example, I simply wrote "Harvey Weinstein" on the board—most of my students at the time either did not know who he was or seemed to have vaguely heard or seen his name before through the media. Each student is given an index card, and on the unlined side they copy what I've written on the board; on the lined side, they have to showcase what they know and are challenged to go beyond surface-level understandings. They are asked to answer the following about what I've presented:

A. What do you know about the issue, person, topic? (I ask students to consider the "Five Ws and an H" of journalism: Who, What, When, Where, Why, and How.)
B. What are various perspectives on the issue?
C. What connections can be made to the issue (contemporary, historical, personal)?
D. What is the greater importance of the issue?—(I refer to this as the "so what?" question where I am looking for the impact or significance it may have on the economy, safety/health, ethics/ values, environment, international relations, etc.)

At times, some (if not, all) students may be unfamiliar with a topic, person, or issue; in that case, it's a learning opportunity and I will provide them with the information associated with point A and, perhaps, point B. Once I do that, it opens up the discussion (in small groups/pairings and/or whole class) for conversations about points C and D. If there are students who have some information about the topic (as many did—in a limited fashion when compared to current times—when I wrote "coronavirus" on the board in early February 2020), they then have the floor to share what they know with their peers; in this case, I take a step back and may simply facilitate with some probing questions. The students take the lead and soon recognize that there are many people and voices in the room who assist in their education. As the year goes on, I attribute points to this activity and, in some classes, it can even become competitive. I also get strategic with the topics or people I present to students so that students may draw a connection to our current unit/texts, like when I highlighted headlines of news articles regarding George Floyd and police brutality during our 10th-grade study of Elie Wiesel's *Night* and the ideas of protest and what may cause one to be a bystander. This highlights the importance of making class material or curriculum relevant to the students, their experiences, and their world, not to mention the fruitful conversations that come out of it, which are revisited at different points in the year. Our students have things to say and perspectives of which we ourselves may not be aware. As I've matured in my career, it's become clear to me that it is our responsibility to give them the platform to share, question, and expand their (and our!) understandings.

Finally, as an ELA teacher, I must branch out with my reading, exploring contemporary authors and the latest Young Adult (YA) texts that address common themes in our students' lives and in the world. And let's be honest—all of this takes a lot of time and energy. And who has that at the end of a day or week of teaching? Or in the midst and aftermath of a pandemic, no less? But I've had to be conscious about making it a priority—for both myself and my students. It's not been perfect, but it's a major step in the right direction, providing a clear answer to the questions, *What am I doing?* and *Why am I even here right now?*

As I currently teach in a district deemed the most diverse in Massachusetts, I've made it a point to provide my students with opportunities to read books with protagonists that look like them, have similar questions, and have overcome similar adversities. Yes, we may still read titles by Shakespeare, Austen, and Dickens, but they also read *American Street* by Ibi Zoboi, *I'm Not Your Perfect Mexican Daughter* by Erika Sánchez, *The Surprising Power of a Good Dumpling* by Wai Chim, *Between the World and Me* by Ta-Nehisi Coates, and *I Was Their American Dream* by Malaka Gharib, to name a few. They read articles that address current events that directly impact them, their families, and their well-being and success in this country. They view clips of spoken word, film, and TV shows and analyze the messages being delivered about specific groups of people, our world, and society. They have become more critical about the information presented to them (even analyzing Superbowl commercials within our societal context), and they appear to be more engaged in a genuine manner than they may have been in the past. My students may not all (or always) be able to explain the difference and purposeful use of a loose sentence when held against a periodic sentence, and they may not be reading some of the deemed "classics" of decades past (well, at least, not in total isolation), but what they are able to do with increasing mastery is insightfully discuss prominent and pertinent issues in our society— issues that matter in their lives—and they are drawing connections across times and texts, recognizing and questioning both patterns and changes. They are invested in the discussion and are sharing their own experiences and perspectives in connection with these topics. In sum, my students are reading and analyzing through a new lens, one that allows them to draw parallels between what we're doing in the classroom and their worlds.

WHERE DOES IT ALL LEAD?

The classroom discussions are growing, both in depth and participation. Students are recognizing the fact that authors (of contemporary or classic texts and nonfiction) write because they have commentary to share about the society and the people of their times, and because they want to awaken something within the reader, within us as citizens. And students are drawing meaningful connections across texts and histories, including their own. What I have personally enjoyed witnessing are the questions students pose and the respectful disagreements they have with one another—not simply orally, but also in writing. One discussion I recall in particular addressed the role of Nanny on Janie's life in *Their Eyes Were Watching God*, by Zora Neale Hurston: One student claimed Nanny was a negative influence on Janie and questioned her love toward Janie based on the expectations Nanny placed on Janie, whereas another student respectfully disagreed, claiming that Nanny wasn't necessarily a bad influence but merely felt responsible for Janie in their world, thus grounding her teachings and expectations on all she had ever known due to her own life experiences. This soon evolved into a broader and richer discussion about the progress of women, various obstacles we've had to overcome and continue to face, and roles we must take in continuing to fight for equality, citing current events (the election of Kamala Harris as vice president of the United States, for example) and various articles regarding gender bias in the workplace. In this way, no longer are students solely looking to me to constantly guide them. I admit that I've also caught myself trying to hold back from interjecting at times. I am proud of the connections made, of their ability to articulate their thoughts, of their maturity and respect when addressing differing opinions while knowing that their point is also important and should be shared.

FINAL REFLECTIONS

Trying to incorporate and balance as much variety of texts as I can within my teaching hasn't been seamless, nor has it been without its flops or remaining gaps, nor is it not (at times) overwhelming, but the bright moments I've described and their benefits far outnumber the challenges. Those challenges are just reminders of the fact that we teachers must continue to evolve as well, and we can always pivot and try again (when feeling refreshed) from a different angle. The most important thing is to do what we can for our students, as even the smallest change can result in an incredibly positive impact. Many times, it's the students themselves who have helped me recognize how it is that I must continue to grow as an educator.

Allowing students to join me in educating and encouraging them to take on more prominent roles in the classroom has been one of the major shifts in my teaching when comparing the start of my career to the present: I'm now a facilitator and perpetual learner within my classroom and no longer a band leader of sorts. This has taken experience, patience, planning (a lot of it!), and the realization that students will surprise you with their abilities if you just provide them with adequate support and respect them for who they are. If what we're truly doing is working together (another highlighted gem and reminder of the past several years) to prepare our students to be independent learners and thinkers outside of school, then we must allow them a welcoming and safe classroom environment in which they can practice, err, share ideas, question, and draw their own conclusions. We must allow this kind of productive struggle in order to allow growth.

For me, the initial engagement this growth requires has come by addressing content from a different angle. I find myself constantly revisiting those questions: What are *we* doing? What's the point? Why are *we* even here right now? With everything we've been navigating as individuals, as a country and in the world, it's imperative for me to fill my day as an educator and those of my students with what I feel genuinely matters to all of us while providing a welcoming space for the variety of individuals who walk through my classroom door. That must come first. All else regarding the specifics of curriculum and content eventually will follow and fall into place.

Students need to feel seen and valued for the knowledge and experiences they, too, bring to the classroom. Thus, maintaining that ideology and combining it with both an understanding of our current world and my expertise in content and pedagogy has fueled my purpose and has enriched my own experience as an educator. Ultimately, what has rooted itself in the forefront of my mind and become of utmost importance when plagued with questions of *what* and *why* is the fact that I can make a difference in how my students feel they are viewed, respected, and valued in society.

My goal is to continue to find ways that bolster students' confidence by allowing them a platform for their identities and voices, as it not only fosters a sense of safety within my classroom, but also empowers them as they step out as citizens who are aware of the impact they can have on others and in our world, adding beautiful colors with the broad strokes of their experiences. Not least of all is the fact that teaching feels much more fun and fulfilling this way, creating a supportive and enriched community with all involved, which is exactly what we need nowadays.

Why I Still Teach

High School Is a Haunted House, but My Students Are Ghostbusters

Seth Peterson

The older I get, the longer I teach, the more I believe in ghosts. The routines—both the comfortable, tried and true ones that fit my style and sense of self like the soft leather of shoes or a broken-in baseball glove, as well as the ones we grudgingly adopt to get by, like the 4:45 a.m. alarm or those seemingly endless, empty PD sessions late into a hot afternoon—all these routines are now regularly interrupted or haunted by the apparitions of memory, admonishing or reminding, never minding their business, sometimes chirping out laughter at my stubborn persistence. I am still at it, still rolling my stone up that hill. I am teaching at the same Boston Public High School where I did my student teaching, six governors ago. I first walked through the wrought iron doors of Snowden International School in September of 1994. Somehow, in the blink of two myopic eyes, I have become the longest serving staff member in any position at my school. I have aged. I have grown wider; I'm not sure I've grown any wiser.

With these still new, uncomfortable, and unsolicited titles of "old-timer," "lifer," or "dinosaur," there comes a ringing in the ethereal ear, the wistful whispering of many haunting voices. Fending off the ghosts has become another part of my job, quieting the restless spirits who dance their macabre jigs in my aging head, kicking up the dust of doubt, hollowly stomping out repetitive rhythms of yesteryear. Some ghosts are friendly, some belong to friends and students we lost along the way, some specters strive to trick the unwary, but all hauntings happen for a reason. If, as the philosophers tell us, questioning is at the root of reason, then it follows that doubts and fears might be part of the ethereal mists that form the reasons we teachers keep at it . . . as much because of, as in spite of, these spirits that haunt us.

Doubts, questions, worries, and frustrations are the spirits that keep us up at night, scheming more than dreaming of something different to try, of some more practical or more ethical way to tackle problems plaguing our students, our schools, and the larger society that surrounds and sometimes suffocates us. By day, we work, making decisions at a blinding rate—some good, some bad, some with which we can only reckon at a later date. By night, in the wee hours, we entertain reveries of grandeur. While others drift off, we become policymakers and dream of practical solutions that respect our students' minds and hopes, ones that are shaped by experience more than the desire to keep up appearances. I have been a teacher the whole of my adult life. I don't know if other professions are haunted so routinely. I'll never know, but I know it's not a competition. I trust there are plenty of ghosts to go around. I do know this: The high school of my mind is haunted ground. I am visited every night by ghosts of high school past, present, and future.

PART I: THE HAUNTED HOUSE

As I wander the hallways of this teaching life, I am regularly reminded of the risks, the losses, the warnings of those who came before, as well as the misdirection and myopia of those in power now. These are the ghosts that haunt the ever-buzzing, whirling, and over-caffeinated corridors of a teacher's mind: lost time with family; painful memories of children who are hurting and fears of what terrors might still find our students; privatizers and corporatizers, politicians, appointees, and policymakers who rarely visit schools, preferring to mandate from afar, who refuse to invest their time or our state's ample resources in educating all our children.

It is the ghost of the future who troubles me most, the one who bellows out sullen warnings about the inhumane sacrifice of time. This is the reaper of regret, the shadowy question mark eternally asking if, in the final analysis, I will have traded irrecoverable minutes with my family for a fantasy this phantasm whispers may be out of reach. Without meaning to sound melodramatic or self-pitying, my fears for the future mean my present is dominated by the bandaged, bleeding ghost of sacrifice. At no point in my teaching career have I ever had enough time to complete my work during the school day. Now, in these pandemic years, teachers are being asked to do entirely new jobs while teaching a whole new way, on multiple new platforms at once, with two hands sanitized behind our backs and a mask over our mouths (the doorway to our skill set of communication). I am all for the necessary safety precautions, but they make a hard job harder. I don't know if my family even misses me anymore since the norm of long days and late nights spent responding to student work was established so long ago. I know I miss them more than ever. The year of mostly remote learning, 2020–2021, was like a mirage, a taunting ghost that beckoned promising time to be together as a family, only to reveal through the fiber-optic haze, a world where we all sat on separate screens. Texting more than talking, lulled into exhaustion by the tiny boxes where our classmates, colleagues, bosses, and even well-wishing friends and family now resided, imprisoned in the Zoomiverse. With students' lives thrown into turmoil and assignments zooming in from cyberspace at all hours, with due dates transformed into windows of expectation, into periods of hope, into accept work whenever it might arrive, the old cycle of grading hell a few times a year eventually grew into a vast purgatory of teacher seeking a connection, feedback-seeking papers, and comment boxes substituting for emotional exchanges and support. The night and its ghosts stretched toward insomnia's incessant shores. The commenting, the responding to creative words and intellectual thoughts, doing far more connecting than correcting of papers is the part of the work I value and invest in most. But it comes at a cost. Like so many of us in this working whirlwind, my greatest source of both doubt and regret is the extent to which my family and my job compete for my time.

It may be the cruelest facet of modern society that it pits our love of other people's children, our commitment to a career-long pursuit of equity, against our time for our own children and families. This is the ghost I have the hardest time quieting, the regret I fear will stare me down and cause me to hang my head in shame when that bell tolls for me. Teachers, we know, live and die by the bell. When it chimes, I genuinely fear the flood of regret that I didn't read a few more pages aloud, couldn't make believe I was another customer at my daughters' imaginary restaurant, couldn't find time for the game of Life, that I was gone before my children's eyes met each new day, or that I was always impatient at bath time because I could not get my mind off the stack of essays that I knew awaited me when the kids were dried off, cozy in bed, and the lights were out everywhere else.

We must remember the teachers of writing-intensive courses when we finally restructure our schools. When the revolution comes, please do not build another system in which the teachers begin their second workday when the rest of their family falls asleep and they must then, unpaid, attend to the writing of other people's children. I don't have all the answers, but I know this: It is not multiple-choice scanners and rubrics; tell that to the Pearson Profit Pundits. Most of the solution lies in smaller class sizes, more unfettered time for teachers during school hours, and a respect for the sacred but labor-intensive exchange of written ideas between students and their teachers.

When all of this is done—the early rising, the late nights of grading, the comments in the margin, the make-up work, and recommendations—I hope the connections I've made with my students, the future paths I hoped to illuminate, and the carefully crafted comments I wrote will seem worth it to my daughters and my wife, who have, for so long, known the fleeting apparition of a father and husband—that teacher ghost that longs to haunt his own home a little more.

Let us dwell a little longer in the shadow lands of the underworld, where the shades who cannot see the lighter side of teaching wait and wail. Teaching can suck the life out of educators, especially in today's classrooms that squeeze out the voices of children and the laughter of learning with perpetual testing seasons and policymakers high on edicts but low on efficacy. Like most public servants, we give so much in hours, emotion, and care that we have fewer hours left for our loved ones and too many of us actually cut years from our lives. I am haunted by the voices of the inspiring but unfortunate souls who helped raise me as a teacher, but left us too soon: Elaine, Joe, and Eddie, who march in a somber procession of colleagues who died too young, who gave so much and never saw the gentle days of retirement, those denied the free time to frolic with their children's children.

Elaine had no children but cared deeply about her students. They were her children, generations of them. Elaine was old guard, but not as old school as the caustic, demanding exterior she presented. She was our math teacher, our registrar for many years, and a leader in both our school and district. As befit her discipline, she was calculating and a trained problem-solver, but always willing to listen and try something new if it might benefit the school community. She knew her students and knew her colleagues equally well, steadfastly representing them for years, standing firm as a voice of reason and respect for her union sisters and brothers. She was a leader in our community and, it seemed, we were mourning her loss so soon after we had celebrated her well-earned retirement.

Joe, too, was a building representative for the union at Snowden. He was my predecessor in that role, my friend and mentor, the reason I became a member of the staff softball team and, later, the reason I became so active in our union. He had a wry sense of humor, a get-it-done attitude, a winning personality, a refreshing supply of common sense, a desire to help, and a family that he left far too soon. Cancer stole Joe from us when he was just about the age I am now. He never had time to retire and travel with his wife, as they had planned. His health made him retire early into an ugly brawl with cancer, which, like teaching and fighting for fair working conditions, took up all his time. Joe's death hit our community particularly hard. He was so stable, so fun and reliable. He was young and talked so openly about his hopes and plans for the last phase of his teaching career and what dreams would follow. He had been a father figure and coach and advocate for many students. They hung onto the rest of us the day he died, clinging and crying as they moved from one class, one hallway to another. We buried him on Valentine's Day 2005, which was at once fitting and all wrong. It made sense to honor the life of one with so much heart on that day, but remains a painful reminder that, even for a teacher with commitment and charisma so easily romanticized, the romance can be so unceremoniously cut short.

Eddie was my first loss. I was young, still one of the "kids" on staff when, healthy as he was, Eddie dropped dead of a heart attack one day while out running. His humor had kept us all afloat through the teaching of 9th-graders. He was a math teacher and a track coach and we all needed both, to run the a race against time and maturity. Among the collection of advice Eddie shared from his trophy case of experience was what he told me as my bandmates and I planned to run our first 5k ever. I asked if he had any advice. He leaned in and said, "I'll tell you the secret to running any race . . ." I waited, eager to learn all I could, I didn't really need or plan to win, but I hoped to gain some confidence for my naive knees. "The secret is: Run faster than the other guys." That was Eddie and he was gone too soon, leaving us mid-year to cry in the back of offices and coax his ghost into inspiring his students to work, as best they could, with the series of substitutes who drifted in and out of our cluster until June. He left so much more behind, though: a loving wife, children, a legacy of wit and wisdom, a scholarship in his honor, and hopes for a life after teaching that he would never know.

Illness, stress, long hours, the cocktail of late nights planning and in-sanely early morning commutes all sharpen the scissors as the Fates spin the threads of our teaching lives. We lost Bennie, Rob, Florence, Maryellen, and George as well. We create scholarships in their memories, we plant trees and dedicate rooms or benches, we endure and we remember, but we grieve the pages left blank and worry about the loss of all that was left undone. I'm sure every school, every organization that lasts, has staff who tally the losses, a collective land of souls who haunt its halls and whose words serve, alternately, as warning and inspiration. But teachers are planners. Our days are spent enacting and adapting the lessons we dreamt up and mapped out in the wee hours. After years on the job, we can't help but plan our lives like our units, in interlocking related and cumulative chunks, knowing the plan will get better with practice and a live audience. The plans we push the farthest off, the lessons that keep us plodding through the duds are the ones we hope to explore in another phase of life, but too many of us never reach that phase or we carry too much disease, ache, doubt, or pain into that final stretch of road. We need our students to hold us up through the grief and fear. Their strength and perseverance, the knowledge that they will walk into a future we will never see and make it a bit better, a bit more just, somehow wiser . . . that belief must serve as the elixir.

Perhaps the ugliest ghouls of them all, the ones with no soul, are the corporate voices who try to privatize education, demonize experience and unions, and minimize the efforts of public school teachers and students.

A deal struck in a dark corner of hell convinced some gullible living souls that schools should be run like businesses. This was a lie, a mismatch from the get-go, but one sold to politicians on both sides of the aisle.

I'm old enough, I've been around long enough now to realize these are the voices who taught and shaped so many administrators of the last decade. They went to schools of education who had tried to stay hip by hiring the charter charlatans and captains of privatizing industry who worshipped at the altar of altered statistics and deified data.

While my generation had learned at the feet of radicals trying to diversify pedagogy and curriculum, they were carved into a mold that placed a premium on standardization, consistency over creativity, a deficit model of urban students (believing they could not handle realities of variation and diverse methods, across different fields of study). The obsession to measure superseded all and led to months of measurement on standardized tests, killing the curriculum through atrophy—death by a thousand dagger points of data. They came into our schools with very little teaching experience and the warped belief that truth could only live on a graph, that pie charts could tell the whole story, so that their very concept of schools and especially of young minds and how they develop was half-baked.

The language of leadership, even in liberal, supposedly progressive Boston—even from sanctified (and sanctimonious?) Harvard, even from card-carrying Democrats, even from my own school administrators—turned from "build it together, with all stakeholders, and you will get buy-in" to "demand buy-in from the beginning or tell those with other ideas that they don't belong." Or, worse yet, tell the public that those who disagree are the enemies of children, out to do harm. The Democratic institutions within our district and schools became rubber stamps—most obviously the rubber stamp farce of the Boston School Committee, but straight on down to School Site Councils and Instructional Leadership Teams. In my experience, teaching at one school through all these shifts and shysters, I see that the legacy of Democrats for Ed Reform and top-down, exclusionary charter school tactics is evident in school cultures that have become more divisive, more encouraging of favoritism that thrives on a climate of "in-crowd" versus "targets." I see adherence to the foolish notion that competition among colleagues and students will breed success or rigor when all it begets is better blurbs and resumés for those looking to use the school as a steppingstone on their way up and out.

Sadly, this brand of school leaders is so steeped in it that they cannot smell their own bullshit. Like the for-profit charter charlatans who claim all their cherry-picking, punishments, and public shaming are innovations, these new school bosses spend the bulk of their time building their own brand, shaping newsletters and upward tilted emails to make themselves and their sacred data look good. They dub themselves innovators, but a simple read through any of the evaluations, newsletters, or discipline reports they "write" reveals them to be the captains of copy and paste, careful crafters of self-promotion.

As is the case in too many school systems across the nation, Boston's district voices of babble build a culture of perpetually shifting sands and double-speak. Through battles to democratize the schools, their site councils, and the machinery of Boston school politics, we soldier on, from hearing to hearing, meeting to meeting, rally to rally. All the while, we feel our voices, educator voices, parent voices, student voices, community voices— the many and well-informed multitudes who live the experience—shut out and shut down by the moneyed and appointed, the mayor's chosen folk (whichever mayor it may be), the superintendent's mouthpieces (whichever superintendent happens to have just swung through that revolving door).

Ghosts and zombies are eternal; they lack soul but will not die. They seem to force us to fight the same battles over and over again. Such is the case with the disempowering, decidedly undemocratic treatment of my district's families and citizenry. Here is an excerpt from testimony I prepared for a hearing held almost a decade ago. We are still trying to fuel this fire, awaken this appetite for an elected school committee in Boston, the largest district in the state and still the only one where constituents are so severely patronized that they are not trusted to elect their own representatives to the school committee.

Testimony Before Boston City Council
Re: Docket 0155—A Home Rule Petition Regarding An Act Reorganizing the School Committee of the City of Boston

The refusal to challenge the ideas of the appointers also disrupts the natural connection between school committee members and the stakeholders in schools. While the appointed committee does hold "public hearings" on major proposals or controversial reforms (such as the current student assignment struggle), those of us who attend these forums know how they are run. Without fail, they open with a two-hour spiel by the superintendent or her designees. We're told it is to guarantee an informed discussion, but the reality is that the parents in attendance, many with young children who are up past bedtime when the meeting opens, have to leave before public comment begins. Those who suffer through the untimed, methodically dull presentation of the mayor-favored ideas, sign-up and line-up for the chance to speak for two minutes. Tense moments ensue when a parent or student—whose school might be on the chopping block—dares to keep talking after the words "Time's Up" are blurted in the middle of their sentence. The chair of the committee is happy to lecture the audience on respect and conduct, eager to promise all ideas will be weighed and questions considered, and then—unfailingly—they vote, allowing each member more minutes of untimed pontification on their vote, which is, you guessed it . . . unanimous. This climate of discourtesy to public outcry, disrespect for the time and commitment of parents, students, and teachers to their schools, and disregard for the will of neighborhoods, of citizens to play active roles in the shaping of their children's schools would not happen if those members were accountable to voters. The disconnect would not reach absurd levels, as it did following the tension of the 2010 school closure hearings, such that the thin-skinned committee, unused to having to hear voices raised in anger or anything remotely like dissent, proposed draconian rules for their own meetings—public by law, mind you—that included refusing to allow students to hold signs, forcing speakers to face only one direction, and the threat of removal for applauding the words of a citizen who rose to speak his/her mind. We cannot continue to have a school committee that tries to limit student voice at their meetings, that hides from public outcry, a committee that lectures on respect while its own members hurl discriminatory remarks from the microphone (see the transcript of the school closing hearings). We cannot continue to have a committee beholden only to the mayor who appointed them, especially when that mayor skips the public forums to attend a chamber of commerce meeting, then calls the angry crowd of students, parents, and teachers who spoke out at that forum "outsiders." We cannot continue to give the head of a foundation, who sends his children to private schools with class sizes of 17, a greater voice in our schools than the parents whose children attend the crowded classrooms he claims are fine at class sizes over 30.

And yet, my students know and understand the role their own voices should play in the decision-making. They not only recognize the absence of that voice, but rail against its exclusion. I am so proud to work at a school that promotes activism, so proud to have had the opportunity to teach some of our region's most rabble-rousing next generation activists. My Snowden pride glows bright when I tell any who will listen that I teach at the school that launched the great walkout of March 7, 2016. Four young women of color, four clever and charismatic Snowden sophomores, devised, promoted, and pulled off a massive walkout of thousands of Boston Public School students to object to budget cuts and the process that left their voices out of the decision to slice and strip the budgets that were designed to provide for their peers and younger relatives. It may not be because our school teaches globalism, that we strive across subject areas to emphasize interconnectivity; it may not be the fact that Baldwin, Morrison, Chavez, and Garcia Lorca are in our curriculum; but then again, it may well be interconnected, interwoven and baked into the nourishing goodness that tells young people that enough string pullers yanking on the purse strings can—and sometimes must—nudge the strong-arms of power hoarders. World history, hours of intellectual debate, and years of human courage tell us so.

Time is another battlefield populated by recurring zombies. Educators are always forced to defend the autonomy of their minutes, to shield the valuable use of our time from the slings and arrows of those who would commandeer it, armed with little knowledge and adorned with blinders to the light of reason. It is hard to stay in a career when one's experience and the extra time one puts in are not valued. Worse yet, in teaching, experience and the desire to be compensated for additional hours of work are scorned and demonized regularly by editorial boards. When the push for an extended day was launched in Boston, we teachers and our union supported the idea of expanding the curriculum, giving our students access to a full arts curriculum and better options for the hours beyond the bell. We did not, however, embrace the idea of adding micro-managed work hours to the teaching day without any meaningful compensation. This battle spawned these words in support of extra pay for extra time . . .

Comments on an Extended Day for Boston Public Schools

Seth Peterson

This is my school bag, full of papers and tests to be graded. I call it "The Bag of Guilt." My wife calls it "The Other Woman." For all those who believe a Boston Teacher's hours are short, I invite you to follow me any day of the week. Get up at 5am, teach 5 classes, attend meetings, stay after school to tutor, give make-up quizzes, plan and prepare the room for tomorrow's lessons, and get home ten or twelve hours after you left the house in time to see your baby daughter for one meal, put her to bed, and then respond to student writing until midnight. Those are the short days of teachers. If you won't follow me, just come hold the other woman . . . appreciate her girth and the hours of unpaid, unacknowledged labor she represents.

I love my job and my students. I'm not here to complain or even to refuse to work a longer day, but I won't stand the indignity of hearing I don't work hard or long enough. Nor will I stand here and accept the ridiculous proposal that teachers in Boston are so well paid they should work additional hours without compensation. The Superintendent is compensated generously as well. She earns $266,750 plus $56,472 in other compensation, for a whopping annual total of $323,222 (according to the Boston Herald's most recent report of the city payroll). That is four times what I earn. I don't really begrudge her the money. I ask, why is the city willing to pay so high a price tag? Because they want to draw excellence. How will Boston recruit, let alone retain, excellent teachers if we don't pay them for their work? At a bare minimum, teachers must be treated as professionals and paid for *their labor. This current proposal to add hours without compensation is an insult to the dignity of all workers and a further attack on the profession of teaching. If a volunteer force is really the answer for Boston's schools, then it should start from the top. If we should all be in it for the greater good alone, then let this superintendent trade in her $322,000 for a starting teacher's salary. Better yet, when her term is done, let the mayor and school committee advertise for the next superintendent simply by hanging a shingle outside Court Street that reads: Wanted: superintendent. Must love children and be willing to work for free. If we really do love our children, we will pay our teachers so we can continue to recruit excellent ones.*

Furthermore, the students of Boston need more than excellent teachers, they need a rich, stimulating array of courses to keep them energized about learning and in school. There is no point in expanding the day if you continue to narrow the curriculum! I work in a school with no music program whatsoever; a school that just cut art out of the budget and the lives of students; a school with no elective courses empowering students to carve out their own niche within the broader academy. This is an intellectually impoverished model of learning and extending the day alone will do nothing to change that. If the day is longer, it should be to provide my students with more opportunities. Will you hire back art teachers? music teachers? Add philosophy, poetry, photography and criminal justice courses, as students have requested? That would actually expand students' learning, not simply extend the minutes they sit in the same underfunded classes. If we love our children, if we really intend to focus on them, we will ask ourselves what an extended school day should add. The answer is clear—look at the districts that succeed: more student choice and more arts in the curriculum!

The ghosts are many and powerful, they come in all shapes and sizes. These are the specters with whom I do battle, the windmills at which we teachers tilt in hope of a better society, a system that will serve not only the needs of our students, but the diversity of their dreams and passions. Many days, the ghosts win and dance their eerie dance over the bones of budgets, collective bargaining sessions, ballot initiatives, and the tired bodies of teachers and students alike, consumed too young by the violence, vitriol, and exploitation. Warding off such powerful ghosts is not easy. I cannot do it all the time and when I can, I am unable to do it alone. Luckily, I know who to call . . .

PART II: THE GHOSTBUSTERS

Staffs splinter and heads of schools who lack leadership skills engage in these sinister charades of who cares most about the students. It is a sick circus, an echo of "Race to the Top," as this era spawns dogfights over who is really "in it for the kids." Stop it! Stop it, damnit. We all are. That is a given, that is the thread that binds us to this work and to each other. The details worth studying, the divergence that could actually form the strength of school communities, is what aspect of students we each love. For me, it is their intellect, their hunger for reason, their almost involuntary will to dissect and reassemble. That is the aspect that so many well-meaning politicians and district leaders—and some not so well-meaning ones—have denied and voided in the name of helping students through these difficult years of the pandemic. The brush is so broad. The assumption is that we are all traumatized (which could have a grain of truth to it) and, the greater error, that we all respond to trauma the same way, with immobilization and inertia. Only a fraction of students I have known become incapacitated by their trauma; those young people should and must be granted the space, time, support, and academic leeway to heal first. Yet, for so many, diverting their attention and converting their intense emotions into the challenge of intellectual growth, the pursuit of relevant, healing knowledge is the path to higher ground, to hope, to belief in self and a secure future. For those of us who have taught for decades, who have been to too many funerals where parents buried their children, seen too many teddy bear memorials on street corners, held too many candles at vigils, exchanged too many letters with incarcerated youth, teaching is trauma-informed by human necessity. I have gritted my teeth through these years of selling out those students' needs and abilities in the name of "putting children first" by replacing teaching with relationship building—never realizing that the two are synonymous. Teaching is relationship building. Luckily, my students hear the patronization in policies that undersell their skills and ambition. My students seek out challenges, not only in classes and books and assignments, but in their own research and organizing, in their refusal to stay quiet or be treated as if their lives or their intellect don't matter.

My students refuse to be de-intellectualized. They reject facile solutions and wisely distrust voices over-saturated in sympathy. If there is one line I cannot cross, it is belittling the human dignity or the minds of my students. I got into this work because of the faith I have in the power of the young mind to develop, the ability to grow morally and intellectually. My administrators have not always understood this. District leaders and politicians rarely do. I wish they could see, as clearly as my students do, that the shortcomings of our education system (and there are many) will not be solved by a rubric or a tiered chart or a not so gently used "new to you" grading system. In the autumn of my teaching years, I am clearing the gimmickry off my plate. It is only through ideas, honest conversations (lots of them), and a trust in young minds' appetite to engage with the difficult stuff of life that we will improve on what we have—through inclusive dialogue with those who engage in public schools on a daily basis.

The insanity and inadequacy of reformers and market testing educational entrepreneurs would drive all of us teachers from the field were it not for the reminders our students graciously offer us—in key moments, in dribs or drabs, in off-hand comments or compositions—that they get why we do what we do . . . and they are here for it as we are here for them.

Amid all the harrowing ghosts that lurk in wait to scare me from this profession, I hear the ghostbuster voices of students, who center me and remind me of my purpose. The promise of community my students offer silences the doubters by reaching across gender, language, race, and even that never shrinking generational divide. It is the students who remain genuine, insightful, interesting even if not always invested . . . who cut through the BS and are always able to talk or write about what matters. The student voices I share here come from writing assignments, letters exchanged in recent years, course evaluations, student comments, and conversations. Even social media, with all the trouble and headaches it causes in school, sometimes comes alive with posts about a teacher who made a difference. These testimonials are among the most welcome apparitions of all, when specific memories or general appreciation for the times we spent together in class appear out of the fiber-optic blue.

The words of my students embolden me, help me shuffle off the shackles of doubt, and second-guessing in the twilight of my career. Like a playlist of old, made to medicate my mood, even years later, their words heal me from the thousands of bureaucratic paper cuts that sting my soul. I find reason and sometimes rage to summon strength for the Herculean tasks of teaching. And so, bolstered by the truth of my students:

"I ain't afraid of no ghost . . ."

After graduating, Nelisha wrote me a beautiful letter, three typed pages recounting the books we read, the units in which we placed them, and the lessons she took from each one over the course of our 2 years together studying World Literature. Teaching books is not about sounding out words nor is it about plots; it is an inner journey into the hidden places in human hearts, the quiet places in our minds where doubts, hopes, and lonely truths live longing to be found out. Nelisha's letter begins:

> Thank you for the last two years in your class. It was one of the most outstanding experiences of my life. With every single lesson you taught from the beginning to the end, it wasn't just for us to learn writing, I also learned life lessons.

She goes on to describe what lessons she pulled from Salmon Rushdie's novel, *Haroun and the Sea of Stories*,

> I also learned that it's possible to lose yourself, your identity, when you have your family members doubting you, but you've got to keep your head up and

continue your own path and you will regain yourself and find out just exactly who you are.

In response to reading Toni Morrison's masterpiece, *Song of Solomon,* Nelisha wrote: "This has taught me that, although I have reasons to be angry at my father, it won't help me. I can't express my anger to a dead body. I have to begin to let go and forgive."

Another student, Kayleen, wrote in her reflection on individual and collective progress in our IB English class:

> I believe that by continuing what we have so far been doing (in-class essays, literary commentaries, and oral presentations) it will gradually become easier to understand how the English language works and how we can best align it with our intentions and opinions, presenting them in the most effective way.

Coming from another country, a different culture's traditions and expectations of schooling, she commented on the environment that we established together at the start of the year as part of our first unit, building a community of writers:

> One thing I love about our classroom is its opening and welcoming qualities. It feels very relaxed which is something I was not accustomed to before I moved here. Had it not been for this, I would not have been able to be vulnerable and share all my ideas, even as I was still developing them.

This idea of vulnerability is one I stress and model often, based on the truism that learning requires trust and trust building mandates vulnerability. It is rewarding when these beliefs and messages get through and the mantle is carried into the future by those more perceptive, more analytical than I ever will be.

Yet amid all this noise, set against the violence and trauma, there is a beauty and a peace that stems from the intense study of language, the quiet, careful intimacy of truly knowing words. In my classes, with the help of my students' engines of curiosity, we try to discover the ways words dance together on pages, the hidden secrets that lurk where sound curls up with meaning. As Peter Pereira writes in his poem *Anagrammer*: "If you believe in the magic of language . . . If you believe the letters themselves contain a power within them, then you understand . . ."

Sammy understood the magic. She was willing to buy into my reverence for the power within letters, the secrets that cleverly written books can whisper to us. Here was a student who dove into those rabbit holes we explored in our windowless basement classroom called G-20:

> Our class has mostly helped me in the area of reading. My time in G-20 made me for sure a better reader. In class, you would bring up a part in our reading

I would've never thought would have a bigger meaning. So now, I keep a close eye on small parts in a book because I really need to read between the lines. It's like playing 'Where's Waldo?'

And that is the magic of books, the wizardry of Toni Morrison and Salman Rushdie and writers who make us turn back pages to see, remember, and visit with the ghosts that were planted there to wake our intellect, to cast their ethereal light on breadcrumbs we barely noticed. That game of "Where's Waldo?" is where it's at. That is the kind of reading I want to teach, not the disjointed extracts from nonfiction texts and manuals that appear on multiple-choice questions from standardized tests.

In the course description for our journey through world literature, I address the desire for our work and words to matter beyond the classroom walls. For students to find and refine their voices, their writing must be aimed at real life, at real audiences. Sometimes that means tackling the topics that are painful, mature, uncomfortable, the kind that rewriters and white-washers of history are trying so hard to censor and ban. Ghostbusting means lunging headlong at the topics that the easy way urges us to shy away from. In their first year of in-person high school learning, still in the awkward midst of pandemic living, my sophomores met me on that trembling ground, taking on the issues that were tearing at the fabric of our society. They boldly wrote their thoughts, fears, frustrations, and observations woven from the headlines and chat rooms that whirled around them all year.

This past year, in our short story unit, we read touchstone texts by authors who tested limits or offered surprising choices regarding particular elements of narrative. In exploring alternative approaches to narrative voice, we read South African journalist and author Don Mattera's chilling short story, *Africa Road*, which tells the story of the Soweto Uprising of 1976 from the perspective of the main road running through the troubled township. Mattera's road provides distanced, bemused details of the awful acts that oppression makes unfold upon it. Each touchstone story began with reading, followed by days of analysis and discussion, and concluded with authoring our own story drafts inspired by specific techniques featured in the story we had just studied. For Mattera's work, I challenged students to write a story narrated by an inanimate, first-person place or object. They did not have to focus on disturbing events from the news or history, but many followed in Mattera's footsteps and chose to do so. There were drafts on the murder of George Floyd, on September 11th and the fall the World Trade Center Towers, one from the perspective of a tree that witnessed domestic abuse across generations in the house it grew behind, and—logically but devastatingly—several students chose to write stories about the horrors that unfolded in Uvalde, TX, during the week we were working on Mattera's anti-apartheid story.

Here is Karina's short story on the shooting at Robb Elementary:

The morning of May 24, 2022 started off as any other morning at Robb Elementary School. The kids rushing into the classrooms to get the day started. The kids usually try to move me around so they can be closer to their friends. I normally stand there and provide the kids support to write or draw their genius thoughts. Never did I think I would be trying to protect the kids and be used as a hiding place, hearing them as they pray that they wouldn't be found. Never did I think I would hear the screams and tears of fear that they might not make it out of the classroom alive.

This day felt off, the kids who were normally excited to be at school seemed as if they didn't want to be there. I felt the tapping of their hands almost as if they were nervous about something but couldn't tell about what. It was around 11:33 am and class was going as normal when all of a sudden there was screaming and yells coming from the other classrooms. As soon as the screams and shots were heard everyone started moving me around, using me and others to barricade the doors, using others like me as hiding places, praying that they wouldn't get shot. I was hoping that I was enough to protect these kids. My job is not supposed to be protecting or being used as a hiding place or a barricade, my job is to help these children when they don't have a place to write or to be a place they can lay their heads on when they are tired. The job to protect is for the police and they were failing them. The police took over an hour and 15 minutes to take some action.

There was blood all over me and all over the classroom. Kids were too scared to leave their hiding spots. They are innocent children they didn't deserve to be in this situation. These kids didn't deserve to be taken from this world in such a tragic way. Imagine the parents sending their kids to school thinking they were safe, that nothing could happen and then they get a phone call saying that their child just perished. The anger and the sorrow they must feel knowing their child wasn't going home that day.

I was never built or fit to protect people. I was never meant to be a hiding place. I hated hearing the screams and tears of these kids. Feeling it as they were trembling in fear. May 24, 2022 was a day where you came in school thinking everything was fine and turned into not knowing if you were gonna make it out the school alive and safe.

As an example of the exchanges that build writer relationships in our class, here are some of the initial comments I wrote in response to Karina's draft:

Karina,
    You have chosen a very timely, very disturbing topic for this draft. There are few things in the world as awful to recount as the violent

deaths of children, yet we live in a society that forces us to contemplate this horror over and over again.

Your choice of a desk to narrate brings out the nightmarish contrast between the desk's regular use and its inadequate, terrifying role as shield from high-powered rifle fire. The empathy and concern expressed by your narrator is moving. This is a powerful draft . . . very hard to read, but necessary reading for our times.

For the same prompt, Jaiden composed a moving story that functions on a more intimate, personal level. In his story he tracks the human life cycle and emotional connections we form with the cuddle toys that bring us comfort. The piece is sentimental in touching ways that remind me of what works so well in many Pixar movies . . .

On a Shelf

I Remember the first time I touched her warm, soft skin. I remember the first time I saw her toothless, chubby cheeked smile, her dirt colored eyes staring at my pitch black ones, I would smile back, but I always smiled back. I was always present, I saw her walk, fall, talk, eat, cry, whine, but I was always there to make her smile.

I Remember the first day in her own room, scared as ever, I could hear her cries from down the hall. I was lifted and brought to her, suddenly there was no more crying, I made her happy, I made her feel safe, I made her feel comfortable.

I Remember the first time she went to school, scared. She wanted me to go along, I wanted me to go along too, but I couldn't. She cried as she went out the door. After that she didn't need me to make her happy anymore. She had made friends, had them come over for little play dates, sometimes I was a part of them but not much.

I remember the first time she was panicking, she looked all over her room, she stopped, stared at my pitch black eyes and my frozen smile, she grabbed me off her shelf, she held me in her arms, I held her back. She started to cry, but not out of sadness, no, but out of joy and comfort and love.

I Remember the first time she was on her own, her room looked different now, smaller. She now had a friend in her room every day, I watched them stay up late, laugh, and enjoy each other's company. They would leave for a few hours then come back. I Remember being put away for a spell, it was dark.

I Remember being taken out of the dark place and placed back on a shelf in a bigger room than the last. The colors of the walls were also different, her friend was also there. I remember them enjoying each other's company even more, they would touch faces a lot, and she would hold her how I was once held. I remember them coming home one night with rings on their fingers. A lot of days went by with the same thing repeating, hugging, touching faces, going to sleep, then I remember the days would repeat over and over for a long time. Then I was moved to a new room, with blue walls and clouds painted on those walls. I was no longer on a shelf, I was on a bed surrounded by bars.

I Remember the first time I touched his warm, soft skin. I remember the first time I saw his toothless smile with his chubby cheeks, his emerald colored eyes staring at my pitch black ones, I would smile back, but I always smiled back. I was always present, I saw him walk, fall, talk, eat, cry, whine, but I was always there to make him smile.

Here are some of the comments I wrote in response to Jaiden's first draft:

Jaiden,
This is an absolutely beautiful story, capturing the cycle of support and comfort that (I assume) a teddy bear can bring. The stages of life, described through the stuffed animal's eyes are simple, but not devoid of emotional impact. The cyclical structure, repeating the opening, but with a new child, a new gender, is artful and delightful to read. The plot is well developed and, while the characters are not well known to the reader, we can feel the connections formed. Excellent draft!

In his exit letter from several years back, my student, Timothy, noted the values and work habits that have kept me busy and bound to this work. His words validated my belief in promoting intellectualism, in the Vygotskian notion that students will aim where we set the targets of challenge, riddle solving, and mystery unraveling. His letter also hits on our desire to train keener eyes, detail-hunting hawks to circle the thermals above literary pages. Most settling to my uneasy mind, Timothy noticed the margins, the hours of my life that I used up on things other than sleep and cuddles and binge-watching all the great shows of the current century. The value of words, offered in earnest, after all the grading and measuring up is done, hold so much value. They—perhaps they alone—can still the restless apparitions that stir and rattle the chains that are linked to my guilt, my fears of what my family missed out on, what I could have done instead of toiling beneath all those stacks of paper.

I remember, in elementary school, being so inspired by the adults who spoke to us like we were young adults and used advanced vocabulary. I felt that I missed that in middle school. But when I came into the 9th Grade English Class, I knew that I was back home with the advanced vocabulary and the respect for students that I had missed. I valued the amount of intellect and specifically the attention to detail that you show. I have striven to emulate that in my own character. One of the things that actually kept me interested in putting forth more effort in the classroom was how much effort you put forth for your students. I remember every piece of writing from 9th grade and IB Literature would have annotations by you, responding to my work. That showed me how much you cared about all of the work that was passed in.

FINAL REFLECTION

To be a memorable and meaningful space for learning, our classrooms need to be places where students feel safe to experiment, free to try on new perspectives, and stumble, knowing the community will catch their fall. Equally important, though, is that it be a space where they are expected to engage, where effort is required, and each member feels accountable for making progress. I find that students sometimes understand this better than adults in supervisory roles. I am able to keep trying, stumbling and succeeding in equal portions, because of my students who understand that trying leads to success and inaction leads nowhere. I am fulfilled and rewarded by my students who know that these expectations and accountability are a form of love. As I write to my seniors in the learning letter I use to launch our year together:

> At times, it may feel like I am asking the world of you, but that is only because I want the world for you. I want this globe of ours to lay down before you and offer up all its riches in the form of opportunities, options, and joy. It is a mathematical equation: my high expectations of you are exactly proportionate to my high hopes for you. I hope that comes through in the work we do together and that we can build an intellectual community on that foundation of mutual trust.

What we read matters. Our reasons for reading matter. We are all looking for solace, comfort, new ways to see the world through our own eyes and ways to reflect our own experiences, to process our pain or bolster our truths with the lives and words of people who came before, who come from other corners of the world. We want to understand and be understood— that is the purpose of writing, the reason we teach literature.

Student voices, with all their angst and anger, all their wonder and weariness, their doubts and daring, student voices keep the ghosts at bay. Even if I am tired some days, bitten by the zombies or lifeless from outrunning my midnight ghosts; even if some of my lessons on etymology or the early Caliphates fall flat or don't awaken the curiosity of every young mind; even if students groan at my dad jokes or don't love my favorite book, the ghosts still retreat and my sense of purpose, my soul is restored every time a student gets the bigger picture of what I am trying to do. When they see that

I ask so much because I want their happiness and success so much; when they say, as Jadah did, that I can come to the big barbecue at the end of the world because she knew how much I wanted a world where her rights and dignity and power were valued as much as mine are privileged . . . in all those blessed moments, the fears subside, the bitterness and doubt recedes, and I am able to remain a teacher, to wake and do the work of making a few more strides toward that world we envisioned together. If they get that I am trying to change lives with words, trying to bring light and joy but also tears and doubt from books into all our lives, if they get this, then they get me . . . and that allows me to step back into the classroom feeling more whole than haunted.

CHAPTER 15

Developing a Humane Pedagogy in Order to Live in the Sticky Promises of Hope

Kerrita K. Mayfield

In my front yard there is a sign typical of the progressive types in the valley where I live. On one side is a reminder that love is love, science is real, and a host of other statements that equate to the basic version of "don't be a d**k[1] to other people!" On the other, homemade, side I have written: Thank Teachers! The "You" in between the thank and teachers has inexplicably faded. It is like the marker read my id and my fatigue and faded away into a more powerful and emphatic statement that, as teachers, we all deserve so much more than we have even acknowledged in our pre- and post-pandemic labors.

I am a social justice–oriented science teacher. *I. Am. A social-justice-oriented. Science. Teacher.* And this chapter is a terrible project to engage in as a public school science teacher in what I hope are the waning days of a global pandemic (now endemic?), during a time when the failures of so many social systems seem both clear and long-lasting. I mean, how dare I promote hope when every school day in October feels like December, and December sucked, and the students feel behind in their behaviors, knowledge, or

225

disposition—not in enthusiasm or promise, but in their sheer ability to regard each other as worthy humans in their daily interactions. Or behind in their ability to simply keep up with their damn academic binders. "Where is your binder?" I ask at least one kid at least every day as they alternatively panic, ask me to look for it, or shrug nonchalantly. Or have panic attacks on the floor behind my desk on the bright red yoga mat with discount carpet squares for a pillow because they cannot feel their legs. Or wander the room begging for hugs as their bodies at the end of the day are simply crying out for connection and release. And I haven't had a professional contract for 18 months, even though my union colleagues and I saved all our families from the indignities of doing science without an actual science room or science supplies—for no additional financial output. My science department redesigned our curriculum, rerouted expenditures and created lessons for hundreds of families, all while filming experiments from our yards, kitchens, and empty classrooms. We delivered standards-based content to hundreds of parents in my school alone by creating over a thousand lab bags of science supplies for pick-up, and in some cases delivery when they were not picked up by families. Day after day, we were/are there: online, in-person, hybrid; laboring and loving the kids[2] while the magnitude of our professional prowesses and generosities disappeared from public view faster than ice on a black car's hood in July. But. And. I am a social justice–oriented science teacher still.

I vacillated about what was the most compelling way to start an essay about what it has been like to continue to teach during the 3 years of a pandemic, while seeing so much tumult in the profession, and so many iterations of the sites of education. Should I mention the number of my friends and colleagues who have quit the field? The number of my students who have had extensive mental health crises over the intervening years? Or what it is like to wonder how many kids you can hide safely in a closed room during a respiratory pandemic if there is a shooter in the building as yet another day in America a White boy, or at least a boy with a grievance, has easy access to an automatic high-powered weapon? Are these examples illustrative enough to get you to see what I do all day, and have for over 30 years?

The simple truth is that this pandemic and its aftermath has been the hardest teaching I have ever done: through 9/11 as I watched the towers fall and wondered where my cousin, the East Coast–based pilot, was; through the unexpected deaths of kids and colleagues; through my own bouts with COVID; and the overwhelming sense of despair that hangs in many K–12 hallways, including my own. The many entanglements of labor that does more than survive, and which provides services to my families is growing more invisible to the publics served by public school. It has been unspeakably hard of late, maybe even before the pandemic. One of my kids asked the other day in the middle of our extra help session, "Dr. M., did you have a happy childhood?" I am pretty sure his father is dead, killed before the family immigrated, and he has complained that his mother, who does not speak, read, or write English, "is scared of everything" but I haven't asked. It has been unbearably heart-wrenching to carry the voices of so many hurt children in my head and heart day after day. The secondary trauma is so, so real for so, so many of us in our chosen profession.

There have been so many students in the last few years who have spent extended time outside of the classroom for a variety of mental health needs that I have taken to calling these sojourns the names of desired trips abroad that we choose together. When we talk about where they've been or what work they need to make up we reference their absence as their time spent in Japan or Mexico City or Paris—the name of some place they'd rather visit rather than the place they have gone to work on their mental health needs away from school or maybe even home. It is an attempt to give power back to children who developmentally experience the emergence of many psychological diseases, concomitant with an equally emergent set of tools for dealing with the world at large. Yet there is hope. Always hope. Under these circumstances hope feels not only like an audacious claim, but maybe one where an observer can rightly assert that I am not cognizant of my current working conditions or those of my colleagues.

I teach, we teach, I posit, because education work is professional labor in three dimensions: past, present, and future, and each mode has its own particular enticements that render us hopeful and committed as educators. Over the last 30 years, I have been moved to develop and exercise, with what I hope is integrity and grace, a modality I am calling Humane Pedagogy. I believe deeply that this particular praxis has the power to make learning spaces tenable. Sustainable. For all of us.

UNDERPINNINGS: TEXTS OF LEARNER AND PERSON POWER

Learning is a space of necessary violence when a person's body interacts with educational systems and structures. That violence is an inevitable outcome when the existing schemata of the learner is actively and constantly disrupted in order to accommodate the needs of an education structure's curricular[3] demands. The learner loses some measure of control, and the feeling of control is necessary for empowerment. I know that the claim of teacher-to-learner violence may be hard to envision, let alone to admit to being a part of, but imagine it like a beloved and crammed bookshelf of texts and knickknacks that the stranger (and there are many in a school calendar) approaches and rearranges without permission or regard. Repeatedly, at almost every encounter. With instructions of dubious consistency, depending upon the stranger, since there are multiple "bookshelf" interrupters that change with scheduled regularity. Because your pre-existing organization isn't serving the stranger's purpose, a purpose only the stranger truly understands as they are understanding's gatekeeper, and assessor. The stranger and their bunch of texts are anointed as they contain knowledges that they will share with you on a schedule of the strangers' choosing because they are interlocuters for another set of dominant structures and systems you may never see. Because, of course, the revelation is good for you. I'd be pissed, and pissed constantly too, if that were my precious construct/bookshelf, and these were the conditions I was powerlessly trapped within for about 180 days.

Humane Pedagogy is intended to positively interrupt the disruptive nature of teaching and learning; to aid in creating learning spaces that soothe, without necessarily ameliorating, the inherent discords of learning. The theories that could potentially underwrite Humane Pedagogy abound. In particular, and to name my subjectivities, I am personally drawn to the work of feminist, womanist, kyriarchal, and critical[4] education theorists because I believe that (my) teaching is an ecclesiastical craft that I engage in as a big in body, queer, Brown woman because public education is the only democratic promise this country has ever consistently kept to its people (Abrahams, 2005; Freire, 1970). I want to participate in making such a ubiquitous state-sponsored system of power and access like schooling work for as many folx in as many kinds of bodies as possible.

I want to go all "deep theory" here. As a Black woman I have treated the phrase as an accusation, because that is how it is wielded against my body by White professors and professor colleagues who squawk: "We don't do (deep) theory here" as if it were a condition too complex for my mere Brown body to handle. But eff that! I deeply believe that every liminal person theorizes their life's conditions in order to grapple with an inherently hostile world. For example, theories like, "If I lay out my clothes the night before, I don't have to rush to catch the bus and will feel better in the morning." "The grocery guy likes me so he puts out the best grapes on the days I stop by." "This teacher cares about me—and I know because she stocks halal candy for me when I come to extra help." A learner can own their liberation from school when they feel seen, heard, valued, and welcome.[5]

I developed *Head, Heart, Guts* (Figure 15.1) as a way of both seeing and teaching my students to explicate the truth of their own bodies of knowledge, and the ways these sites interact with other learners' spaces of comfort and knowledge. The long list of words on the right are simple synonyms for how the lefthand locations appear. Head, Heart, Guts illumes the ways every person's access to curriculum and social–emotional self-awareness

Figure 15.1. Head, Heart, Guts

HEAD	Superego; cerebral; being "heady"; brainy, smart, praxis; text; theoretical; knowledge; cold; separate; data; factual; masculinity; evidence; theory; observation; language, etc.
HEART	Ego; passion; praxis; emotion; feeling; movement; warmth; desire; risk; knowledge; "good at already"; would do for free; faith; hope; observation; language, etc.
GUTS	Id; praxis; passion; "gut instinct"; emotion; femininity; darkness; truth; knowledge with less language; belief; faith; ancestors' knowledge practices; observation; languages, etc.

interacts in school. Just like every person theorizes, every person has sites of awareness and knowledge. Make what you like out of the fact that some terms repeat.

Theory Into Praxis—Living the Talk in the Classroom

It is easy to state formational theory for me—the systemic rewards for a certain kind of intellectual production abound when you speak the language of deep reading and theoretical interlacing. But faith without works is dead—and in true postmodern fashion—theory without praxis is simply onanistic. Humane Pedagogy looks like a classroom that feels good most of the time because it is student-aware in its approach to knowledge building, has rich sound landscapes, visual vibrancy, and assessment structures that honor multiple ways of knowing (Esteban-Guitard & Moll, 2014). We will tackle each in turn in the ensuing paragraphs. A student-centered approach is nothing without student voices as testimony.

Every day starts with 2 minutes of quiet time. Quiet Time is a battle against fidgety feet, my closed eyes, surreptitious cell phones, and friendly whispers. But once the kids sink into the peace of the solitude, the ability to put one's head down to rest becomes so pleasant they often ask to extend the time to 3 minutes. Nothing is so urgent—no lab, no test—that cannot be introduced with 2 minutes of quiet reflection while listening to the radiator rattle. What continually surprises me is how my own body reacts to the quiet. I have a tiny bit of time to assess myself: Are my arms crossed? Am I leaning my head on the board because I am tired? Is my body open to my students? What am I carrying from my prior experiences in the day? Even when Quiet Time does not help us transition into the science class—quiet time analysis gives us a chance to reflect upon its purpose and what we as a collective can gain from the practice.

The most important assertion in my classroom is the learner's voice of experience. Almost every day we explore content through the expertise of their outside-of-class interests and encounters. First, the student-aware Humane pedagogical space asks that students, as people with their own interests and skills, bring themselves to the table as part of their content understanding. This is a simple example, but we use a modality I created called *TKCC*. Before we dive into any content or concept, we start the conversation with the child's *built* worlds. What do you THINK? What do you know about the world? What is your history, what are your home languages around this term or topic? Do you know the *carne* root of carnivore and how do you use it away from school? Do you like what we are about to do? Do you believe what we are about to do is going to work? Is what we are about to do smelly, weird, or complicated in your august opinion? The richness that is the student's lived experience is integrated into the curriculum because everyone can THINK, and thus everyone has a potential point of curriculum entry.

KNOW allows us to bring in the formal and rewarded languages of schooling. This space rewards the student who has traditionally received props for grades and exemplary school performance. We ponder the standard languages of school success. Where have you seen this concept in academic spaces? In what systemic settings have you had an encounter with this concept or idea? In short, What have you been taught in formal schooling?

The other space in TKCC where students insert their own worlds of knowledge is when they are asked to connect the in-class content world with whatever worlds the students experience: the first C, CONNECTION. Where in your worlds do you see connections between and among? Where and how does the scientific concept have legs beyond these walls for you as a learner? Where are you inserting, individually or collectively, the disparate possibilities before you? CONNECTION is a site of reflection upon process and growth, impediments, successes, in school, and in the wider world.

CONCLUSION is the hardest because it asks that the students, who work in table communities called Research Pods, have a collective conversation about the meaning of their engagement with the task, text, vocabulary, or idea. How would you summarize the experience? Reflect upon your initial ideas in THINK—how have you moved (or not) since then? What do you know now? How has your knowledge changed since we started? Can you reflect on your growth in the topic and demonstrate knowledge? What's something your group wants to put in its pocket about this experience? What was the point of engagement with this material anyway?

We also spend considerable time in my science class analyzing how we do and how we know. After lab experiences, especially the ones that push them out of their comfort zones, we spend time on whole class talk using these three prompts: What went well in the lab (or encounter)? What could we do better as individuals or as a community? What was a limiting factor (a thing outside of your control) that impeded your progress? We sit around and reflect on the who, and what, and how of our knowledge creation. There are no illegitimate topics or claims. Students can blame me for creating difficult conditions. I can reflect out loud about future possible changes or my own design assumptions. Oddly, learners struggle the most with asserting how skilled they are at a task or mode of thinking. This process works so well that I use it in my intimate relationship life to process how my partner and I are engaging with each other.

In a bid to better understand the impact and receipt of the Humane Pedagogy, I interviewed former master's and doctoral level education graduate students years after their matriculation in a social justice education program where I was their praxis and pedagogy professor. It is important that you hear from y/our professional peers—fellow social justice-oriented educators whose understanding and implementation of praxis and pedagogy is critically collegial. People with similar professional languages, sites of practice, and possible aspiration. All respondents have gender neutral pseudonyms of my choosing.

To combine the space occupation of K–12 and graduate students, there are elements about physically owning the space: leaving a stamp and making a mark upon walls that have been potentially inhospitable to you. Next, the "Best of Wall," or prodigious wall and display work, which is not about the competition for grades but about acknowledging the ways students struggle with individual tasks and to promote their mastery over difficult systemic conditions. Every child will make the wall. Students' successes occupy the perimeters in and outside the classroom. The wall is not only academic work. Students can make drawings or signs or vocabulary that also go up in the space. They occupy the walls and state clearly that learners and their myriad voices are welcome here. It is easy to cast music and paper as simple sops, as soft skills with marshmallow meaning. But it is in the subtle welcome that student-centered relationships are built. Mo notes that,

> All of these elements have to do with creating spaces. Taking the time to ask us what kind of music we wanted to listen to, providing things like tea and candy are nurturing elements to a space. Walking into your classroom offset a traditional dynamic. You were there to do more than just teach us and we were there to do more than just learn from you. It felt full. It felt whole. I wanted to be there even if I was having a bad day or felt unsure about what we were doing, I knew that I mattered. My existence mattered and you wanted me to be there. You showed me that in more ways than one . . . I absolutely consider these elements pedagogy.

Then, the classroom's sonic landscape is built by the students themselves from what comforts and buoys them. In my classroom students are asked to submit songs or genres for our mutual listening while we do tasks that do not require deep concentration or deep listening to others. The rule is any music you like, but no bitch or ho or fuck in the tunes. It is a signal that we are shifting away from the intensity of performance into a space co-created (Esteban-Guitart & Moll, 2014; Moll et al., 1992) by the learners. No genre is unwelcome. Everyone present in the learning space participates in the submission of music, and no student has ever balked at submission even as they think it is weird. Cam notes that, "In the classroom, the use of music helped me feel grounded, and sometimes inspired me to push my boundaries and explore 'learning edges.' I appreciated that the music we listened to in class was "of the students" in the community . . . it was a fun and insightful way for us to creatively share a piece of ourselves, while learning about others."

Humane Pedagogy is trauma aware. My work designing gendered hegemony disruptive *Interruptions* workshops, training teachers and educators on gender norm interrogations and disruptions and creating spaces in my classrooms for children to remove themselves safely from the action matter. There is no student-centered room if students do not have moments of power and reflection. And there is no trauma resilience without the exercise of learner power to overcome adversity and risk (hooks, 2004). There should be moments *designed* into the content where a child has access to their power as a learner and moments where they can reflect upon their successes and the work yet to come.

My own K–12 students note, when asked, that the seeming ephemerals also make a difference to them: sanitary napkins from a Black-owned company are available without question or limit. There is tea for students to drink when we are not in lab (safety first!), ramen or oatmeal if they miss breakfast or lunch.

Charli reported that,

> Those elements absolutely made the space more humane and welcoming and safe, which is certainly not always the case in higher Ed settings (or any level of Ed). I'm not sure if I considered them pedagogy at the time, because I just appreciated them but didn't think too too much about them, but looking back I can see how that was indeed the case. It's funny because I remember thinking that those things (tea, music, treats, etc.) must have been things you appreciated and wanted in your classroom, not just as something nice for your students. That is so rare, isn't it?
>
> Thinking about the well-being of everyone in the room at once? And the class soundtrack was wonderful because it was so inclusive and also fun. Honestly, the warmth of your pedagogy helped me complete graduate school, when I wasn't sure I would be able to.

Finally, assessments that are about encouraging multiple ways of knowing and demonstrating mastery. Group quizzes of your choosing or singleton with notes, choose your own adventure assortment of prompts. Video reports and diagrammatic posters. Students are asked to apply their burgeoning academic self-awareness to make choices that fit their lives, desires, and skill sets. We are making a more holistic learning space.

THE PERILOUS BEAUTY OF HUMANE PEDAGOGY

This is lovely! Who could hate a thing based simply on love and a deep belief about the power of a student? Do not get me wrong, while Humane Pedagogy is based upon theories that are liberatory and person-first, you will likely face pushback from systems and structures when you implement it. Challenging systemic power norms is not the way to make systemic friends. A senior academic colleague once accused me of "currying favor" with students by its implementation and articulation with graduate-level education students. This silly accusation was in the context of an education program whose stated purpose was inculcation into the art of creating learning spaces shorn up by a pedagogy of empowerment and justice. It is easy as an educator to become acculturated, even rewarded, for maintaining the violent status quo within systems that depend upon our inured and continual subscription to structures of violence for our, and their, legitimacy. We get our checks as willing participants in, and agents of, this system.

It is messy. So, so messy to change systems that do not want to change. It is hard to work mindfully and humanely within institutions that do not see the need for change as it grinds along, taking us with it. It is hard to do this work in places where well-meaning people assure you the work is already, and has already been, done. Humane Pedagogy is dissonant in its appearance when you are evaluated professionally. You have to be an articulate ally for it in order to survive in a world of rewarded regularity.

Humane Pedagogy is as messy as people are when they bring their true selves to the table. The co- part of co-created curricular spaces means that people are dragging their nonsense with them into the classroom. Every day. Because it is safe, because they are seen, because they have been invited, every part of the learner shows up. As an educator you have to be ready. In the postmodern it is dangerous to focus simply on the deconstruction and haruspication of various systems and structures. The next and most important step is to take that knowledge constructed of educator expertise and to build something new; to create knowledge beyond cell models and meiosis.

Am I good at it all the time, year after year? Absolutely not. This year, even as I write this, I see how I have fallen short from my own high standards. I see how if I dialed it up and did even a bit more of what I am writing about we could have had better relationships in my classroom. I am stating clearly that part of engaging in Humane Pedagogy as essential and sustaining praxis is saying that I am human, too: tired, striving, disrespected, unwavering in my belief in the possible.

And to be honest, this is a system that is also hard to be a student in, too. Not everyone wants power—some people enjoy being told who and how and when and why on their way to social reward and acceptance. It is difficult to be asked, at 12 or 34 to take ownership of one's learning when you may never have had that invitation before. Humane Pedagogy is exhausting to manage, because it is not just content; Humane Pedagogy asks that the teacher truly invest in the social and emotional aspects of the learning craft. That the educator be invested in and careful of the humanity of every person who enters the room (Buber, 1996). Every smelly kid, recalcitrant jerk, or dubious participant. And sometimes that person is your department head, evaluator, principal, or colleague whose curricular and pedagogical choices are easier to understand. All these things are true and have happened to me at some point over my 30-plus-year career. But a learning space where the discoveries are mutual is so, so nice to keep getting out of bed for.

It is much easier to talk about bringing light unto the darkness without acknowledging that once a darkness is illuminated—at best the giant dust bunnies in the corner are revealed and at worst the roaches will run over your feet as they scatter in all directions away from revelation. I believe that every person—every body[6]—can theorize. We create seas of meaning daily in order to move successfully through built worlds that are often not to our making. Humane Pedagogy is not just for this post-pandemic moment—but it is a way to approach the potentials of all learners. And I believe that every learner has some sense, for good or ill, how learning for them is constructed. Humane Pedagogy is a radical retelling of what and who school may be for. It will bring you problems, but may it also bring you peace. And unimaginable joy at school.

NOTES

1. You are welcome, Mother, on my working not to swear in professional settings!

2. I use kids here not as an adultist grab – but because the word illumes the contract of care every school-based adult and teacher has for the children in their charge.

3. When I reference systems, I mean larger social structures comprised of federal, state, and local governments and community curricular expectations, whether overt, covert, hidden, or null. The system called (public) school exists in every

county, city, district, or university structure touched by colonialism, and each has its own modalities and rhythms.

4. "Critical" is used here to reference Critical Education Theory - a postmodern reflection upon the praxis, purpose, and pedagogy of education structures institutions that reside within larger social systems. See also Mayfield, 2008, for a review of the literature.

5. I am using liberation instead of emancipation, as liberation is an act freeing oneself from the worst effects of systems to create new systems and structures and means, while emancipation is a physical and psychic release.

6. Every body is an intentional way of acknowledging that every person in their corporeal form has embodied contexts, and those contexts drive how we move through or arrange systems to deal with our body-world/s.

REFERENCES

Abrahams, L. A-L. (2005). *A critical comparison of Elizabeth Schüssler Fiorenza's notion of Christian ministry as a 'discipleship of equals' and Mercy Amba Oduyoye's notion as a 'partnership of both men and women'* [Minithesis submitted in partial fulfillment of the requirements for the degree of Magister Theologiae, University of the Western Cape]. UWCScholar—ETD Repository. https://etd.uwc.ac.za/handle/11394/1446?show=full

Buber, M. (1996). *I and Thou* (W. Kaufmann, Trans., 1st Touchstone ed.). Touchstone. (Original work published 1923).

Esteban-Guitart, M., & Moll, L. (2014). Lived experience, funds of identity and education. *Culture and Society 20*(1). https://doi.org/10.1177/1354067X13515940.

Freire, P. (1970). *Pedagogy of the oppressed*. Herder and Herder.

hooks, b. (1994). *Teaching to transgress: Education as the practice of freedom*. Routledge.

Mayfield, K. (2008). *"I love being a freak." Exploring the ways adolescent girls on the margins create worlds of power in high school classrooms* (Order No. 3358847) [Doctoral Dissertation]. ProQuest Dissertations & Theses Global.

Moll, L. C., Amanti, C., Neff, D., & González, N. (1992). Funds of knowledge for teaching: Using a qualitative approach to connect homes and classrooms. *Theory into Practice, 31*(2), 132–141.

CHAPTER 16

Love, Hope, Empathy, and the Way Forward

Alicia López Nieto

The essays in this book bring to life the words of a wide range of teachers and other educators of various ethnicities and backgrounds, subjects and grades taught, geographical locations, gender identities, and years of experience. They give us fresh insights into pedagogy, and reinforce what we, as longtime educators, have tried to practice as well. While there are recurring themes that describe the challenges in education today, there are also many nuggets of hope for us to absorb and move ahead with, reminding us that teaching is also joyful and spirit-filling.

In this educational climate—book-banning, the assault on transgender people/students, the racial reckoning we are still dealing with, the after-effects of the COVID-19 pandemic, union-busting, the increasing load on teachers and the mental health crises in our schools—it can be easy to simply leave the teaching profession. But our schools need great teachers, and the alternative can be to lead with love, hope, and empathy first. This is not to say that's all that educators need to have. Supportive administrators and school boards, forward-thinking superintendents, excellent curriculum, materials and supplies, and quality professional development are all essential too. Nevertheless, the ideas that sustain me as an educator—love, hope and empathy—are clear throughout this book.

In this chapter I focus on these three themes, reminding us how our authors have touched on them in their essays. Additionally, I include the words of other scholars and some suggestions for ways in which we can practice love, hope, and empathy.

LOVE

After reading a recent issue of *Learning for Justice*, this quote resonated with me:

> We are in another iteration of the great exchange of power and justice. And we will fight for both and not concede for less. As we grapple with the phase of the reckoning and reconstructing of our democracy, let's be inspired by the words of Martin Luther King Jr: "Power at its best is love implementing the demands of justice, and justice at its best is power correcting everything that stands against love." (Dunn, 2023, p. 6)

Love—for teaching, for our students, for designing curriculum—is a recurring theme in the essays. I had a student from Brazil, who, every time she left my classroom, told me that she loved me. "I love you, Miss Loaps" (being from Brazil, she pronounced Lopez the Portuguese way, swallowing the "e") she would say in a matter-of-fact tone of voice. And I would say to her, "I love you, too, Ana—see you tomorrow!" This is partially due to the similarities in our cultural backgrounds, where showing love for teachers is a normal expression including for Ana. I realize that not all teachers would be comfortable explicitly saying this to their students or hearing it from their students, but the underlying sentiment of caring for the well-being of a student is one that many teachers would share. When I taught large groups of Spanish and French students, totaling 100+ students a day, I would sometimes become frustrated with the noise in class or the side conversations and would sigh, exasperated. Inevitably, a student would ask me, "Ms. López, do you hate us?" I would answer, "Of course not! I don't hate you. Do you sometimes drive me crazy? Yes! But I love you all, and if I hated you, I definitely should not be a teacher anymore." These conversations made me realize that my students needed to see and feel that I cared about them in more tangible ways than previously. For instance, I started doing things like not having any reaction when a student didn't have their homework—often they already felt badly, so why should I make them feel worse? Also, I tried to stop calling out individual students over disruptive behavior in front of the whole class, instead taking them to the hallway to chat. I made more of an attempt to understand the students' contexts and figure out why they were exhibiting certain behaviors. And, importantly, I had more fun with my teaching and took some things less seriously. None of this happened overnight, but gradually throughout my years of teaching.

Years ago, I wrote about love and teaching in my blog, Maestra Teacher (www.maestrateacher.com). I reflected on how, when I began teaching at the age of 25, I desperately wanted my students to like me. Finally, after some years I realized that I was looking at teaching the wrong way. I wrote:

> It wasn't until years later that I realized that it doesn't matter so much whether or not your students LIKE you. More importantly, do you love them? And do they feel YOU care about THEM? . . . . Now I believe that while it's great if you also LIKE your students, and they like you, it's more important for them to feel you care about their learning, their future, and their well-being. (Lopez, 2015)

In her essay, Odalis, a Latina who teaches in an urban dual language school, expresses her views on love and teaching. She writes, "Education is love in action. Love in education is multifaceted." Odalis's words especially resonate with us, since we understand that as teachers, love for our students is essential. Abolitionist scholar Bettina Love agrees, writing, "To love all children, we must struggle together to create the schools we are taught to believe are impossible: Schools built on justice, love, joy, and anti-racism" (Love, 2019). By empowering her students, Yahaira, a high school English teacher, embodies these words. In her essay, she writes:

> And so, in these tumultuous, unpredictable, and emotionally charged times, I choose to fuel my own uncertainties, anguish, and frustrations into what I believe to be my calling; I've aimed to use my time in the classroom to make it all as relevant as possible—for both me and the students, to connect real life with the content (which for me is English language arts), and to help empower my students in a way that helps them recognize the importance of their experiences and their voices as propellers of change and growth.

Love also means finding creative ways to care about and fold families into the education of their children. In her essay, Nadla, an elementary school ELL teacher, writes "we need to have a less White-middle-class lens when examining the realities of low-income families. Many of my students' parents work two or three jobs to provide for their children and help their families back in their home country. They might not be checking their children's backpacks every day or able to attend school functions. However, they show up for their children every day by sending them to school, entrusting educators with their children's future, and providing for their families." Opening our hearts to the families of our students is another way for educators to show that we truly love and care about their children. Schools need to understand the home lives and contexts of their students in order to find diverse ways for families to be engaged in their children's education.

For many educators, love for the profession and for the students is what keeps them going in the face of the increasing challenges they face. I have heard many retired teachers state that they would have retired later if they only had the students to worry about, and I have also overheard practicing teachers say that their frustration is almost never about the students. And every teacher can recall with fondness names of students, years after they are gone—even the most challenging students (sometimes those are the ones who come back to visit, surprising us with their changes and their development into amazing young people). Love is ever present in this profession, though some educators may not use that exact word for it. In a 2016 blog post, I wrote, "Our kids drive us crazy, test our limits, scream, whine, demand, and do things they are not supposed to do—even the best of kids. Even so, we keep loving them. In fact, I find that my love for my children grows each time we jump a hurdle of difficulty" (Lopez, 2016). While I wrote this about children in general, not students, in that blog post I continued by writing about how this applied to our students as well. I think often of my son's 2nd-grade teacher, who at our parent–teacher conference told me that she had not yet found something to love about my son. At first, I was shocked! But she explained that she knew she WOULD find something. And by the spring, she had found several things to love about him, most notably that he always knew how to fix any technology issues in the classroom, and that he endearingly called Wi-fi "wee-fee" as if in Spanish.

HOPE

Post-COVID teaching has brought with it new challenges for students, teachers, and administrators alike. While schools in some areas had already left online teaching by the beginning of the 2021 school year, my Massachusetts district was one of the more cautious ones. We returned to full in-person teaching in September of 2021, fully masked and bracing ourselves for whatever the school year would bring. That October, I wrote in my blog:

Statements I keep hearing and reading from teachers this fall:

"It's only October and I feel like it's May!"
"I've never been so tired in my life."
"I'm more tired this year than any other year."
"I go home and collapse on the couch/bed."
"I can't read anymore; I just zone out watching stupid tv or videos."

We know many students are not okay, but many teachers are also not okay. What is happening this year that makes it feel unlike any other? I can't quite put my finger on one cause, but I can speak about some of what I am experiencing. (Lopez, 2021)

That blog post was called "Check in with your teacher friends—we are not all right." I went on to write about the difficulties of that fall: lack of communication with a new administration, a loss of community, a shortage of substitute teachers, and dysregulated students, not to mention the ongoing racial violence and other crises in the country and world.

In this *Washington Post* article, Valerie Strauss outlines some of the challenges facing educators:

> Teachers have tolerated far too many indignities in the latest manufactured culture wars over pandemic health measures, fetishized parental rights, anti-racism censorship, LGBTQ book bans, teacher loyalty oaths, demands for cameras in the classroom to surveil against the supposed teaching of dangerous ideas even as we expect the same teachers, armed, to prevent mass shootings—all to fit a narrative of failing public schools to provoke the privatization of education. Meanwhile, the same forces attempt to undercut teachers by deprofessionalizing them, purportedly to address teacher shortages. (Strauss, 2023)

Nevertheless, having hope may be the thing that helps us get through every day, every year. Mary Jade, a public school librarian, offers a message of hope in her essay. She writes, "I am an educator because of the intersectionality of my nontraditional and traditional learning spaces where I was celebrated as a learner, leader and visionary . . . being free to learn and create and create while making mistakes along the way."

I ended my October 2021 blog post with words of hope:

> While I find a lot of things challenging and exhausting about this school year, I look to my students for moments of hope and happiness. Little things such as watching 7th and 8th grade students play on a playground with abandon during a field trip; seeing them engage in a lesson with focus and willingness; hearing their shouts of joy when they get ahead during a game of Kahoot; taking mask breaks outside, and playing ball or picking up gorgeous fallen leaves as we walk around the school; teaching about el Día de los Muertos. And thankfully, there are also people and moments that help . . . I let everything else fall away and stick with these people and moments to help me keep going. (Lopez, 2021)

One amazing aspect of teaching is that you get to start over at the beginning of every year. The first days of school are a time of optimism and hope, and of knowing that whatever happened the previous year can change and improve. New students arrive, with excitement and hope in their eyes; teachers redesign units and lessons, keeping in mind the failures of the previous year and finding different ways to teach to make learning happen for their students. Some of the essays in this book may serve as a balm to tired teachers, helping them remember that there IS always hope. As Kerrita writes in her essay, "I teach, we teach, I posit, because education work is professional labor in three dimensions: past, present, and future, and each mode has its own particular enticements that render us hopeful and committed as educators."

Teachers are incredible people. It is astounding to me every time I talk with my colleagues at the beginning of the year; they are excited, planning, prepping, nervous for the first day of school. Regardless of the challenges they know they will be facing—the difficulties with administration, stress, lack of time, trying to keep a work-life balance, students who test their limits—every beginning of school year there are happy faces who look forward to it all, keeping hope at the center of what they do.

EMPATHY

Empathy is about understanding our students' emotional and physical contexts and responding to them. It means not blaming them for their challenges, and instead trying to understand where behaviors are coming from and why they are happening. I am a person with a lot of empathy, yet I always say that when my first child started kindergarten, my empathy level as a teacher exploded. Suddenly, I saw all my students in a different light, understanding that every single one of them was someone's special little person—whether that someone was their parent, grandparent, aunt, foster parent, older sibling, or family friend. Even the most exigent, defiant student who might make my day tougher was the apple of someone's eye. I felt that in my soul, and it changed how I viewed all my students and my teaching practice. Research backs up these feelings. In a research study about empathy and discipline, the authors found that "the quality of students' relationships with teachers is one of the strongest predictors of classroom behavior" (Okonofua et al., 2016, p. 116). This is unlikely to be surprising to educators.

The year I transitioned from teaching Spanish to teaching ELL, one of my English learners was a girl, Aline, who arrived from Cape Verde; her entry into our school was delayed due to a New England March snowstorm. Aline's 13th birthday happened shortly after she started school. She spoke no English other than "hello," and I had to quickly learn some words in Portuguese (Cape Verde's official language is Portuguese, though the language commonly spoken is Kriolu. Aline was comfortable speaking both). One of the first words I learned was "bolo," or cake, as I asked her what kind of cake she liked. She was stunned when I brought in a chocolate cake I had made for her 13th birthday. About a month after she arrived, Aline started attending our afterschool program, which offered homework help. One afternoon, she came to my classroom in the middle of the after-school session with a distraught look on her face. Aline sat down and told me that a staff member in the afterschool program said they couldn't help her because they didn't understand her. Aline cried with frustration; in her country she had been an excellent student, outgoing and friendly, and suddenly here she was, silent and silen*ced*. I sat next to her and cried with her. When Aline moved on from 8th grade to high school, we both cried again, and she left me notes on the board. One of them said "Thanks you for help me." I took a photo of it and still look at it when I need inspiration, and when I need reminders of the importance of having real empathy for our students.

Having empathy, and teaching students empathy, can have profound effects on students. In an article about how a strong Latinx identity can help these students thrive in school, the authors cite empathy as one of the values taught at home as an essential piece of their identity: "Latinx children receive strong lessons in empathy. A recent qualitative study found that when Latinx mothers talk to their children about sibling conflicts, they use other-oriented language to present the other sibling's perspective" (Carlo & Roos, 2023). Empathy is also key for teachers to place at the center of their teaching, along with love and hope. The authors in the research study about empathy and discipline write that "The more teachers understand how students perceive teachers' actions, the better equipped teachers are to interact with students in ways that nurture their growth into responsible, motivated young adults" (Carlos & Roos, 2023). This research study suggests that the use of empathic discipline can reduce challenging behaviors and increase student engagement.

There is no set way to be an empathic educator, but one major focus in many schools has been to include more social–emotional awareness across the curriculum. Social–emotional learning is not new, but its importance has grown since the COVID-19 pandemic. The Collaborative for Academic, Social, and Emotional Learning (CASEL) is one of the most influential organizations in this work in schools. The framework they developed "is organized around five competence clusters that include thoughts, attitudes, and behaviors related to self-awareness, self-management, social awareness, relationship skills, and responsible decision-making" (Greenberg, 2023).

A simple way for teachers to include social–emotional learning in their teaching is by having some sort of daily check-in at the beginning of class. Students can self-reflect, have a few moments to transition, regulate themselves and be more present for learning. One teacher uses a check-in chart, which is a large poster board with the question "How are you feeling today" and then various statements under it, such as "I'm okay" or "I'm struggling." Then "students are encouraged to grab a Post-it, write their name on the back and place it next to the statement that best matches their feelings for the day" (Pelletiere, 2023).

Other teachers begin class with a short meditation or a mindful minute. At the school where I have been teaching for many years, teachers adopted these routines long before COVID, about 10 years ago. A number of teachers close their doors at the start of class and begin a mindfulness practice right away; this means the students who are late must wait outside so as to not interrupt this time. Some teachers use guided meditations from YouTube; others simply play relaxing music while students close their eyes, calm their bodies, and ready themselves for class. I always begin class with writing, a practice I adopted after participating in the Western Massachusetts Writing Project Summer Institute many years ago. In this workshop taught by teachers for teachers (which is the National Writing Project's model), every day began with "writing into the day." In my class, I sometimes give students a prompt; at other times, they can just write what is on their mind. I have found that as a teacher of mostly beginner English learners, providing both a prompt and a model, as well as sentence starters, can help them be successful with this practice. After writing, I ask students if they want to share. At the beginning of the year, they tend to be more timid, but as we get to know each other, even the shyer ones exclaim, "Can I share first?" Even greeting students by name at the door of the classroom as they come in is a great way to set the stage for that class. As Adi wrote in her essay, "The point of greeting them doesn't have to do with training them in basic courtesies, or making myself feel seen, but rather it is to make sure they know I see them individually."

Having an empathic practice and creating social–emotional learning opportunities in our classrooms can set our students up for success. As Seth writes in his essay,

> To be a memorable and meaningful space for learning, our classrooms need to be places where students feel safe to experiment, free to try on new perspectives, and stumble, knowing the community will catch their fall. Equally important, though, is that it be a space where they are expected to engage, where effort is required, and each member feels accountable for making progress.

The start of the school year is another wonderful moment to share ourselves with our students and lay the groundwork for a teacher's values and goals in the classroom. Odalis, one of the essay authors, begins every year with a slideshow entitled, "Get to know your teacher." She reflected that being vulnerable and open as a teacher showed students they could do the same:

> It felt *good* to share that English was my second language, and that I knew exactly how some of them felt. It felt *good* to share that I was a mom, daughter, and sister. It felt *good* to share that I was Dominican and talk about my first name being Odalis and how to pronounce it.

As education and our student populations evolve, many teachers, like Odalis, have experienced how this opening of oneself is also a kind of empathy, trying to share our context so we can better understand our students' contexts.

Nevertheless, being open and vulnerable with our students is difficult for some educators. Years ago, teachers were told not to smile until wintertime, and to never divulge personal information. While this attitude has evolved over the years, many schools are still not doing enough to help equip teachers to be fluent in SEL practices: "Teachers need training to understand how to effectively implement SEL programs for children but focusing on teachers' own SEL is also beneficial for their own well-being, teaching quality, and for improving outcomes for students" (Greenberg, 2023). This article also suggests that there should be a public health approach to implementing SEL by integrating it more widely in schools, coordinating with mental health counselors and partnering with families. In today's educational climate, this seems like a wise approach.

This is a good segue to consider other policies and practices that go beyond the purview of one teacher and instead include a broader range of people in and out of the field of education, an issue we address below.

LOOKING AHEAD

We have made clear in this book that we admire and respect educators and the work they do to teach, love, inspire, and keep students safe in schools. However, we reject the notion that teachers *alone* must be responsible for creating all the changes needed to do the job. This book has largely focused on valiant individual and collective efforts within classrooms and schools to promote changes to create schools that are nurturing, secure, and unscathed from the sometimes troubling sociopolitical context in which they exist. The criticisms, harassment, and lack of respect that many teachers have endured in the past several years make it obvious that without support, educators are not equipped to handle all the problems by themselves. Schools are, after all, a reflection of the society they serve. So, we end with a note of caution and some helpful research that might shine a light on broader perspectives and practices that can lead the way for others to do their part in addition to teachers and other practitioners.

One example comes from other education institutions. The word "courage" in the title of this book comes from our view that teachers are extraordinarily valiant, something they have demonstrated time and again over the years and particularly in the past several years. Certainly, the teachers in this book have shown tremendous courage. Their courage is evident in their ongoing commitment to students despite the many trials they face every day; their will to continue in the field even when it is life-sucking; their decision to challenge what they consider absurd laws, rules, and regulations that rob them of their authority and dignity. There are numerous examples of courage in, for instance, Seth Peterson's public comments to the Boston City Council concerning a change in the reorganization of the school committee, or his indignity at the school committee's request that teachers work extra hours for no commensurate compensation. We see courage in the teachers—immigrants and children of immigrants and refugees such as Nadla Tavares Smith, Jorge Lopez, and the Cabo Verdean Center for Applied Research collective who stand up to protect their native language and community.

On a broader level, teachers fight back, for example, by refusing to accept a recent state law in Tennessee that limits the discussion of race and gender in the classroom (Sargent, 2023). The law claims that such discussions allow teachers to focus on so-called "impartial facts" and that without it, males and White students would feel guilt or discomfort. Instead, the result of the law is to stifle dissent in classroom discussions, silencing talk that would most benefit marginalized communities. The Tennessee Teachers Association lawsuit claims that there is no simple way to avoid addressing the history of the extermination of Indigenous societies in what is now the United States, or the violent nature of slavery, or other historical facts or issues that may upset some students. In these circumstances, it is no wonder that many teachers feel besieged. But teachers alone cannot take on every state legislature or every angry school board.

Another way that other institutions—schools, towns, cities, and the federal government—can address their commitment to students and the adults who work with them is by doing something about school safety. A recent study suggests that combining trauma-informed care, restorative justice, and multicultural education would go a long way toward healing schools where both students and staff have suffered the consequences of trauma and neglect; this is particularly true for, but not limited to, urban schools (Parameswaran et al., 2023). While there have been many recommendations for making schools safer—from arming teachers to posting guards at every entrance—a recent study from the Learning Policy Institute looked at two key approaches, one focusing on investing in *physical* security such as guards, metal detectors, and security cameras and the other on investing in *other means of student support* through mental health, SEL, restorative practices, and structures that support positive developmental relationships. In their extensive review of both these approaches, the LPI found that the approach that emphasizes the policing of students often makes schools *less* safe, while the approaches that personalize supports and promote caring school communities lead to *improved* behavior, safety, and better academic outcomes (Greenberg, 2023).

We believe that everyone, at every level of our society, has a role to play in creating schools that students want to attend, that educators love going to every day, and that communities can be proud of.

FINAL THOUGHTS

We hope that the essays in this book have provided the readers with a sense of hope, along with reminders of how love and empathy are crucial for modern pedagogy. The way forward for educators will not be easy; the challenges seem to be increasing as the support for educators decreases across the country. Every year brings new policies and initiatives from policymakers and administrators who have little knowledge of what happens inside a classroom. Teachers' salaries do not nearly match the amount of work they do, requiring many to get second jobs. Teachers complain of the very real work creep that happens every year. There is a dearth of mental health support in our schools. Fewer young people are choosing teaching as a profession, and who can blame them? It is not an easy road. People who say that teachers are so lucky to have the summers off do not realize that many teachers work at other jobs in the summer to supplement their income. And students all over the country continue to face many difficulties as well, increasing their stress and that of their teachers.

Yet, in the face of all of this, we remain positive. We must—for ourselves and for our kids. Our students' education is at stake, and thus the future of our country. The essays in this book are a reminder to us to put our students at the center of their own learning; to remain hopeful; to include joy in our teaching; to be critical thinkers and to teach critical thinking; to hold high expectations for them; to recognize all that our students and families bring with them to school, acknowledging their funds of knowledge; to foster wonder, spark imagination and to be creative ourselves; to share ourselves with them so that they may open up to us, too; to value the multitude of languages and cultures and learning styles our students bring to us; and above all, to love, inspire, engage with, and teach them with our whole selves.

REFERENCES

Carlo, G., & Roos, J. (2023, February 7). How a strong Latinx identity helps kids thrive. *Greater Good Magazine.* https://greatergood.berkeley.edu/article/item/how_a_strong_latinx_identity_helps_kids_thrive#:~:text=Additionally%2C%20Latinx%20values%20promote%20the,account%20for%20the%20group's%20needs

Dunn, J. L. (2023, Spring). The power of place. *Learning for Justice, 4,* 6.

Greenberg, M. T. (2023, March 6). *Evidence for social and emotional learning in schools.* Learning Policy Institute Brief. https://doi.org/10.54300/928.269

López, A. (2015, March 26). Opting out: Better late than never. *Maestra Teacher.* https://www.maestrateacher.com/blog/opting-out-better-late-than-never

López, A. (2016, March 27). Teaching and love, revisited. *Maestra Teacher.* https://www.maestrateacher.com/blog/teaching-and-love-revisited

López, A. (2021, October 30). Check in with your teacher friends - We are not all right. *Maestra Teacher.* https://www.maestrateacher.com/blog/check-in-with-your -teacher-friends-we-are-not-all-right

Love, B. (2019). Dear White Teachers: You can't love your Black students if you don't know them. *Education Week.* https://www.edweek.org/teaching-learning /opinion-dear-white-teachers-you-cant-love-your-black-students-if-you-dont -know-them/2019/03

Okonofua, J. A., Paunesku, D., & Walton, G. M. (2016). Brief intervention to en- courage empathic discipline cuts suspension rates in half among adolescents. *The Proceedings of the National Academy of Sciences (PNAS), 113*(19), 5221– 5226. https://doi.org/10.1073/pnas.1523698113

Parameswaran, U. D., Molloy, J., & Kuttner, Paul (2023). Healing schools: A frame- work for joining trauma-informed care, restorative justice, and multicultural education for whole school reform. *The Urban Review.* https://doi.org/10.1007 /s11256-023-00666-5

Pelletiere, N. (2023, May 9). *This teacher created a mental health check-in chart for her students and now teachers around the world are doing the same.* ABC News. https://abcnews.go.com/GMA/Wellness/teacher-created-mental-health- check-chart-students-now/story?id=62169283

Sargent, G. (2023, July 27). Fed-up teachers in Tennessee find a novel answer to anti- woke hysteria [Opinion]. *The Washington Post.* https://www.washingtonpost .com/opinions/2023/07/27/tennessee-teachers-lawsuit-antiwoke-restrictions -race-slavery/

Strauss, V. (2023, January 26). The basic rights teachers don't have. *The Washington Post.* https://www.washingtonpost.com/education/2023/01/26/basic-rights -teachers-dont-have/

About the Editors and Contributors

Abel Djassi Amado is an assistant professor of political science and international relations at Simmons University. He holds a PhD in political science/African studies from Boston University. He researches and has published on the politics of language in West Africa/Cabo Verde and the political history of national liberation in Cabo Verde and Guinea-Bissau. His works have been published in *Lusotopie, The Journal of Cape Verdean Studies, Desafios,* and *Portuguese Literary and Cultural Studies.* Amado is the current chair of the Cabo Verdean Center for Applied Research (CVCAR).

Odalis Amparo is a first-generation educator who is highly committed to elevating the voice and supporting the achievement of students and teachers in historically marginalized communities. She is fiercely passionate about the intersection between language learning, equitable mathematics instruction, and culturally sustaining pedagogy. Odalis resides in western MA and enjoys spending time with her son Elijah, family, and friends.

Marlyse Baptista is the Distinguished Presidential Professor of Linguistics in the Linguistics Department and MindCore at the University of Pennsylvania. She specializes in the morpho-syntax of Creole languages and in theories of creole genesis. In addition to conducting generative and descriptive analyses of a variety of Creoles, she is involved in several collaborations using experimental methods and agent-based modeling to examine cognitive processes involved in language emergence. She is deeply committed to the study of Creoles in education and has been collaborating with members of the Cabo Verdean Center for Applied Research in designing K–12 heritage language and culture curricula.

Suzanna Dali-Parker is a K–12 teacher of multilingual learners in a small urban setting. Her academic and professional areas of interests are in the nexus between language, literacy, and culture. She has been teaching for 30 years across grade levels, including adult learners, and is passionate about creating memorable learning experiences that promote bicultural and biliterate identities for her students. Her background in the performing arts plays an important role in her desire to approach curriculum development and language instruction through an equity and inclusion lens. Suzanna has also been a teacher educator and is currently a school equity leader at her school.

Sonie Felix is the head of school at Community Academy and has served in various capacities throughout the Boston Public Schools system to promote literacy, access, and achievement for *all* students and structured teacher professional development sessions. Sonie was born in Haiti and grew up in Boston, MA, where she attended Pine Manor College (as an undergraduate) and earned a masters in educational leadership at Simmons College in Boston, MA. She is committed to high student achievement and is passionate about helping others explore the importance of the work and figuring out their "Why." She often references her experiences as an English language learner and as a BPS student as a foundation for her love of the work.

Lourenço García is the assistant superintendent of equity and inclusion in Revere Public Schools. He provides leadership on critical issues in diversity, inclusion, and equity throughout the district to ensure anti-racism education, programs, policies, practices, and resources are thoughtfully constructed and implemented to build a more inclusive school system for all stakeholders. Dr. Garcia coauthored the "Schools of Opportunity: 10 Research-Based Models of Equity in Action" book and has been featured in two books, *Five Practices for Improving the Success of Latino Students* and *The Human Side of Changing Education: How to Lead Change with Clarity, Conviction, and Courage*, as well as numerous other case studies on urban education, leadership, and school reform. Dr. Garcia's areas of expertise include human rights, urban education, leadership, and policy studies, special education, second-language acquisition, critical pedagogy, culturally responsive teaching, restorative justice, equity audits, and systems thinking and design thinking. He is proficient in Cape Verdean, Portuguese, English, Spanish, Russian, and French languages.

Mary Jade Haney was born to live the life of an educator. She served as a classroom teacher, visual arts teacher, reading teacher, reading interventionist, literacy coach, teacher educator, professional developer, founder of a summer literacy camp, and is currently a librarian in an elementary public school. With over 25 years of service in the public school system and a heart for the profession, Mary Jade reflects, reclaims, reignites, and recreates her passion to sustain joyfully as an educator. Reflections from the field of education is a constant motivator to journey onward as a beloved educator.

Alicia López Nieto is a teacher and administrator. Her 29 years in the classroom span two states and three subjects (French, Spanish, ESL). She is a doctoral student in the College of Education at UMass, Amherst, and a lecturer in the ESL licensure program in the Professional and Graduate Education program at Mount Holyoke College. Alicia is the coauthor with Sonia Nieto of the book *Teaching, A Life's Work, A Mother-Daughter Dialogue* (Teachers College Press). She lives in Western Massachusetts with her family, including husband of 25 years, three wonderful children, two dogs, and two cats.

Jorge Lopez has been teaching history–social science and ethnic studies for over 20 years at Roosevelt High School in Boyle Heights, Los Angeles. He received his PhD in education, teaching, learning, and culture. His research focuses on the impact of critical ethnic studies on high school Latinx youth and examines ethnic studies curriculum and pedagogy that centers youth narratives and *testimonios*. His interests also include community muralism, activism, social justice education, critical race theory, and humanizing pedagogies. Dr. López has coauthored a book, articles, and chapters on ethnic studies and critical pedagogies. He is also a lecturer in Chicana(o) Latina(o) Studies at California State University, Los Angeles.

Ambrizeth H. Lima is an educator in Boston. Her research areas of interest include urban education, race, ethnicity, class, gender, and culture in education, first and second language acquisition, and immigrant studies. She has presented at numerous workshops that focus on the integration of immigrant communities in the United States. She received her master's and doctorate in education at Harvard Graduate School of Education. She is also the author of her newly published book, *The Socialization of Cabo Verdean Immigrant Men in Urban America*. She is an active member of the Cabo Verdean Center for Applied Research.

Yahaira D. Márquez, raised by her Puerto Rican parents in New York City, was a student of New York City public schools before attending Boston University, where she earned her BA in English, and Old Dominion University, where she obtained her MS in education. Besides her love for travel and adventure, Yahaira has always been passionate about educating youth and has been a public urban school educator for 20 years, spanning three states. For the last 15 years her tenure has been in a diverse Massachusetts high school where she's taught a wide variety of courses, including a teacher development course for teenage students, and is currently the lead teacher of her English department.

Adriana Martinez, daughter to Mexican immigrants and migrant farm workers, is a high school English department chair and is in her 9th year of teaching. She is pursuing her PhD and is exploring issues within critical literacies and equitable policy and praxis.

Kerrita K. Mayfield is a middle school science teacher with a PhD in secondary curriculum and instruction from the University of Wyoming. Her work incorporates social justice principles into standards-based science curriculum design and considers global climate change implications for disenfranchised communities. She believes that everybody has a story; she tells stories about science, communities, and people. Kerrita lives, makes art, and gardens in Western Massachusetts.

Sonia Nieto is a member of the National Academy of Education and professor emerita of language, literacy, and culture, College of Education, University of Massachusetts, Amherst. Her research on multicultural education, teacher education, literacy, and the education of students of culturally and linguistically diverse backgrounds has resulted in dozens of journal articles and book chapters, 13 books, including a memoir, *Brooklyn Dreams: My Life in Public Education* (Harvard Education Press, 2015), and she has coauthored a book with her daughter Alicia López. She is the editor of the Visions of Practice series (Teachers College Press). The first edition (1992) of her classic text, *Affirming Diversity: The Sociopolitical Context of Multicultural Education*, was selected for the Museum of Education Readers' Guide as "one of the 100 books that helped define the field of education in the 20th century." Dr. Nieto has received many awards for her scholarly work, teaching, activism, and advocacy, including nine honorary doctorates.

Seth Peterson was born into a family of educators and swore he would not join the family trade. Time, fate, and the right people and experiences saw otherwise. Seth is in his 26th year as a high school English teacher in the Boston Public Schools. These years have convinced Seth that our schools must use teacher inquiry and teacher–student collaboration—not pie charts and deified data—to spearhead their reforms. In 2013, Seth was named one of Boston's Educators of the Year. A deep believer in the power of words and the growing need for both passion and precision in language, Seth sees literacy and literature as students' ticket to a broader, more complete world. The hopes, worries, and expectations he foists upon his students are the same ones he has for his own daughters. Seth lives with them and his dynamic, civic-minded wife in the Mattapan neighborhood of Boston. Along with the love and support of his family, he is sustained by the great talent and commitment of his colleagues and his students at Snowden International School, all of whom inspire Seth to challenge the convenient lie that high standards require standardization. He is tired of the demonization of teachers and their unions, but remains inspired by the classroom community and the next generation's desire to do better by each other.

Heather Robertson-Devine is the founder and general manager of Books del Sur. She has been involved in the education field for 17 years as a bilingual teacher, a Spanish teacher, a District Professional Development teacher leader, and an Instructional Resource teacher. Her experience acquiring and instructing with Spanish children's literature and her love of Latin America drove her to make Books del Sur a resource for teachers, librarians, administrators, and parents to access and understand Latin American literature. Heather has a BA in International Relations and Latin American Studies and a master's degree in Educational Leadership and Administration.

Nadla Tavares Smith is a Brazilian immigrant, mother, and equity-focused educator. She teaches English language and literacy to elementary school multilingual learners in Massachusetts. For her commitment to social justice and equity for multilingual learners, she received the Roger L. Wallace Excellence in Teaching Award. Nadla has also served on several committees as part of her district's school improvement plan, and she has facilitated in-district professional development on scientifically based research and evidence-based instructional strategies to develop multilingual learners' literacy skills.

Dawna Marie Thomas is a professor and the chair of the Critical Race, Gender, and Cultural Studies Department at the Gwen Ifill College of Media, Arts & Humanities, a member of the Sociology Department, and the director of the Law and Justice minor at Simmons University. Dr. Thomas's research is grounded in her Cabo Verdean and African American cultural roots. Her latest study, *The Cabo Verdean Women's Project,* includes four generations of Cabo Verdean women throughout New England; she explored their experiences with domestic violence, healthcare and disability, and their concepts of womanhood.

Beth Wohlleb Adel has been honored to work alongside and learn among truly dedicated and wise teachers and courageous, thoughtful students in many educational settings: at a free school in Scotland; at Zhejiang University, China; in Revere, MA; as a 6th-grade social studies teacher at the Springfield Renaissance School in Springfield, MA; and most recently as a humanities teacher in Easthampton, MA. As a descendent of settler-colonials from Europe, Beth strives to continue to deepen her understanding of her privilege, and to use her privilege to collaboratively work toward untangling the racist underpinnings of our educational systems and interrupt the current practices that benefit White people and perpetuate White supremacy. Beth considers her students, colleagues, life partner, and family to be precious and profound teachers, who help her grow, whether she likes it or not.

Index

The letter *f*, *n*, or *p* following a page number represents a figure, note or photo, respectively.